George Trevor

The catholic doctrine of the sacrifice and participation of the Holy Eucharist

George Trevor

The catholic doctrine of the sacrifice and participation of the Holy Eucharist

ISBN/EAN: 9783742861719

Manufactured in Europe, USA, Canada, Australia, Japa

Cover: Foto ©Lupo / pixelio.de

Manufactured and distributed by brebook publishing software (www.brebook.com)

George Trevor

The catholic doctrine of the sacrifice and participation of the Holy Eucharist

THE CATHOLIC DOCTRINE

OF THE

SACRIFICE AND PARTICIPATION

OF

THE HOLY EUCHARIST.

BY

GEORGE TREVOR, M.A.

CANON OF YORK;
RECTOR OF BURTON S. PETER'S, HOLDERNESS.

LONDON:
J. AND C. MOZLEY, 6, PATERNOSTER ROW;
OXFORD: PARKER AND CO.
1869.

PREFACE.

These pages are not designed to attempt a new exposition of the Sacred Mysteries, but to vindicate from recent misconceptions the old Catholic Doctrine of the Memorial Sacrifice, and Real Participation, of the Body and Blood of Christ in the Holy Eucharist. The authorities adduced, in exposition of Holy Scripture, are the Councils, Liturgies, and Fathers before the division of East and West, together with the Liturgy and standard Divines of the Church of England.

The same authorities have been lately claimed for conclusions to which they are, in truth, strongly opposed. The old Catholic phraseology is unhappily being more and more limited to the Tridentine interpretation. The Real Presence, which Bishop Cosin affirms and proves to be common to all Protestant Confessions, is now sought to be restrained to the Church of Rome, and one section of the Anglican Communion. The Eucharistic Sacrifice, taught by all our great theologians, is to a large extent confounded with the Sacrifice of the Mass. It is a natural though startling sequel, that one of these miscalled High Churchmen at last reaches the conclusion, that England and Rome are absolutely at one on the very doctrine which historically formed the chief ground of their separation!

These reactionary paradoxes are aided rather than restrained by indiscriminate opposition. The churchmanship of our day happily revolts from all that goes to lower or rationalise the Christian mysteries. In view of the secular tendencies of the age, it clings the more fervently to the Catholic tradition, which may soon be our only bond of union, when temporal Establishments shall have ceased to exist. The present Essay is an appeal to Catholic tradition; to Church authority against private judgement; to the simplicity of the universal Faith against an overbearing Scholasticism, which, in seeking to localize the spiritual, darkens what it affects to define, and desecrates the ark it presumes to uphold.

It is the diversity of Doctrine which creates, and gives importance to our Ritual diversities; these can never be satisfactorily adjusted while the standards of teaching are misunderstood.

I have long hoped to see the task of restoring the balance undertaken by some more competent writer; but perhaps an imperfect attempt may be less dangerous, than a delay which has already been too long for the peace of the Church.

Happily no new and independent exploration of the Fathers is required: on the contrary, the citation is best limited to the beaten path of our own theology. It is not what the private judgment of learned men may now find in antiquity, but what the Church of England has taken from it as Catholic truth, that her children require to be told.

The publication of this Essay is due to the encouragement derived from the subscriptions of the late lamented Archbishop of Canterbury; of my diocesan, the Archbishop of York; of the Lord Primate of Ireland; the Bishop Primus of Scotland; the Presiding Bishop of the Protestant Episcopal Church in the United States of America; and Twenty-one other Bishops of the Anglican Communion. To these Prelates, with the several Dignitaries and Professors who have been pleased to honour me with the same mark of confidence, my grateful thanks are due.

To Archdeacon Freeman I am further indebted, not only for easy access to the valuable stores collected in his *Principles of Divine Service,* but for much assistance in the laborious task of verifying the references, and for his most kind and careful revision of the proof sheets of this Publication.

Burton S. Peter's, December, 1868.

CONTENTS.

SECTION I.—THE EUCHARISTIC SACRIFICE.

	Page
The Eucharist the Christian Liturgy . . .	1
Term 'Sacrifice' used both of the whole celebration and the material elements	2
Argument from Scripture	3
Sin-offerings and Burnt-offerings abrogated in New Testament	4
Not Peace-offerings, which alone admitted of Communion	5
Use of the Memorial	,,
Eucharist a Memorial	6
S. Augustine	,,
S. Chrysostom	7
Theophylact	,,
Peter Lombard	,,
Thomas Aquinas	,,
Question of a *true* Sacrifice	8
Scripture use of the word	9
Note on altars	10
Spiritual worship required in Old Testament no less than the New	,,
Primitive interpretation of Malachi i. 11, and Leviticus ii. 2; xxiv. 9	11
Participation essential to the Sacrifice . .	12
The Sacrifice *commemorative*, the Participation *real* .	13

SECTION II.—THE SACRIFICE OF THE MASS.

	Page
Decree of Council of Trent	14
Meaning of 'Body and Blood:'—not contained in the Sacrament, but represented by it	15
New idea introduced by Transubstantiation	16
Sacrifice declared identical with that of the Cross	17
Confusion of the 'Body and Blood' with the Body glorified	”
Contradictory assertions	18
Sacrament exhibits the Body and Blood sundered in death; the means of communion with His glorified Manhood	19
Means not to be confounded with the end	20
Novelty of Concomitancy	”
Bishop Andrewes—*ad Cadaver*	21
Melchisedek's sacrifice	”
True superiority of his order	22
His sacrifice unknown to Apostolic Fathers	23
Not in Liturgies or Canons till Trent	24
Refutes Transubstantiation	”
S. Cyprian	”
S. Augustine	”
Our Lord's oblation before Consecration	25
Question in what the Sacrifice consists	”
Thomas Aquinas	26
Mutilation in the Missal	”
Bishop of Meaux, Suarez, Vasquez, Bellarmine, Melchior Canus	”
Question at Trent whether Christ sacrificed in the Supper	27
Inconsistent conclusion	28
Five points involved in the Sacrifice of the Mass	29
Corporal Presence	”
Transubstantiation	”
Identity with the Sacrifice of the Cross	”
Participation of Christ by unworthy Communicants	”
Adoration of the Host	”

	Page
All impossible in the original Institution . .	30
Consecration not separable from Communion .	31
Novel and illicit uses of the Sacrament . . .	,,

SECTION III.—THE LUTHERAN HYPOTHESIS.

Corporal Presence, without Transubstantiation and the Sacrifice of the Mass	33
Unworthy receiving, and Eucharistic Adoration .	,,
Protestant canon *nihil extra usum* . . .	,,
Difficulty of Lutheran Presence . . .	34
Consubstantial Adoration	,,
Inconsistency of Luther's demand of the Cup .	35
Suppression of the Sacrifice	,,
Weakness of Lutheranism	36
Recent revival of 'co-existent' theory . .	,,
Its authorized statements	37
Sacramental union	38
Gerhard and Pfaff	39
Practical approximation to Hooker . . .	40
Corporal Presence heretical	41
Irreconcilable with Scripture and antiquity .	42
Of no use to communion with Christ . .	,,
Contradiction in terms	43
The Real Presence *mystical* and *spiritual* . .	44

SECTION IV.—THE ANGLICAN DOCTRINE.

Sacrifice of the Mass rests on two errors: Corporal Presence and Oblation after Consecration . .	44
Catholic teaching recovered by Anglican divines .	45
Eucharistic Sacrifice not identical with Sacrifice of the Cross	,,
Elements *offered* as Memorials, *received* as Realities .	46
In what sense propitiatory	,,

	Page
Objects of the Sacrifice	46
Limited to worthy Communicants	”
Christ adored in heaven	47
Phrase 'Real Presence'	”
No presence without Communion	”
Christ received by faith	48
Sacrament is the *Dead* Body	”
Christ in the receiver	49
Question of *Blood* in the glorified Body	”
Romish objection of Nestorianism	50
English divines :—	
Elfric	51
Corporal Presence introduced by Lanfranc	53
Wiclif	”
Cranmer	”
Ridley	54
Cooke's Diallacticon	58
Ponet	60
Bilson	62
Andrewes	63
Lake	64
Laud	”
Cosin	65
Patrick	66
Bull	67
Burnet	68
Aldrich	”
Real Presence fourfold	69
Universal agreement on the *Spiritual* Presence	71
Diversity on the *mystical*	72
Rationalistic arguments	73
Significance of Consecration	74
Divine action on matter	75
Invocation of the Holy Ghost	76
Power of Sacraments	”
Effect of Christ's Commission	77
Peculiarity of Johnson's Unbloody Sacrifice	78
Denies the Real Presence	81
Based on the same error with Transubstantiation	”

SECTION V.—THE NEW OBJECTIVE THEORY.

	Page
Deprecation of new theories	82
'Objective' a novel term, metaphysical and ambiguous	83
Inapplicable to the Divine Presence	84
Signification already changing	,,
Archd. Wilberforce	85
Mr. Keble	86
Profession of faith by twenty-one clergymen	87
First article evades the question of corporal or spiritual	88
Repudiates what no one asserts	,,
Not what the Church repudiates	,,
Doubtful if it exclude Transubstantiation	89
Romish phrase, 'under the form of bread and wine'	90
Not in the Homilies	,,
Rejected by the Church of England	,,
Not in the Catechism	91
Irrelevancy of the corporal view	92
Participation omitted	93
'Objective' Presence probably corporal	95
Second article ambiguous	96
Oblation of consecrated elements	,,
Repudiation falls short of Article XXXI.	97
May agree with the Mass	,,
Another interpretation ends in Zuinglianism	98
Third explanation makes it commemorative	99
This requires participation	,,
Field	,,
Jeremy Taylor	,,
Forbes	100
Brevint	,,
Overall	,,
Andrewes	101
Cosin	,,
White	,,
Bramhall	102
Patrick	,,
Mede	,,

	Page
Sacrifice representative and commemorative	102
Third article also ambiguous	,,
Question of adoration	103
Idolatry an act	104
Hooker on the worship of the Cross	105
Such adoration implies Transubstantiation	106
Against the mind of the Church of England	107
At best an unauthorized inference	108
Unknown to antiquity	,,
S. Augustine	109
Sacramental Presence not hypostatic	,,
Bilson	,,
Andrewes	110
Sursum Corda	111
Jeremy Taylor	,,
Johnson	112
The new theory eclectic not Catholic	,,
Impossible in the best ages	113

SECTION VI.—TEACHING OF HOLY SCRIPTURE.

John vi. anciently interpreted of the Eucharist	113
So understood in our Communion Service	114
General Exposition	115
Double figure of eating and drinking	116
Blood drunk in the Eucharist only	117
Bengel	,,
Distinction between Christ and the Sacrament	118
Retained in our Liturgy	119
Not Nestorianism	120
History of the Institution	121
Consecration, distribution, communion; all equally necessary	125
Originally intertwined and contemporaneous	,,
Question of Christ's words in consecration	126
John xviii.	127
Sacrifice begun in the Supper: finished on the Cross	128

CONTENTS.   xiii

	Page
Nature of the Memorial-offering	129
Peace-offerings	,,
Shew-bread	130
Sin-offering	,,
Memorial representative and communicative	,,
So the Eucharist	131
Communion of the Blood a new feature	,,
Privilege of the Christian Sacrifice, Heb. xiii. 10	132
Christ our Passover	,,
No Presence but to faith	133
Profane Reception not real	,,

SECTION VII.—THE CANONS AND LITURGIES.

No body of divinity in Catholic Church	134
Decrees of Councils to the end of the seventh century	,,
No reservation	136
Nor non-communicating attendance	137
The *consistentes*	138
S. Chrysostom	139
Subsequent relaxation	140
Earliest Liturgies	141
No apostolic Liturgy extant	,,
No written forms before Constantine	,,
Number of after Liturgies	142
Substance of Ante-Nicene Offices gathered from points of agreement	143
Evidence weakened by interpolations	,,
The Clementine the best type	144
Substance stated	145
Six common elements	146
Collation of the three great features, Institution, Oblation, and Benediction	147
Clementine	,,
S. James's	148
S. Basil's	150
S. Chrysostom's	152

	Page
S. Mark's	153
Other Offices	155
Consecration not effected by the words of Institution, but by the Invocation of the Holy Ghost	,,
Oblation unconsecrated	155
Not a Sacrifice of Christ, or of His Body and Blood, but of their symbols	156
Consecration designed only for communion	,,
Seventh General Council	,,
Objection of the Image worshippers	157
Latin Church originally in accord with the Greek	,,
Difference at Council of Florence	158
Virtual doctrine of Mark of Ephesus	,,
Participation of the Sacrifice indispensable	159
Mixed chalice universal	160
Union of the elements a corrupt innovation	,,
Forbidden by the Council in Trullo	161
Prayers for the dead not a sacramental oblation	162
No trace of Purgatory	164
Note on 'Lord's Supper'	,,
Example of S. Paul	165
Incense of later introduction	166
Not derived from Jewish Liturgy	,,
Replaced by Prayer	,,

SECTION VIII.—THE WESTERN LITURGIES.

Inferior in age and authority	167
S. Peter's Liturgy translated from Roman Canon	,,
Charged with innovation at the Council of Trent	,,
Other Latin Liturgies agree with the Oriental	,,
Gothic	,,
Gallican	168
Mozarabic	,,
Ambrosian	,,
Language of Roman Church originally Greek	,,
Origin of present Missal	,,
Gelasius	,,

CONTENTS.

	Page
Gregory the Great	168
Early corruption	169
Present contents	"
Canon of the Mass	170
No sacrifice of Christ or of His Body and Blood	178
Peculiarity of *two* oblations	173
Omission of the Invocation	174
Probably due to Gregory	"
His account of it	175
Distinction between *preces* and *orationes*	176
Later interpolations	"
Inconsistencies	"
Elements made the Body and Blood relatively, not absolutely	177
Origin of Consecration by the words of Institution	"
Differences in the Fathers	178
Chrysostom	179
Greek prelates at Florence	"
Corruption of dark ages	181
Transubstantiation invented to explain the corporal view	"
Profane results	"

SECTION IX.—THE FATHERS.

Insufficiency of patristic catenas	183
Fathers witnesses to fact rather than truth	"
Value of their consent	"
Superior authority of the Church	184
Present improved state of criticism	185
Nature of the evidence	"
Clement of Rome	186
Parallel of Levitical sacrifices	187
Oblation attributed to Christ's Institution	188
Ignatius	189
Unity of the altar	"
Justin Martyr	"
First account of the celebration	"

CONTENTS.

	Page
Offering for the leper	191
Prophecy of Malachi	,,
Christian priesthood and sacrifice	,,
Irenæus	,,
Reality of the bread and the Body	192
The New Oblation	193
Sacrifice not abolished	,,
Eucharistic Sacrifice	194
Fragment published by Pfaff	195
Disclaimer of sacrifice in heathen sense	196
Two parts in the Eucharist	,,
Inconsistent with transubstantiation	,,
Bellarmine's explanation	197
Massuet	,,
Pfaff	,,
Not two substances, but one	,,
Athenagoras, 'unbloody sacrifice'	198
Tertullian, Sacrament a figure	199
All who attend the sacrifice must communicate	200
Elements when reserved not adored	,,
Origen, Type of the Shew-bread	,,
Wicked do not receive Christ	201
S. Cyprian	,,
Eucharistic oblation not identical with that of the Cross	202
Not for remission of sins to the dead	203
Christ's Body withdrawn from the unworthy	204
Private masses unknown	,,
Mixed chalice, new allegory	205
Type of Melchisedek	206
The Supper perpetuated in the Eucharist	207
Eusebius of Cæsarea	208
Oblation effective through prayer	,,
Not the identical Body, but the symbol and remembrance	209
Cyril of Jerusalem	,,
Confirms the Greek Liturgies	,,
Benefit to departed souls ascribed to the prayers, not the Sacrifice	210
The Oblation not Christ	211

CONTENTS.

	Page
Manner of receiving in both kinds	211
No Corporal or Co-existent Presence	212
S. Ambrose	,,
Sacramental Body spiritual not natural	,,
The Shadow, the Image, and the Truth	,,
S. Augustine	213
Sign and representation of the True Sacrifice	,,
Sacrament of remembrance	,,
Christ corporally absent	,,
His Body only in one place	,,
African Liturgy agreed with the Greek	214
Species means substance, not 'form'	,,
The true bread is spiritual	,,
S. Chrysostom	215
The Sacrifice a memorial	,,
Exhibits the Dead Body, not the Glorified	,,
Summary	216
Fathers not infallible	,,
Growth of error in the decay of letters	,,
Abuse of Church authority	217
Aim of the Church of England at the Reformation	,,
Her authority over her members	,,

SECTION X.—THE ANGLICAN LITURGY.

Two great landmarks	218
Three modes of worship	,,
Anglican more Catholic than the Roman	219
Eucharist the central rite	220
No withdrawal in present Book	221
Common difficulty from decay of piety	222
Anglican solution	223
No forsaking of antiquity	224
Liberty and authority of the Church	225
Need of a National Liturgy	,,
Standard of doctrine	226
Exclusion of private judgment	,,

CONTENTS.

	Page
First Book of Edward VI. not different in doctrine from the Second	227
Injurious reflections	229
Both Books Parliamentary: Church little consulted	230
Their brief authority	231
Present Liturgy the voice of the Church	,,
Perversity of recurring to Book of 1549	,,
Incompleteness of that Office	232
Elevation and reservation prohibited	,,
Communion enjoined	,,
Entire abrogation of the Mass	222
Consecration Prayer	233
Corrections in later revisions	236
Omission of prayer for the Spirit	,,
Not in accordance with Eastern Liturgies	237
Elevation still prohibited	238
Portions removed to the Post Communion	,,
Little objected to at the time	,,
Scottish Liturgy of 1637	239
No oblation of the Gifts in 1549	240
Not proper after Consecration	241
Non-jurors' New Communion Office	242
Abandons the Western doctrine of Consecration	243
Scottish Liturgy of 1765	244
American Liturgy	245
Based on Oriental not Western view of Consecration	246
Serious reflection	247
True oblation in present Liturgy	248
Post Communion Sacrifice	249
Advantage of present arrangement	250
Best represents the original Institution	,,
Excludes corruptions	,,
Mixed chalice ancient but not essential	251
No uniform tradition of its significance	252
Question of its prohibition	253
Prayers for the departed lawful but not necessary	254
Object and abuse	255
All Liturgical forms in the discretion of the living Church	256

	Page
English Liturgy as Catholic as any, and more Scriptural	256
Danger of altering received uses	257
Interpretation belongs to the Bishop	258
Private action uncatholic and sinful	260
Duty of the Bishop	"
Spurious demand for liberty	"
Without parallel in Catholic Church	262
Italian ceremonial inferior to our own	263
Real truth and beauty	264
NOTE ON VESTMENTS	266

ERRATA.

Page 44, line 11, for 'on' read 'only.'

Page 179. The extract from Chrysostom here borrowed from Pfaff is in Hom. de Prod. Jud. i. s. 6. The translation was printed off before I had found the original. The second sentence should run thus: 'The priest (at the Eucharist) stands executing the form ($\sigma\chi\tilde{\eta}\mu\alpha$ $\pi\lambda\eta\rho\tilde{\omega}\nu$) and pronouncing the words, "This is My Body," but the grace and power,' &c.

SACRIFICE AND PARTICIPATION

OF

THE HOLY EUCHARIST.

I.—THE EUCHARISTIC SACRIFICE.

THE HOLY EUCHARIST is universally acknowledged to be not only the principal means of grace, but the highest act of worship, in the Christian Church. It is the divinely ordained 'liturgy' of the spiritual Israel;—the service which, like that of the altar at Jerusalem, unites the many members, scattered in place, to present them before God as one body in Christ.[1] Comprehending the prayers and praises and thanksgivings of the Church below, it offers them to God in union with the Sacrifice of His dear Son upon the cross, of which it is the appointed Remembrance, till He come to translate us to the Church above.[2]

When it is disputed whether this service be

---
[1] 1 Cor. x. 17.   [2] 1 Cor. xi. 26.

itself a 'sacrifice,' the question turns wholly upon the meaning of the word. It arises, in fact, out of the erroneous conception of sacrifice in the modern Church of Rome. Nothing is more certain than that in the Catholic Church, before the division of East and West, the Holy Eucharist was universally regarded as a sacrifice. This is its common appellation in the Liturgies and Canons; and no one point of doctrine or discipline is more firmly established by the consent of the Fathers. Primarily and principally the term was used of the whole service as 'a sacrifice of praise and thanksgiving;'—a phrase still retained in our own Liturgy. It was the same under the Old Testament, where the 'sacrifice,' properly speaking, meant the whole act of worship, including the spiritual devotion of the worshipper, and not only the material symbol by which it was presented.[1] But as under the Law the material offerings were called in a secondary sense 'sacrifices,' as expressing the true inward sacrifice of the man, so the Church applied the same word to the visible elements in the Eucharistic Sacrifice.

The bread and wine were solemnly 'offered,' before they were partaken of; this liturgical act was termed the 'Oblation;' and the things offered were called 'oblations,' 'gifts,' and 'sacrifices.' The true intent and meaning of these expressions

[1] 'Illud quod ab omnibus appellatur sacrificium, signum est veri sacrificii,' (sc. misericordiæ, &c.)—*S. August. De Civ. Dei.* x. 5.

is a main article in our long controversy with Rome; to reject them altogether would be to cut away from under our feet the whole body of evidence on which we appeal to the primitive Church.

To the objection that the Eucharist is not called a sacrifice in the New Testament, the answer is obvious, that neither is it there called a *sacrament*. If it be rejoined that the qualities of a sacrament are affirmed of it, so also are the qualities of a sacrifice. The two words, in fact, come from the same original, and are distinguished only in the use. A sacrifice is an offering from man to God; a sacrament is a gift from God to man; and communion means a partaking of the same thing by God and man.

In the New Testament the bread and wine are declared to be the Body broken and the Blood shed, *i. e.* the Flesh of Christ offered in sacrifice on the cross. The participation of them is a participation of that Sacrifice; and the whole celebration is a 'showing forth of the Lord's Death.' Now these are the qualities of a sacrifice under the Old Testament. The Levitical offerings were all designed to represent, more or less directly, the one True Sacrifice of the Lamb of God, and minister participation in its benefits. To whatever extent these purposes are fulfilled in the Eucharist—and it is certain that they are more truly and beneficially realized in the Commemoration than in the Type—to the same extent the Eucharist must be a sacrifice.

The word, in short, is a scriptural one; and by Scripture, not by modern prejudice, its use and meaning must be determined. It is nowhere affirmed in the New Testament (as some appear to suppose) that all material sacrifice is abolished under the Gospel. On the contrary, gifts bestowed in charity are declared to be 'sacrifices with which God is well pleased;' and we offer them as such on the Holy Table at every Communion. Again, words of thanksgiving, —the fruit (or, as the prophet called it, the *calves*) of our lips—are a sacrifice of praise.[1] What the apostle teaches is, that 'there remaineth no more sacrifice *for sin.*' But the Sin-offering was only one kind of sacrifice under the law, and one which admitted of no participation either by priests or people. The body was burned without the camp, and the blood was poured away into the cavities under the altar. Hence it is a great point of superiority in the Gospel dispensation, that 'we have an altar whereof they have no right to eat who serve the Tabernacle.'[2] Communion in the Sin-offering, always inexorably denied to the Jew, is the prerogative of the Christian in the Holy Eucharist.

Again, the daily sacrifice of the law—the Holocaust, or whole burnt-offering, which was renewed morning and evening, and continually burning on the altar formed the root and ground of acceptance to all other services—disappeared in the

---

[1] Heb. xiii. 15; Hosea, xiv. 2.   [2] Heb. xiii. 10.

offering of the true Lamb, and finds no counterpart in the evangelical liturgy. But neither of this sacrifice did the law afford direct participation, seeing it was all consumed in the sacred fire.

The sacrifices by which the Israelites 'partook of the altar' were of a third kind, and the most numerous of all. These were the *Peace-offerings*, or as the Septuagint renders it, 'sacrifices of salvation.' Their peculiar feature was the oblation of a choice morsel to God, which was consumed on the altar along with the Holocaust, while the remnant was feasted upon by the priests and people. The choice morsel was called the 'memorial,' or 'remembrance' of the sacrifice; and its office was two-fold;—first, to represent the sacrifice before God; and secondly, to be a means of communion between the Holocaust and the worshippers. Mingling with the Burnt-offering in the fire, and going up in the sweet savour to God, it was held to acquire the value of that sacrifice, and communicate it to the remnant which was eaten by the worshippers. Hence they were said to 'partake of the altar,' though no part of the offering actually on the altar was ever given back, but all was consumed in the fire.

These Peace-offerings, then, had no virtue in themselves: they derived all their value from the Holocaust, by means of the Memorial, and were generally preceded by a Sin-offering. To this class the Passover belonged; and so far from abolishing this kind of sacrifice, the Eucharist was given to make it 'new in the kingdom of God.'[1] Hence the apostle, referring to this rite, says, 'Christ our Passover is sacrificed for us; therefore let us keep the Feast.'[2]

Further, it is to be observed that the 'memorial,' which distinguished this class of sacrifice, is the very name assigned by our Lord Himself to the Holy Eucharist: 'Do this in remembrance of Me,' or more literally, 'for My remembrance,' (or memorial,) εἰς τὴν ἐμὴν ἀνάμνησιν. These words we shall return to hereafter. Meantime, we note that this was the precise character of the Eucharistic Sacrifice in the Primitive Church. The Fathers uniformly represent the Sacrifice of the cross as the one true meritorious Sin-offering, or satisfaction for the sins of the world: and the Eucharist as a commemorative, representative rite to apply its virtue.

'What men call sacrifice,' says Augustine, in the general proposition already referred to, 'is the outward sign of the sacrifice.' And again, 'The Memorial of a thing, on account of its resemblance to that of which it is the memorial, receives the same name; just as we say, tomorrow, or next day, is the Passion of Christ, when in fact He suffered only once, many years ago; and on the Lord's Day we say, Christ arose to-day: the day is said to be what really it is not, on account of the similitude.'[3]

[1] Matt. xxvi. 29.   [2] 1 Cor. v. 7, 8.
[3] Ep. ad Bonifac.

So Chrysostom: 'We offer not another sacrifice, but the same; or rather, we celebrate the Memorial of the Sacrifice.'[1]

And after him Theophylact: 'Him we offer always; or rather, we make the Memorial of that offering.'[2]

Similar too was the original doctrine of the mediæval schools. Peter Lombard says: 'That which is offered and consecrated by the priest is called a sacrifice and oblation, because it is the memory and representation of the True Sacrifice and holy immolation, made on the altar of the cross.'[3]

Even Thomas Aquinas writes: 'The celebration of this sacrament is aptly called the immolation of Christ, both because it is a sort of an image of His Passion, and because by the sacrament we are made partakers of the fruits of the Passion.'[4]

Now a Memorial rite is obviously not the identical sacrifice, nor necessarily the same kind of sacrifice, with that which it commemorates: yet it may be a true and proper sacrifice of its own kind, as the Peace-offerings under the Law were sacrifices, though very different from the Sin-offering and the Holocaust.

Protestant controversialists spend their pains to little purpose in insisting that a commemorative

---

[1] 'Οὐκ ἄλλην θυσίαν, ἀλλὰ τὴν αὐτὴν ἀεὶ ποιοῦμεν, μᾶλλον δὲ ἀνάμνησιν ἐργαζόμεθα θυσίας.—Chrys. in Heb. x. Hom. xvii.

[2] Τὸν γὰρ αὐτὸν ἀεὶ προσφέρομεν, μᾶλλον δὲ ἀνάμνησιν τῆς προσφορᾶς ἐκείνης ποιοῦμεν.

[3] Lombard, iv. Dist. 12.   [4] Sum. iii. qu. 83. art. 1.

celebration is not a sacrifice, or not a sacrifice 'properly so called.' They mean that it is not a *sin-offering*, efficacious by its own merit, but only a means of communicating the Sacrifice of the cross. This is unquestionably true, and may be easily proved from the Fathers. Still the Peace-offerings were sacrifices, though deriving all their value from the Holocaust; and the early Church uniformly gave the same appellation to the commemorative sacrament, as standing in a similar relation to the Lamb of God which taketh away the sins of the world.

It is a mistake to suppose that 'sacrifice' implies an animal victim, and 'offering' an inanimate one. No such distinction is known to Scripture or antiquity. The apostle uses sacrifice ($\theta\upsilon\sigma\iota\alpha$) of alms and thanksgiving, and offering ($\pi\rho o\sigma\phi o\rho\grave{a}$) of the Sacrifice of Christ.[1] The Greek Fathers also apply both words indiscriminately to the Holy Eucharist. The true distinction is, that 'offering' means simply a gift, whether to God or man, while 'sacrifice' is confined to holy things. Thus in the Old Testament *mincha*, which means a gift, and is used even of presents to men, is also the general name for sacrifice, whether animate or inanimate. Another word, *zebach*, is indeed restrained to animal victims; and when this word occurs (as in Psalm xl. 6.) in contrast with *mincha*, the former is translated 'sacrifice,' and the other 'offering.' But in general *mincha* is used of both. It is the

[1] Heb. x. 10, 14, 18.

word employed of the sacrifices both of Cain and Abel.¹ Both are called sacrifices (θυσίαι) by the apostle;² while the Septuagint uses 'sacrifice' of the unbloody offering of Cain, and designates Abel's lamb by the common word (δῶρα) 'gifts.'

Again, *mincha* is used of animal sacrifices in 1 Sam. ii. 17; xxvi. 19; and Mal. i. 13; and of the oblation of fine flour in Lev. ii. 2; though rendered 'offering' in our version, the Septuagint has in all these places (θυσία) 'sacrifice.' That the offering of fine flour was a sacrifice is clear, not only from the 'memorial' being burned on the altar, but from the remainder, which was eaten by the priests in the holy place, being designated 'a thing most holy of the offerings (θυσίαι) of the Lord made by fire.'³

The same character is ascribed to the shewbread, (which some of the Fathers held to be a type of the Eucharist,) though no part of it was consumed by fire.⁴ Indeed, the greater part of the Jewish sacrifices were unbloody, and that neither altar nor fire were essential, is shown in the two greatest examples, the 'sacrifice of the Lord's Passover,'⁵ and the grand Sacrifice of the cross; neither of which were either offered on an altar, or consumed by fire.⁶

¹ Gen. iv. 3-5.   ² Heb. x. 4.   ³ Lev. ii. 3.
⁴ Lev. xxiv. 9.   ⁵ Exod. xii. 27.
⁶ These examples are equally conclusive against the objection made to the Catholic usage of calling the Lord's Table the

In the scriptural meaning of the term, then, a sacrifice is anything, animate or inanimate, which is offered to God in worship, and disposed of according to His direction. The apostle applies the name to almsgiving, to prayers and thanksgivings, and to the self-dedication of the worshipper as 'a living sacrifice to God.' These were always included in the true use of Jewish sacrifice: consequently, they cannot be taken to imply, either that no material offerings are to be made under the Gospel, or that such offerings are not to be considered sacrifices. That external sacrifice is worthless, in comparison with moral and spiritual devotion, is the doctrine of the Old Testament no less than the New. In fact, it is from the Psalms and the Prophets that our Lord and His apostles urge the superiority of spiritual worship. This is no new commandment peculiar

---

Altar. It is a verbal objection, founded on a mistake of the meaning and use of the word. It is not true, that in Holy Scripture *altar* is simply the correlative of *sacrifice*. The Passover is called the Lord's sacrifice in Egypt, (Exod. xii.) where we read of no altar. The Cross is never called an altar, nor the table of shew-bread, though the bread was a sacrifice. On the other hand, the incense is never called a sacrifice, though the table on which it was burnt was the holiest of altars.

Moses built an altar in remembrance of perpetual war with Amalek; (Exod. xvii. 15, 16.) Gideon, of peace with God; and the tribes beyond Jordan, of their right in the national sacrifice at Jerusalem. On none of these was any sacrifice actually offered. In Malachi, i. 12, and 1 Cor. x. 18, 21, altar is clearly equivalent to the Lord's Table, as it is in the Liturgies and Fathers of the Christian Church.

to the Gospel, but the only acceptable worship from the beginning; yet the assertion of this truth by the prophets was not meant to abolish the sacrifices of the Law; nor do similar exhortations abolish external acts of worship under the Gospel. Our Lord Himself ordained the use of material elements in Baptism and the Holy Eucharist; if these can be made channels of grace to man without injury to spiritual religion, it does not appear why they may not be also the visible signs of a holy and spiritual Sacrifice.

To deny a *sin-offering (zebach)* is not to exclude a *mincha*, or Eucharistic Sacrifice. But to say there is no sacrifice at all in the Eucharist, is to make a gratuitous and dangerous concession to the very error we mean to oppose. For if it be granted that no rite is properly called a sacrifice but a sin-offering, the Romanist will triumphantly produce the unanimous testimony of the early Church—not without support from Scripture itself—that the Eucharist is a sacrifice, and so conclude for the Mass.

The Fathers were so far from thinking there was no external sacrifice under the Gospel, that they almost unanimously refer Malachi's prophecy[1] of a pure offering (*mincha*, θυσία,) to the Holy Eucharist; and Justin Martyr had no doubt that the leper's[2] *mincha* was a type of it. These interpretations may be right, or they may be wrong; but they were at least consistent with

[1] Mal. i. 11.   [2] Lev. xiv. 10, 21.

the Eucharistic doctrine of the age immediately succeeding the apostles; when the language of the New Testament was the Christian vernacular, and the usages of sacrifice, both Jewish and Gentile, were familiar as household words. Surely it is idle to dispute with these writers the meaning of their own language.

The Church of England solemnly appeals to that early age in vindication of her Reformation, and of her claim to be a genuine branch of the Catholic Church. For private persons to put their own construction on antiquity, and then affirm that such is the mind of our Church, in defiance of the contrary utterance, or the not less significant silence, of her actual formularies, is a grievous insult to her authority. But it is hardly less disrespectful to disallow the appeal to antiquity altogether.

That the object of the Reformation was to convert the Sacrament 'from a sacrifice to a communion,' is a Lutheran, not an Anglican conception. Both characters are inalienable from the Eucharist; when the Church of Rome had perverted the one and mutilated the other, the aim of our Church was to restore them to their true relations. In Scripture and antiquity the Sacrifice and the Participation are inseparable. The apostle says that we '.show the Lord's death' —which is the office of the Sacrifice—'when we eat this bread and drink this cup.'[1] S. Augustine

---

[1] 1 Cor. xi. 26.

expressly observes that 'to eat bread is the sacrifice of Christians;'[1] and Bishop Andrewes, pointing out that the sacrifice is Eucharistic, remarks, 'Of that sacrifice it was ever the law that he who offers it should partake of it.' 'He partakes,' he continues, 'by eating and drinking, as the Lord commanded: for participation in the prayers only is a novel and illicit sort of participation.'[2]

What our Church sought, then, was to restore the Sacrifice and the Participation to their original unity. What Christ has joined together, let not man put asunder. The Sacrifice is not denied, but vindicated, by insisting on Communion. For it is in eating and drinking, that we show forth the Lord's death; and without eating and drinking there is no sacrifice. 'The Sacrament of the Lord's Supper was ordained (we say) for the continual remembrance of the Sacrifice of the death of Christ, and of the benefits which we receive thereby.' In the first aspect it is a Memorial Sacrifice, in the second a Real Participation, of the Body and Blood of Christ.

To distinguish the full force of this teaching, in the primitive Church and our own, it is necessary to consider in detail the erroneous constructions of the Church of Rome and the manner in which they were dealt with at the Reformation.

[1] *Civ. Dei.* Ideo hic dixit manducare panem, quod est in N. T. sacrificium Christianorum.

[2] Adv. Bell.

II.—THE SACRIFICE OF THE MASS.

THE Decree of the Council of Trent concerning the Sacrifice of the Mass is as follows.

1. That on account of the imperfection of the Levitical Priesthood, it was necessary to establish another Priest after the order of Melchisedek, that is to say Jesus Christ; Who though He offered Himself but once on the cross, nevertheless, in order to leave His Church a visible Sacrifice, *representative of that of the cross, and applicatory of its virtue*, did in quality of Priest after the order of Melchisedek, offer to God His Father His Body and His Blood under the forms of bread and wine, and gave it to His apostles, commanding them and their successors to offer it. And this was that pure offering foretold by Malachi, which S. Paul calls the Table of the Lord, and which was prefigured in divers sacrifices under the law of nature and of Moses.

2. That since Jesus Christ, who was immolated after a bloody manner on the cross, is the same who is sacrificed after an unbloody manner in the Mass, this sacrifice is propitiatory;[1] and God being appeased by this offering, accords us the gift of repentance, and remits all our sins; because it is the same Victim which is offered, and He who offered Himself on the cross is the same who still offers Himself by the hands of His priests. So that the sacrifice of the Mass is so far from derogating from the Oblation of the cross, that on the contrary it is by this that the fruits of the other are applied to us. The Mass may be offered not only for the sins, pains, and needs of the faithful living, but

---

[1] This word is allowed to be ambiguous. If it mean that the propitiation of the cross is *applied* in the Eucharist to all faithful communicants, no one would deny it. Practically, however, the Roman teaching imputes a power of *effecting* propitiation to the Sacrifice of the Mass; and this gives it its pecuniary value, as an offering for departed souls.

also for the benefit of the dead who are not yet wholly purified.

6. That the Council, far from condemning as unlawful private Masses in which the priest alone communicates, approves them, and declares they ought to be regarded as public Masses, both because the people present communicate spiritually, and because they are celebrated by a public minister, and offered for all the faithful.

To the first article of this Decree the objections may be reduced to a question of words rather than things. The 'Body and Blood' of Christ mean in Scripture, and all Catholic antiquity, the crucified Body and outshed Blood of the Sacrifice of the Cross; and it is admitted by Roman Catholic divines that ' in this condition they are not really contained in the sacrament but represented by it.'[1] Consequently, notwithstanding the expression, 'under the forms of bread and wine,' the sacrifice according to this article is only ' representative of the Sacrifice of the Cross, and applicatory of its virtue;'—an application undoubtedly made to the faithful in partaking of the Communion.

The language of the second article, though open to more exception, might also (with the

---

[1] 'The sacrament is not really the Body of Christ constituted in the actual state of one slain, dead, and inanimate; neither in that respect does it contain it, but so far represents it only.' —*Card. Perron, de loc. Aug.* iii. (*Patrick's Full View*, 213.)

'It is evident that the real separation of the Flesh and Blood of Christ in the sacrament is represented only; but in the death of Christ it was actual, and according to the thing itself. He discourses of the Flesh and Blood which were parted in His death, *as they are to be embraced by the mind, being the meat and drink of the soul.*'—*Card. Cajetan. In Johann.* vi. 53.

omission of the last sentence) be reconciled with primitive and Catholic doctrine; understanding first, that the Sacrifice really offered on the cross is mystically commemorated in the Mass, and that this is the meaning of offering the same victim after an unbloody manner; and secondly, that it is the Real Sacrifice, not the commemorative one, which 'appeases God' and procures remission of sins.

The last sentence of this article, and the whole of the sixth, are mere inferences, unsupported by Scripture or Catholic antiquity.

Setting these inferences aside, it will be found that it is not so much the Decree of the Mass,—and still less (as we shall find hereafter) the Canon of the Mass,—as the tenet of Transubstantiation, which determines the character of the sacrifice in the Church of Rome. The Council of Trent further lays down

'That by the consecration of the bread and wine there is made a conversion of these two substances into the substance of the Body and Blood of Jesus Christ, which conversion the Church justly and properly calls Transubstantiation.'[1]

And again,

'That the Body of Christ is under the species of bread, and His Blood under the species of wine, by virtue of the consecration; but that by concomitancy the one and the other are under each of the species, and every part of them, equally as under the two together.'[2]

---

[1] Conc. Trid. Sep. xiii. Art. 4.   [2] Ibid. Art. 3.

These limitations define the general statement, that 'after consecration Jesus Christ is truly, really, and substantially, contained under the appearances of things sensible.'[1] This presence is declared indeed to be after a sacramental manner, no way impugning His being in Heaven after a natural manner; still an anathema is pronounced against all who shall deny that 'the Eucharist contains truly, really, and substantially, the Body and Blood with the Soul and Divinity of Jesus Christ—that is to say, whole Christ;'—or who shall assert 'that He is present in it only in symbol, figure, and virtue.'[2]

Now in the Roman Mass the oblation is held to consist of the consecrated elements, thus converted from the symbols of Christ's crucified Body and Blood, into the reality of His living Person. This conception destroys the original character of the sacrifice as 'representative of the cross and applicatory of its virtue,' and introduces a totally different one in its place. The second article affirms the sacrifice of the Mass to be the same with that of the cross. The same Victim, *i.e.* Jesus Christ Himself, is offered, only after another manner; an expression which is no longer allowed to mean, that then He was offered in reality, and now by representation and figure. It is insisted —at whatever hazard to reason and consistency— that the cross and its commemoration are *one and the same Sacrifice*. The oblation which represents

[1] Ibid. Art. 1.   [2] Ibid. Can. i.

Christ crucified, is really and substantially the living Person of Christ glorified. This interpretation plunges everything into contradiction.

It is a contradiction in terms to say that a sacrifice, continually repeated in thousands of places, is the same sacrifice with one of which the distinguishing characteristic is that it was offered once for all upon the cross;—that an unbloody sacrifice is the same with a bloody one;—and a representative one the same with that which it represents and applies. If it were true that both Victim and Offerer were the same, yet the repetition of the *act* would constitute another sacrifice, and a *difference* in the action, or manner of offering, makes a different sacrifice. Bellarmine rightly maintains that 'it is not the thing but the offering of the thing which is properly the sacrifice; for sacrifice is an action, not a thing.'[1] It is a further contradiction in terms to call a sacrifice unbloody, in which one of the things offered is the actual Blood of Christ; for blood cannot be offered after an unbloody manner, unless it be in figure and by representation.

These are only a few of the contradictions which result from identifying the Body and Blood of Christ crucified with the living Person of Christ glorified. It is admitted that the sacra-

[1] Nam non res illa, sed rei illius oblatio, proprie est sacrificium: sacrificium enim est actio, non res permanens.—*De Miss.* ii. 4. Yet this distinction is not always maintained in Scripture or the Fathers, where the thing offered bears the name of sacrifice, no less than the action of offering it.

ment represents the Sacrifice of Christ's Death. It exhibits His Body and Blood sundered in two elements, as in the hour when the one hung lifeless on the cross, and the other lay poured upon the ground below. Now, if it were true that these—whether by transubstantiation or otherwise—could be corporally and substantially contained in or under the sacrament, yet they are not 'whole Christ.' The Soul was certainly then absent from the Body, in Paradise. And though we believe the Divinity of the Word to have remained united to each by hypostatic union, even when the vital union was dissolved, yet there is no hypostatic union with bread and wine. Hence, neither can the Divinity of Christ be contained in the sacrament. Transubstantiation itself could result in nothing but a dead Christ, and that apart from the Living Word: which savours in truth of Nestorianism. But the Lord is risen: His Body and Blood are no longer in a state of death in fact, and can only be so in the sacrament by remembrance and representation.

True it is, that in partaking of them we partake of His life. The living Manhood of Jesus Christ in heaven is the channel of all grace and life to men; and the object and result of the Holy Eucharist is to incorporate us more and more into Him, who is the First-fruits from the dead. But means are not identical with the end. The means are Christ Crucified, the end is Christ Glorified.

The sacrament exhibits the means by way of representation and symbol; for this it is indispensable to retain bread and wine; *it is no sacrament without them.* In *receiving* these, we receive indeed the Body and Blood, Soul and Divinity, of our ascended Lord, in spirit and in faith; but it is a clumsy contradiction to put the unseen reality in the place of the visible element;— to make the same object, at the same instant, bread and not bread—the symbol of Christ slain, and the reality of Christ risen.

The novelty of this doctrine is shown by its involving the suppression of the Cup in the administration of the Communion. If Christ be received 'whole' under the bread, the cup is not only superfluous, but its ministration implies a separation of the Body and Blood, which is inconsistent with the unity of Christ's Living Manhood. Hence the doctrine of *concomitancy,* which retaining the cup in the consecration excludes it from communion, is a necessary consequence of the corporal Presence. And as the cup was undoubtedly administered in all churches for a thousand years after Christ, it follows that 'whole Christ' was not then believed to be in or under the bread.

The root of all this error seems to lie in confounding the phrase 'Body and Blood,' as relating to our Lord's death, with the word 'Body,' as denoting His glorified Manhood in Heaven. To offer the memorials of the first is the Eucharistic

Sacrifice of antiquity. Transubstantiation, in seeking to present the other, would not only require Christ to die again, but make His *Divinity* part of the Sacrifice;—a heresy confounding the whole doctrine of the atonement. Bishop Andrewes remarks that 'if a host could be turned into Him now glorified as He is, *it would not serve*, Christ offered is it; thither must we look —to the serpent lift up—even *ad cadaver*.'[1] Because it is the atonement made by His Death which enables us to partake of His Life.

But to proceed. If the Eucharistic sacrifice were instituted by our Blessed Lord in His capacity of Priest after the order of Melchisedek, the material oblation again must be bread and wine, since nothing else is attributed to Melchisedek. That this personage offered 'the Body and Blood of Christ under the forms of bread and wine,' can be true in no other sense than that he offered bread and wine, as types of Christ's future Sacrifice of Himself. If this were the fact, the Eucharist might be called an 'antitype' of Melchisedek's sacrifice, because it is a commemoration *in the same material substances* of that which the other prefigured. And this is the general doctrine of the later Fathers.

In point of fact, however, there is no mention in Scripture of any *sacrifice* by Melchisedek. The bread and wine which he brought forth were

[1] Serm. vii. On Resurrection.

for the refreshment of Abram and his followers; and the only priestly act recorded is his blessing the father of the faithful. It is true that some of the Fathers *applied* this incident—first to the participation, and afterwards to the oblation—of the Eucharist. In so doing they *inferred* Melchisedek's oblation from their own, since of the historical fact they could know no more than we do. That there was no apostolic tradition on the point is evident from the silence of the author of the epistle to the Hebrews. When expressly treating on the Melchisedekian priesthood, he has no allusion whatever to the Eucharist, but represents our Lord's priesthood, after this order, as commencing at the ascension, and having its sphere exclusively in Heaven.[1]

S. Jerome would account for the omission by the reserve which it was usual to employ, when speaking of the sacraments to the uninitiated; for he maintains that the Hebrews addressed were Jews and not Christians.[2] The apostle, however, not only calls them 'holy brethren, partakers of the heavenly calling,' but directs them to 'Jesus the Apostle and High Priest of their profession;' moreover, he distinctly alludes to the Christian altar, with other much deeper mysteries in relation to Melchisedek, than this supposed oblation of bread and wine.

Further, if such sacrifices existed in the patriarchal age, they would constitute no distinction

[1] Heb. viii. 4.   [2] Ad Evagr. iii. 27.

from the priesthood of Aaron, since fine flour and wine were common among the oblations of the law. Again, our Lord's priesthood in Heaven is exercised by appearing within the veil, with the Blood shed upon the Cross; this is a bloody, not an unbloody sacrifice. The superiority of the order of Melchisedek does not consist in the absence of blood, but as the apostle expressly states, in the eternity and singularity of the Priest, who is Himself the entire order.

It is idle to argue from what is *not* stated in Scripture against what *is*. The Fathers, if they had been unanimous, could not make a type out of a rite neither recorded in the Old Testament, nor expounded in the New. But the Fathers are not unanimous. S. Clement of Rome, Ignatius, and Polycarp, have no mention of this type. It is not found among the numerous similitudes of Barnabas and Hermas. Irenæus is ignorant of it; and Justin Martyr, who ransacked the Old Testament for types, and found the Eucharist in the law and in the prophets, never lighted upon it in the more obvious symbols of Melchisedek.

The first to apply the incident to the Eucharist was Clement of Alexandria, and he limits the type to the communion, without reference to any sacrifice.[1] Tertullian, who speaks of Mel-

---

[1] 'Melchisedek, King of Salem, priest of the Most High God, who gave bread and wine *as hallowed food* in type of the Eucharist.'—*Strom.* iv.

chisedek's sacrifice,¹ does not expound it of
the Eucharist. Origen, the most learned Hebraist
of all, supposed Melchisedek to be an angel, and
knows nothing of his sacrifice. S. Cyprian is the
first to adduce it as a type of the Eucharistic
sacrifice. After him it was held by Eusebius,
Athanasius, and Jerome, and so passed into a
common opinion. It was never inserted, however,
in the Liturgies or decrees of faith till the Council
of Trent, and there it was long stoutly denied.²
Jeremy Taylor admits it, but Bishop Andrewes
confidently affirms of Melchisedek, 'sacrificium
nullum obtulit.'

Be the fact, however, as it may, the Fathers
who adduced this type undoubtedly supposed the
oblation, which our Lord made in the Eucharist,
to be bread and wine, as symbols of His Body
and Blood. Cyprian expressly says that 'He
offered the same thing which Melchisedek had
offered, that is bread and wine—to wit, His Body
and Blood.'³ He calls Melchisedek's oblation 'an
image of Christ's Sacrifice constituted in Bread
and Wine,' and says, 'the Lord fulfilled the type
when He offered the bread and the cup.' Augustine testifies the same of the Latin Church:
'He is our Priest for ever after the order of
Melchisedek, who offered Himself a holocaust for

¹ Adv. Jud.
² Fra Paolo mentions an *anthem* which asserted it; but we
have still too much experience how often such compositions
contradict the doctrine of the Church.
³ Ep. lxii. (Oxford Ed. lxiii.) ad Cæc.

our sins, and directed the similitude of His Sacrifice to be celebrated in memory of His Passion; so that we see that which Melchisedek offered to God now offered in the Church of Christ throughout the whole world.'[1]

There is yet a further contradiction involved in the words 'under the forms of bread and wine,' implying the tenet of Transubstantiation. The oblation which our Lord made in the Eucharist was performed by taking bread and wine, giving thanks, and blessing them; and all this preceded the utterance of the words, 'This is My Body,' to which the change of substance is attributed. What our Lord took, and gave thanks over, and blessed, is confessed to have been bread and wine; but these acts of His constituted the oblation;—the words of Institution belong to the distribution which followed. Unless, therefore, we are prepared to receive the gratuitous *dictum* of Bellarmine, that these words were spoken *twice*—another specimen of the argument from what is not in Scripture against what is—it is certain that what Christ offered was bread and wine, as symbols of His Body and Blood then self-devoted to the Cross.

These conflicting views render it difficult for Roman Catholic divines to define in what the sacrifice really consists. The Tridentine Decree seems to place it in the oblation of the host. Thomas Aquinas expressly teaches that 'the

[1] Lib. de divers. quæst. 88.

sacrifice is finished before the fraction of the host, and the receiving properly belongs to the sacrament, but the oblation to the sacrifice.'[1]

This would make the oblation precede the consecration, and such was the uniform order of the ancient Liturgies. Hence the things offered must be bread and wine, not Christ or His Body and Blood. To escape this consequence the Roman Missal removes the breaking of the bread from the proper place—when our Lord's breaking is recited—and places it *after* the consecration, so sustaining the pretence of sacrificing Christ Himself.

The Bishop of Meaux, with Suarez and Vasquez, found it safer to place the sacrifice in the consecration itself. Bellarmine and Melchior Canus rightly include *manducation* also, without which it is certain that no sacrifice of peace-offerings was ever complete. All these logically exclude non-communicants from any part in the sacrifice; but this, though in strict accordance with the primitive Church, is in opposition to the Tridentine Decree.

The Council had a narrow escape from the further contradiction of declaring that Christ commanded His apostles to offer what He never offered Himself. The clause 'that He offered

---

[1] 'Docuisse Thomam sacrificium ante fractionem hostiæ esse peractum, sumptionemque spectare proprie ad sacramentum, oblationem vero ad sacrificium.'—*Can. Loc. Theol.* xii. 883. *Gibson's Preser. against Popery*, ii. 79.

His Body and Blood under the forms of bread and wine,' was warmly opposed, though all were ready to decree that He commanded His apostles to do so. During several congregations the theologians were almost equally divided on this question, and the opposition was so strong, that the Cardinal Legate Seripand at one time agreed to omit the assertion.

One of the weightiest arguments was that of a Portuguese divine, who said it could not be doubted that the Mass was a sacrifice, since all the Greek and Latin Fathers called it so; but that Christ offered Himself in the supper was not proved by the example of Melchisedek, or by the Paschal Lamb which was rather a type of the Sacrifice of the cross. To this also the words of Institution plainly referred. He urged that Christ's Sacrifice in the supper was a point which theologians were not agreed upon, and it was equally Catholic to assert or deny it. Hence he desired its omission from the decree, and the sacrifice to be rested on apostolical tradition.[1] The archbishop of Grenada was earnest to the same effect, and the bishop of Veglia insisted that to admit a propitiatory sacrifice in the last supper was to deny the ransom of the cross, since it was absurd to say that the Supper and the Cross were the same sacrifice.[2] Yet these very divines agreed that the Mass was the same with the Cross, and that Christ gave it to His apostles as a propitiatory sacrifice!

[1] Fra P. ii. 246.   [2] Ibid. 260.

It was this predetermined resolution, in fact, that occasioned all the confusion. The sacrifice of the Mass was at all hazards to be held propitiatory, in the sense of a satisfaction for sin— the then popular conception of a sacrifice. It was impossible to deny this character to the Sacrifice of the cross, and equally so to admit that Christ offered Himself *twice*. Neither could it be said that the Supper and the Crucifixion were one and the same transaction. Hence the proposal to assert *upon tradition* that our Lord commanded His apostles to do what He never did Himself, though the essence of the rite is confessed to be in perpetuating His Institution. Hence, too, the unanimous declaration that the Sacrifice of the Mass is the same with that of the Cross, though it is beyond all question the same with the Supper, which many held to be quite a different thing!

These intolerable contradictions are not imputable to the doctrine of S. Cyprian, that Christ offered bread and wine in the supper as symbols of His Body and Blood then freely surrendered for the Sacrifice, and left the same to be the communion of His Body and Blood when the Sacrifice should have been actually consummated on the cross. But this true and ancient doctrine would deprive the Mass of the peculiar value, which it was determined to maintain, as a sin-offering for the quick and the dead. It would have overthrown the whole fabric of obituary

Masses, and abolished at a stroke the Indulgences which first lighted the candle of the Reformation. Hence it was rejected at the Council of Trent. The battle there was not for Scripture truth or Catholic antiquity, but for the existing privileges and practices of the Roman See. As long as these could be defended, by whatever show of argument or expediency, the Council seems to have been little careful for the consistency of its decrees. In fact, an amount of compromise was admitted in that famous assembly, far exceeding anything that can be fairly imputed to any Protestant community.

Wading through its cloud of contradictions as best we may, the Sacrifice of the Mass, as now held in the Church of Rome, rests upon the following propositions:—

1. That under each consecrated element is contained the glorified Body and Blood, with the Soul and Divinity of our Blessed Lord, in a spiritual immaterial way.

2. That the natural substance of the Bread and Wine is displaced, or annihilated, by consecration, so that only the 'forms' or accidents remain; that this conversion or transubstantiation continues so long as the 'forms' remain entire, and constitutes the Sacrament to all intents and purposes the Person of Christ.

3. It follows that in the oblation of the host, the whole living Person of Christ is really sacrificed, not in the same manner but to the same

effect as on the cross, it being indeed one and the same Sacrifice.

4. That this Sacrifice is available to the absent and the dead, and that by those who communicate, worthily or unworthily, Christ is received whole in the Host; so that the Cup is superfluous, and may be withdrawn.

5. That the consecrated Host, whether in the oblation, the communion, or otherwise, while remaining undissolved by natural decay, is to be worshipped with the worship due to Christ Himself.

These dogmas, though wholly unprimitive, unscriptural, and therefore in themselves false and pernicious, might be comparatively harmless if the ministration were retained according to the Institution of Christ. He administered the Sacrament in both parts to everyone present at the consecration, and left nothing of either element unconsumed. Nay, it would appear that the Bread was thus disposed of, before the Cup was taken and blessed. The consecration, delivery, and communion were one act, of which the parts overlapped each other. There was in fact no moment of time in which the Tridentine Presence could be affirmed, or the Sacrifice of the Mass be performed, or the consecrated elements be exhibited for adoration. These startling dogmas are all crowded into an interval *which had absolutely no existence in the original Institution.* Neither is any interval between oblation and communion recognized by the apostle when he says, 'As often as ye eat this bread and drink this cup ye do show the Lord's death till He come.' The oblation and the manducation are concurrent parts of the Sacrifice; or rather, manducation implies oblation, while oblation without manducation is nothing.

In the Liturgies, it is true, the consecration was completed before the distribution began; still everyone present at the one partook of the other, and nothing was reserved save the portions allotted to the sick, and conveyed to them at the time. While this primitive practice remained undisturbed, the character assigned to the gifts affected chiefly the private faith of the receiver. There was no controversy to divide the Church; and there might be none now but for the indefensible violation of the main object of the Institution, which subsequently ensued.

In allowing non-communicating attendance, and reserving the consecrated elements for other and alien purposes, an entirely new and unauthorized train of thought was introduced. The host was kept in churches, carried about in processions, exposed for adoration, and in fact regarded as a material embodiment of the Redeemer,—an actual visible God. Then came the novelty of assisting at the sacrifice without receiving the communion, and finally of the priest offering it on behalf of the absent or the dead, to whom receiving is impossible. All was the result of disobeying the one original injunction to eat and drink. The churches are still everywhere agreed, that 'the Body and Blood of Christ are verily and indeed taken and received by the faithful in the Lord's Supper.' What destroys our Catholic unity, is the perverse ingenuity which demands, What is that of which Christ said, 'Take, eat,' when it is *not* eaten?

III.—THE LUTHERAN HYPOTHESIS.

THE peculiarity of the hypothesis adopted by Martin Luther, and the majority of the subscribers to the Confession of Augsburg, is the retention of the Corporal Presence, rejecting Transubstantiation and the Sacrifice of the Mass.

This view includes the reception of Christ by the unworthy communicant, though to condemnation, and the adoration, not of the Sacrament, but 'of Christ in the Sacrament.' It maintains, on the other hand, the continuance of the natural substances of the bread and wine,[1] and insists on the administration of the cup.

[1] According to Mosheim, Consubstantiation was substituted for Transubstantiation, in a treatise by John of Paris, surnamed the *Pungens Asinus*, towards the end of the thirteenth century.—*Eccl. Hist. Cent.* xiii. *part* 2. His treatise, which certainly denies Transubstantiation, was reprinted at London A.D. 1686, and is included in the *Bibliothèque Universelle*, tom. iii.

Some practical abuses were guarded against by attributing the consecration to the prayer of the Church, instead of the priest's utterance of the words of Institution; and above all, by the great Protestant canon,—cited and accepted by Bishop Cosin,—that a sacrament has no sacramental effect beyond the use assigned to it in the Divine Institution. '*Nihil habet rationem sacramenti, extra usum seu actionem divinitus institutam.*'[1] Hence, the Presence was restrained to the time of celebration; which Luther defined to be from the Lord's Prayer and the words of Institution, till all had communicated in both kinds, consumed the remains, and left the altar. He allowed no Presence but in communion, citing 1 Cor. x. 16, as importing that the Body is present only in the breaking and eating. In fact, the words of Institution are recited among the Lutherans during the act of distribution, and not before it as in the Missal. Still Luther believed in the Corporal Presence, and in token of it long retained the elevation of the host at Wittenberg. The same practice, though disapproved by the other leaders of the German Reformation, is said to continue among the high Lutherans to the present time.

Luther rested his doctrine, as the Romanists rest theirs, on the literal force of the words of Institution; but in fact his interpretation was *further* from the letter than any other. The

---

[1] Form. Concord. Art. vii. de Cœna Dom. Cosin, Hist. of Transubstantiation. Pfaff de Cons. Vet. Euch. xv.

words of Institution may mean, 'This is My Body' in *substance*, in *effect*, or in *figure;* as the words, 'this is my estate,' may denote the land itself, the value of it, the title-deeds, or a drawing or plan of the property, according to the nature of the object indicated by the pronoun 'this.' But on the Lutheran hypothesis the bread is *not* the Body, but accompanies the Body; which is a direct contradiction to the words of Institution.

This hypothesis involved the further difficulty of presenting *two* objects to the adoration of the attendants instead of one; a difficulty which the schoolmen escaped by the invention of transubstantiation. For, although the Lutherans profess to worship, not the sacrament but 'Christ in the sacrament,' yet if the two are corporally united, it is impossible to exhibit external homage to one, without doing the same to the other. On this point, as on some others, the Lutheran practice seems to have wavered; and certainly the adoration might consistently be rejected on the principle of *extra usum divinitus institutum*.

The same remark is applicable to the unworthy receiving, than which nothing could be more foreign to the Divine Institution. Olshausen, himself a Lutheran, denies that this inference is contained in 1 Cor. xi. 27; and the better opinion was always, that the Presence is withdrawn from the sacrament when it touches the lips of the unworthy.[1]

---

[1] See Palmer's Treatise of the Church, quoted in Pusey's Letter to Bishop of London, p. 66.

In insisting on the ministration of the cup, Luther considered all debate to be silenced by the words of Institution. But this great Protestant demand was clearly inconsistent with his admission of the Corporal Presence, since, if Christ be in the bread, there is nothing more to receive in the cup. Moreover, the ministration of the Body and Blood, in two separate elements, is absolutely contradictory to the Presence of His whole Person in either.

In regard to the Eucharistic Sacrifice, Luther was obliged to confine it to the general sacrifice of praise and prayer, offered in the entire action, and implied in consecration and communion. He could not make an oblation of the *consecrated* elements, as in the Canon of the Mass, because, with his view of the Presence, that would be to repeat the very error he protested against, of sacrificing Christ afresh. And he seems to have overlooked the true oblation of the bread and wine, made in the ancient Liturgies previous to consecration, and in the consecration itself.

Pfaff admits that such an oblation was practised *in some churches* by the apostles themselves, and even continued by their direction; but he maintains, without a particle of evidence, that it was neither universal nor necessary;[1]—a summary disposal of antiquity which has been too readily resorted to by German Protestants.

Cranmer with some others were at first inclined to the Lutheran hypothesis. Its inconsistencies,

[1] Note on Fragment of S. Irenæus, and Diss. de Oblat. Vet. Euch.

however, being exposed by the sounder learning of Ridley and Ponet, it was never formally held by any party in England. Even in Germany, the authority of the great Reformer proved unequal to sustain so crude a theory. The Corporal Presence was questioned by not a few of those who subscribed the first Confession of Augsburg. The Tridentine phrase, 'under the forms of bread and wine,' though retained in the original German, disappeared from the authorized Latin version of 1531; and the strongest statement left, only asserts the Presence in *reception*, and is compared by Pfaff to that of our own Church Catechism.

The revised Confession of Melancthon substitutes the word 'exhibited' for 'present;' and notwithstanding the effort made in the misnamed *Formula Concordiæ* to restore the high Lutheran view, it has everywhere yielded to the Calvinist and Zwinglian interpretations. According to a late eminent authority, hardly any genuine Lutherans are now to be found in Germany.[1]

A disposition has lately been manifested among ourselves, to revive the 'co-existent' theory, as less opposed than transubstantiation to the letter of the Article. It becomes important, therefore, to see how this theory of the Presence is defined by the Lutheran divines.

They repudiate the word *consubstantiation*, commonly applied to it by others, as implying a fusion of two substances into one; whereas they

---

[1] Dr. Dollinger's 'Church and the Churches.'

assert a 'sacramental union' of Body and bread, each retaining its own nature distinct. The *Formula Concordiæ* lays it down that 'the Body and Blood of Christ are taken not only spiritually and by faith, but also with the mouth; not *capernaiticè*, but after a supernatural and heavenly manner, by reason of the sacramental union with the bread and wine.' It even disclaims the word *corporal*, insisting only that the Body is truly, though spiritually, present.[1] Bellarmine uses exactly the same language of the Roman hypothesis: the Body is really present, but spiritually, or after the manner of a spirit, *i.e.* without matter, form, colour, weight, &c. This language might correctly describe a mystical Presence of Christ crucified in the elements, or a spiritual Presence of Christ glorified in the soul; but when used, as the Romanists and Lutherans use it, to assert the Presence of our Lord's glorified Body in the material sacrament, it confounds the essential distinction between body and spirit, and goes to deny the reality of Christ's Body altogether.

In like manner the phrase, 'sacramental union,' might properly describe a spiritual union of the *operation and efficacy* of Christ's Body with the visible element, which is the Real Presence of Catholic antiquity. But in the mouth of a Lutheran, this phrase implies a union of the *substance* of Christ's Body with the bread and wine. Gerhard explains it in this way:

---

[1] Pfaff, de Cons. xvii.

'We believe that in the sacrament of the Eucharist there is a true, real, and *substantial* presence, exhibition, eating and drinking, of Christ's Body and Blood; which Presence is not an essential conversion of the bread into the Body, and of the wine into the Blood of Christ, which they call transubstantiation;—neither is it a local or permanent affixion of the Body to the bread, and of the Blood to the wine;—neither is it a personal union of the bread and the Body, such as is the union of the Divine and human natures in Christ;—neither is it a local inclusion of the Body in the bread;—neither is it impanation or incorporation into bread;—neither is it consubstantiation, by which the bread coalesces in one physical mass with the Body, and the wine with the Blood;—neither is it natural inexistence, or hiding of a corpuscle under the bread;—nor any carnal or physical thing of this kind. But it is a sacramental Presence and union, which is so effected, that to the bread and wine, when blessed according to the institution of our most true, wise, and omnipotent Saviour, as to a medium thereunto divinely ordained, the Body and Blood of Christ are united, in a manner incomprehensible to us, so that in a sublime mystery we take, eat, and drink, by one sacramental eating and drinking, the Body of Christ with that bread, and His Blood with that wine. In short, it is not absence, (ἀπουσίαν) not inexistence, (ἐνουσίαν) not consubstantiation, (συνουσίαν) not transubstantiation, (μετουσίαν) but the Presence (παρουσίαν) of the Body and Blood of Christ, which we declare in the Supper.'[1]

This elaborate explanation certainly obviates many objections, and might leave little controversy, if the words 'Body and Blood' be allowed to retain their scriptural and proper application to the *crucified* Body and Blood *shed* for our sins. These are indeed 'sacramentally united' to the bread and wine, and 'in a sublime mystery' eaten and drunk by the faithful communicant. But in this condition, as the Romanists themselves allow, Christ is not contained in the Sacrament, but represented by it.

[1] Pfaff, de Cons. xvii.

The objection to the Lutheran as to the Roman hypothesis, is the confounding the *substance* of Christ's Body in heaven with the sacramental operation of His Body and Blood on the cross.

The objection is greatly mitigated by the Protestant canon of *nihil extra usum,* on which Pfaff observes that—

'There is no sacrament in the Old or New Testament which does not consist in action; and it is not the baptismal water which is properly called the sacrament, but rather the action by which the baptism is performed.' Moreover, the very words of Institution restrain the real Presence to the use and whole action; For Christ said, 'this is My Body, this is My Blood,' after He had said, 'eat,' 'drink,' to show that His Body would not be present, but in the use and action which He Himself prescribed. .... Hence, in our churches, the words, this is the 'Body of Jesus Christ,' are said only in the act of distribution and reception.'

This view he supports from 1 Cor. x. 16, on which Luther's comment is—

'When we distribute and eat the bread, then we receive and eat not mere bread, but also the Body of Christ.'

Referring, further, to the Canon of the Mass, in the petition, 'that they may be made *to us* the Body and Blood of Thy most beloved Son,' Pfaff acutely insists that the pronoun *nobis* indicates the Real Presence to be vouchsafed only in the use.'[2]

These explanations, while they do not justify the Lutheran phraseology, go far to deprive it of any very dangerous consequence. Practically

---

[1] This double use of the word 'sacrament,' no less than of 'sacrifice' and 'Eucharist,' is always to be borne in mind.

[2] Pfaff, Diss. de Cons. Vet. Euch.

the modern Lutheran differs little from Hooker; that 'the real Presence of Christ's most blessed Body and Blood is not to be sought for in the sacrament, but in the worthy receiver of the sacrament.'[1] Luther, it is true, seated it substantially in the sacrament, which the riper theology of the English divine scrupled to affirm. But both regarded the sacramental presence only as a means to the Spiritual Presence in the communicant. Both recoiled from the Tridentine conception of a deified host, with which communion is the last thing desired,—which is offered to the adoration of those who never communicate, and even sacrificed for souls no longer in the flesh. Luther's hypothesis was purely speculative, and for that reason probably took but little hold of practical religion. Its advantage lay in getting rid of the grosser evils attendant on transubstantiation. This common-sense rational reform, a mind like Luther's would eagerly grasp; but he overlooked other errors scarcely less objectionable.

To locate Christ's glorified Body in the elements *along with* bread and wine, is not less injurious to a right faith in the Incarnation, than to imagine it in the paten and the cup *instead* of them. That Body (our Church affirms) 'is in heaven, and not here;' whatever glory it has acquired in the exaltation, it is still a real human Body; and of all bodies the distinguishing characteristic, as opposed to spirit, is that they are bounded by

[1] Eccl. Pol. v. lxvii. 6.

form and place. Hence it is 'against the truth of Christ's natural Body to be at one time in more places than one.' This capital heresy is not avoided by saying the Presence is immaterial, spiritual, supernatural, or superlocal. Multiply epithets as it may, the 'co-existent' teaching cannot escape the censure, which Hooker urges from S. Augustine: 'that majestical Body, which we make to be everywhere present, doth thereby cease to have the substance of a true Body.'[1]

As for Scripture and antiquity, it has been already pointed out that they are harder to reconcile with the Lutheran hypothesis than with the Roman. It is true, that the sacrament is called bread and called Body, but that it therefore contains the two substances united, is a very shallow theology. The expression, 'that is Pompey,' may refer either to the Roman general or to his statue; but no one would ever understand it of a *union* of the man and the marble together. In like manner, the words, 'this is My Body,' can only mean one of two things;—either, this is My Body under the form or appearance of bread;—or, this bread is My Body in mystical signification and power. A union of two original substances, Body and bread, cannot with any propriety of language be got out of the singular, '*this is:*' Bellarmine himself admits that if the pronoun *this* have bread for its subject, then it can be Body only in figure.

[1] Eccl. Pol. v. lv. 6.

Neither do the fathers ever speak of the sacrament as containing two subjects united. In their language, the bread *is* the Body, it is *made* the Body, it *becomes* the Body; but it is never *united* or joined to the Body. The ancient Liturgies invoke the Holy Ghost to make the bread the Body; but nowhere in antiquity shall we find the Lutheran petition, 'ut Deus elementa externa cum Corpore et Sanguine J. C. uniat.'[1]

This novel conception, originated by Luther in the first pressure of the Roman controversy, contributes nothing towards the solution of the question. That the Human Nature of our Lord in glory should be united to innumerable pieces of material bread, is quite as objectionable as that it should take the place of their natural substance, and be present under their forms or accidents. And what is more;—neither hypothesis in the least advances the true object of the sacrament—communion with Christ in the heart by faith.

It has been observed that both Lutheran and Roman divines sometimes disclaim the word *corporal*, by which their doctrine of the Presence is commonly described. They repudiate a natural, material, organic, or local presence, asserting that the Body is present after the manner of a spirit, and this they choose to call a Spiritual Presence.[2]

---

[1] Pfaff, de Cons. xxi.

[2] So Bellarmine: 'Vere et realiter, non dicemus *corporaliter*, *i.e.* eo modo quo *sua natura* existunt corpora.'—*De Euch.* l. 2. So the Form. Conc. vii.: 'Dicimus Corpus et Sanguinem Christi in S. Cœna spiritualiter accipi, edi, et bibi. Tametsi enim

But in our ideas, body is distinguished from spirit as being material, organic, and local. To deny these qualities of the Body of Christ, is to deny the truth of His Humanity; to say that He is present without them, is what *we* say, that He is present in Spirit with the *power*, operation, and efficacy of the Body, but not the *substance*. To assert the substantial presence of a body without the qualities which make it body, is a mere contradiction in terms.

What the fathers teach is, that Christ's Body is in heaven, and its presence upon earth is due to the hypostatic union with His omnipresent Godhead. In this 'heavenly, spiritual, and immaterial way,' the glorified Humanity of our exalted Lord is indeed peculiarly present, and partaken of by the faithful, in the Holy Eucharist. This is not the presence of a body contained in or united to another body, but a presence in spirit and effect of a Body locally absent. The elements remain in substance what they always were; what they acquire by consecration is the

---

participatio illa *ore* fiat : tamen modus spiritualis est.' Just before a *corporalis præsentia* is denied, ' quæ tamen ea ratione adstruitur ut Corpus Christi vere, licet spiritualiter præsens esse credatur.' This Body is declared to be one and the same with the Body of Christ in glory, and therefore His Divinity is also present. 'Loquimur de præsentia Christi *vivi.*'—*Apol. Aug. Confess. Art.* iv. (*Pfaff de Cons. Vet. Euch.*)

Yet Bellarmine writes in the same treatise : 'Quod autem *corporaliter* et proprie sumatur Sanguis et Caro,' &c. And this is the common language of both Churches.—*See Laud's Conference with Fisher,* s. 85.

power of communicating to the faithful receiver the Body and Blood of Christ; and for this reason the Fathers called the bread the Body, and the wine the Blood, 'in a mystery,' and 'by spiritual effect.'

IV.—THE ANGLICAN DOCTRINE.

THE Sacrifice of the Mass is built on two fundamental corruptions of Catholic antiquity; a doctrinal error concerning the Presence, and a liturgical one of oblation *after* consecration. Luther, grappling on with a portion of the confusion, failed to recover the entire truth on either point. He deprived the corporal theory of its most palpable evils, by limiting the Presence to the duration of the sacramental action, culminating in communion; and he restored the forgotten truth that the Eucharistic Sacrifice in its largest sense includes the entire rite. But the primitive oblation of the elements, which the Romanists had distorted, he altogether discarded, and thus the issue was joined on the question of sacrifice *or* communion.[1] It was

[1] 'All the Reformed Churches have dropped the formal oblation of bread and wine, as foreign to our customs, (?) incurring the danger of misrepresentation after so much abuse.'—*Baron Bunsen, Memoirs*, vol. i., p. 422. This accom-

essentially a false issue, but so long as Rome bore exclusively on the one scale, the Protestants did well to throw their weight into the other. A valid communion *implies* the Eucharistic Sacrifice, whatever be the form of celebration; whereas oblation *without* eating and drinking is no Christian sacrifice at all.

In England, where the Reformation always aimed at restoring the faith and worship of the primitive Church, the sacrificial character of the Eucharist gradually rose to the surface, as soon as the more urgent matter of communion had been secured. In the Anglican view the Eucharistic Sacrifice is a commemorative and representative rite, and therefore *not* the same with the Sacrifice of the cross, either in the whole action or the material oblation. On the cross Jesus Christ offered Himself a sacrifice for the sins of the world;—in the Eucharist the Church offers a sacrifice of praise and thanksgiving, to commemorate and plead before God that atoning sacrifice, and to apply its benefits to the faithful communicant. On the cross the great High Priest offered His Human Nature as the one

---

plished and profoundly pious scholar candidly allows that this symbolical act 'certainly was in the most ancient Church,' and he desires to see it restored. Singularly enough, however, Bunsen regards the thing symbolically indicated in this oblation to be 'the self-sacrifice of the Christian believer;' whereas the Liturgies certainly presented the *oblation* as a symbol of Christ's Sacrifice: the self-sacrifice of the believer is expressed in the act of *communion*. (1 Cor. x. 17.)

Sacrifice for all human sin;—in the Eucharist, an oblation of bread and wine, the appointed symbols of that crucified Body and Blood, is presented on the altar, 'to show the Lord's Death till He come.' These are then received from that Holy Table, consecrated into the Real Communion of that which they represent. This sacrifice and peace offering, which Christ left to His Church in remembrance of Him, is propitiatory in the sense of pleading, and applying to the worthy communicant, the propitiation once made for all on the cross. But it is not a sin-offering or satisfaction for sin, not propitiatory in the sense of meriting or working remission, either for communicants or any others.

The true objects of the Eucharistic Sacrifice are—

1. To praise God for the mercies of Creation, Providence, and Redemption.

2. To plead and commemorate the Sacrifice of the cross, communicating the Body and Blood, there offered, to the faithful receiver.

3. To offer ourselves, in union with Christ, a living sacrifice unto God.

It follows that none who do not communicate, or who communicate unworthily, either assist in the sacrifice, or partake of the Lord's Body and Blood; since these are not substantially contained in, or united to, the elements, but exhibited in mystery, and realized in faithful reception. For the same reason, though 'no one eats without adoring Christ,'[1] our adoration is not offered to anything in the paten or the chalice, but to His glorified Body, which 'is in Heaven and not here.'

The phrase 'Real Presence,' though not adopted in the Anglican formularies,—perhaps on account of the ambiguity introduced into it by the Church of Rome,—is received by our divines in its true and original meaning; viz. that Christ is really present to the faithful communicant in the eating and drinking of the consecrated gifts, and that not by the internal action of his own mind,—or faith alone, (which some call a subjective presence,) but by a real Presence, from without, of the Person of the God-man. In this sense the Real Presence is held not only by the Anglican Church, but, as Bishop Cosin shows, by all Protestant confessions, as firmly as by the Church of Rome or the Lutherans. The peculiarity of the two latter is the seating Christ's *Person* in the material elements, apart from communion, and even when there is no communion save of the priest.[2] This the Church of England, in common with all other Protestants, steadfastly denies.

Now on the controversy so raised it is important

---

[1] St. Augustine's 'nemo manducat nisi prius adoraverit illam carnem,' has reference to the acknowledgment of our Lord's Divinity, not to any particular act of adoration. The Romish interpolation of *id* is exposed in Dr. Pusey's Letter to the Bishop of London, p. 76.

[2] Eccl. Pol. v. lxvii. 12.

to remark at the outset, that Scripture and antiquity are wholly ignorant of it. The Eucharist is never mentioned in Scripture, or any Catholic Liturgy, but with a view to communion; *all* that is said of it by apostles or fathers is said in relation to a rite culminating in oral participation. Consequently nothing in their testimony can apply to consecrated elements which are not eaten, or to a worshipper who does not communicate.

In the next place, it is a mistake to suppose that the communicant receives only what he orally eats and drinks. Even the Romanist allows that Christ must dwell in the heart by faith; but He is no nearer to the heart or soul in the hand of the priest, than at the right Hand of the Father. He does not enter the soul by corporal contact, but by spiritual union; and to this nothing is gained by diminishing the local distance between His Body and ours: so that all have recourse to the Spiritual Presence in the end.

Thirdly, it is obvious that the Sacrament represents and communicates the *slain* Body and Blood, sundered in two elements, which therefore cannot be at the same moment the living Body of the Resurrection: nor are they ever called so in Holy Scripture. It is true, that in partaking of Christ's Death we are quickened with His life. He Himself is not absent (as St. Cyprian notes[1]) from the sacrament of His death; but His Presence is the privilege of the

[1] De Cœn. vii. Eccl. Pol. v. lxvii. 11.

faithful receiver, not of inanimate bread and wine. Our Lord's own words are, 'He that eateth My Flesh, and drinketh My Blood, (he only) dwelleth in Me and I in him.' The Flesh in the bread, the outshed Blood in the cup,—each really though in a mystery,—each with its distinct virtue and operation,—and then, as the *effect* of eating and drinking these, Christ the God-Man personally and spiritually dwelling in *us* and we in Him.

Some ambiguity may occasionally arise, to a careless reader, from the name *Christ* being given to His slain Body, as well as to His living Person in heaven. But this is a common usage, which can deceive no one who will attend to what is spoken. When Augustus was offered his rival's head, with the words, 'this is Pompey,' no one mistook the meaning. So the Body and Blood, separated in two elements, plainly relate to a state of death: and the ancient Church was so far from referring them to the glorified Body, that it was long a question (which cannot even yet be said to be decided) whether our Lord's Body in heaven has any *blood* in it at all. The blood shed on the cross was not buried in the sepulchre, and after the Resurrection we hear only of 'flesh and bones.'[1] The apostle's expression, 'by His own

---

[1] Luke, xxiv. 39; John, vi. 51; and xx. 27: see Alford *in loc*. Augustine seems rather perplexed with this question, which is discussed at length in Allix's treatise 'de sanguine Christi.' See also Wake's Discourse in Gibson's Preservative Tit. vii. cap. 4.

blood' (Heb. ix. 12.) refers not to living blood now in His veins, but to the sacrificial bloodshedding on the cross; and this beyond question is the mystery of the Blood in the Holy Eucharist.

That the sacrament exhibits the dead Body, is the doctrine both of Scripture and antiquity; but when restored in England it was objected to by the Romanists,[1]—and the cavil has been recently revived among ourselves,[2]—that it tends to Nestorianism, as implying a separation between the Flesh and the Divinity of the Son of God. The objection supposes—what the Church of England denies—a natural presence of Christ's Flesh in the sacrament. From His natural Body, living or dead, no one believes the Godhead to have been severed for an instant.[3] But that Body, we insist,

---

[1] 'For either they hold no more than an imaginary presence, or else they believe His Body is present abstracted from His Divinity; and thus they fall into the wicked heresy of Nestorius.' Speech of Scott, Bishop of Chester, in the House of Lords against Queen Elizabeth's Act of Uniformity. Collier, Eccl. Hist. p. ii. book vi.

[2] Medd on the Eucharistic Sacrifice in Church and the World, p. 356. In a postscript to this otherwise unexceptionable treatise the author inserts and adopts a protest by Mr. Bright, charging Archdeacon Freeman's timely re-assertion of the Catholic truth with singularity (!) and Nestorianism.

[3] Quid fecit passio, quid fecit mors, nisi corpus ab anima separavit? Animam vero a Verbo non separavit. *S. Aug. Tract. in Johan.* 47. The argument applies with equal force to the Body; indeed it was the union of the indivisible Deity with each that effected the Resurrection. 'Quoniam Deitas, quæ

THE HOLY EUCHARIST.   51

is living in heaven. The sacrament exhibits the dead Body, not in substance, for it is no longer dead in fact, but mystically to faith, that the communicant may partake, through the Spirit, of the living Body united evermore to the Godhead in heaven. There is no hypostatic union with the sacrament.

This distinction is so important, that it may be well to illustrate it from some of our best authors, before we proceed to establish it from Scripture and Catholic antiquity.

To begin with the well-known Homily of Archbishop *Elfric,* whether of Canterbury or York;[1]—

'Great is the difference between the invisible might of the holy housel and the visible appearance of its own nature. By nature it is corruptible bread and corruptible wine, and is by power of the divine word truly Christ's Body and His Blood: not however bodily, but spiritually. Great is the difference between the Body in which Christ suffered and the Body which is hallowed for housel. The body verily in which Christ suffered was born of Mary's flesh, with blood and bones, with skin and sinews, with human limbs, quickened by a rational soul. His ghostly Body, which we call

---

ab utraque suscepti hominis substantia non recessit, quod potestate divisit, potestate conjunxit.' *Leo, Serm.* i. *de Resurr.* See *Pearson, Exposition of the Creed,* Art. iv., where is also a fine passage from Gregory Nyss: ἐπεὶ διπλοῦν μὲν τὸ ἀνθρώπινον σύγκραμα, ἁπλῆ δὲ καὶ μονοειδὴς ἡ τῆς Θειότητος φύσις, ἐν τῷ καιρῷ τῆς τοῦ σώματος ἀπὸ τῆς ψυχῆς διαζεύξεως, οὐ συνδιασχίζεται τῷ συνθέτῳ τὸ ἀδιαίρετον, ἀλλὰ τὸ ἔμπαλιν γίνεται· τῇ γὰρ ἑνότητι τῆς θείας φύσεως, τῆς κατὰ τὸ ἴσον ἐν ἀμφοτέροις οὔσης, πάλιν πρὸς ἄλληλα τὰ διαστῶτα συμφύεται.

[1] See Collier's Eccl. Hist. book iii.

housel, is gathered of many corns, without blood and bone, limbless and soulless, and there is therefore nothing therein to be understood bodily, but all is to be understood spiritually. Whatsoever there is in the housel which gives us the substance of life, that is from its ghostly power and invisible efficacy; therefore is the holy housel called a mystery, because one thing is seen therein, and another thing understood. That which is there seen has a bodily appearance, and that which we understand therein has ghostly might. Verily Christ's Body, which suffered death, and from death arose, will henceforth never die, but is eternal and impassible. . . . This mystery is a pledge and a *symbol;* Christ's Body is *truth*. The pledge we hold mystically until we come to the truth, and then will this pledge be ended. But it is, as we said, Christ's Body and His Blood, not bodily but spiritually.'

On this Homily Dr. Hook remarks that it bears traces of the Eastern Church, (derived through Archbishop Theodorus,) where transubstantiation was unknown. 'Nor did the adoration of the blessed sacrament ever obtain in the Greek Church.'[1]

Collier, who gives the Homily at greater length, adds a similar passage from one of Elfric's letters to the clergy.

'The sacrifice of the Eucharist is not our Saviour's Body in which He suffered for us, nor His Blood which He shed upon our account. But it is made His Body and Blood in a spiritual way, as the manna was which fell from the sky, and the water which flowed from the rock in the wilderness.'

Hence it is plain that the English Church before the Conquest held the consecrated elements to be the Body and Blood of Christ, not by any substitution of His Body under their forms, or its

---

[1] Hook's Lives of the Abps. of Cant. i. 443.

presence as another substance along with them, but by a spiritual power and efficacy imparted to the bread and wine, and making *them* the Body and Blood for the sacramental use.

The worst result of the Norman invasion was the subjugation of our National Church. Lanfranc came over a pledged supporter of the Corporal Presence; still the cup was ministered to the laity for two centuries later. Wiclif, like Luther, though rejecting transubstantiation, was unable to emancipate himself from the corporal error; and we must pass to the Reformation for a renewal of the independent testimony of the English Church.[1]

Cranmer writes—

'The oblation and sacrifice of Christ in the Mass is not so called because Christ indeed is there offered and sacrificed by the priest and the people, (for that was done but once by Himself on the cross,) but it is so called because it is a Memory and representation of that very true Sacrifice and immolation which before was made upon the cross.'[2]

---

[1] Most of the following references are collected in a Catena published at Oxford and London, 1855, under the title of the 'Doctrine of the Real Presence,' &c. And again in the late Dean of Ripon's copious publication in reply, on the 'Nature of Christ's Presence in the Eucharist.' The latter appears to be the more correctly executed; but, as is too much the case in controversy, it may be doubted whether either publication fairly and *fully* represents the Anglican view. The present author gladly acknowledges his obligations to the industry and accuracy of the learned Dean for the references taken from his volumes.

[2] Collier, Eccl. Hist. part ii. book iv.

In the *participation*, he maintained the real reception of Christ's own Body and Blood:—

'If you understand by this word 'really' *reipsa*, that is in very deed and effectually; so Christ by the grace and efficacy of His Passion is indeed and truly present, &c. But if by this word 'really' you understand *corporaliter*, in His natural and organical body, under the forms of bread and wine, it is contrary to the Holy Word of God.'[1]

Again:

'The same visible and palpable Flesh that was for us crucified, &c., is eaten of Christian people at His Holy Supper.... The diversity is not in the body but in the eating thereof, no man eating it carnally, but the good eating it both sacramentally and spiritually, and the evil only sacramentally, *that is to say figuratively*.'[2]

In another place Cranmer explains the word 'sacrament' to mean sometimes the *sacramentum* or outward sign, and sometimes the whole ministration and receiving of the sacraments. Hence, by Christ's Presence in the sacrament he means either His 'sacramental presence,' *i.e.* His Body and Blood figured and represented in the *sacramentum*,—or the Real and True Presence of Himself 'by power, virtue, and grace, in all them that worthily receive the same;' and this he maintains is the meaning of the old writers and holy doctors.[3]

Ridley testifies, in opposition to the Lutheran doctrine, that 'all learned men in England grant there to be but *one substance*,'[4] which is the sign

---

[1] Laud's Conference with Fisher, s. xxxv. No. 6, p. 4.
[2] Cranmer's Remains, iii. 340.
[3] Answer to Gardiner. Dean Goode, p. 771.
[4] Brief Declaration. Ibid. 767.

or sacrament. The 'matter of the sacrament' (or the thing signified) is received only by faith. Hence, he writes, 'Evil men do eat the Body of Christ sacramentally, but good men eat both the sacrament and the matter of the sacrament.'[1]

It will be borne in mind that 'sacramental' then meant 'figurative:' even the Council of Trent uses the word in this sense, when it defines unworthy reception to be 'sacramental,' while the faithful receive both 'sacramentally and spiritually,'[2] words which properly mean that the latter only receive Christ, and receive Him spiritually not corporally. Ridley says,

'We confess all one thing to be in the sacrament, and dissent in the manner of being there. I confess Christ's natural Body to be in the sacrament by spirit and grace, &c.; you make a grosser kind of being, inclosing a natural body under the shape and form of bread and wine.'[3]

Again:

'The representation and commemoration of Christ's Death and Passion said and done in the Mass is called the sacrifice, oblation, or immolation of Christ, *non rei veritate*, (as learned men do write,) sed *significandi mysterio*.'

And again:

'I know that all these places of the Scripture are avoided by two manner of subtle shifts: the one is by the distinction of the bloody and unbloody sacrifice, as though our unbloody sacrifice of the Church were any other than the sacrifice of praise and thanksgiving, than a commemoration, a sacramental representation of that one only bloody Sacrifice

---

[1] Remains, Goode, p. 768.   [2] Conc. Trid. Sess. xiii. Euch. s. 8.
[3] Laud's Conf. s. xxxv. No. 6, p. 4.

offered up once for all; the other is by depraving and wresting the sayings of the ancient fathers into such a strange kind of sense as the fathers themselves never indeed meant.'[1]

To Ridley probably is due the introduction of a figure often repeated by English divines:—

'The substance of the natural Body and Blood of Christ is only remaining in heaven, and so shall be unto the latter day;—but by grace the same Body of Christ is here present with us; even as, for example, we say the same sun, which in substance never removeth his place out of the heavens, is yet present here, by his beams, light, and natural influence, where it shineth upon the earth. For God's Word and His Sacraments be as it were the beams of Christ, which is *Sol justitiæ*, the Sun of Righteousness.'[2]

In his reply to the three articles propounded to him at Oxford, Ridley complains of the ambiguity of the word *realiter*, 'which may be taken *transcendenter* and so signify whatever in any way belongs to the Body of Christ; in which sense we grant the Body of Christ to be really in the sacrament of the Lord's Supper;'—or for 'the living corporal thing itself, (*rem ipsam corpoream animatam*,) which has been taken into unity of person by the Word of God; according to which signification the Body of Christ, since it is really in heaven after the true mode of a body, cannot be said to be here in earth.'[3]

[1] Works, Cambridge, 1841, p. 209-10.
[2] Remains, p. 13. Goode, p. 766.
[3] He says in another place, 'The sacrament of the Blood is the Blood, and that is attributed to the sacrament which is spoken of the *res sacramenti*.—The Blood of Christ is in the chalice indeed, but not in the Real Presence, but by grace and in a sacrament.'—*Remains*, p. 238. *Goode*, 768.

That the Body of Christ is really contained in the sacrament he maintains to be a monstrous and absurd position, founded upon transubstantiation. He grants its presence by virtue and grace, but denies it as to the whole essence and substance of the Body. Such an opinion he shows to be injurious to the truth of Christ's human nature, contrary to the fathers, the Scripture, and the creed, which assert His Ascension into heaven only to come again at the last day. Such a presence evacuates the institution of the sacrament as a *memorial,* 'commemoratio non est rei præsentis, sed *præteritæ et absentis*,' (clearly referring to the *sacrificed* Body and Blood.) It makes the real and corporal Body of our Lord, in which dwells the fullness of Spirit, Light, and Grace, to be received by wicked men, and even mice and dogs. It necessitates concomitancy and the denial of the cup.

Of the true Presence he concludes with the orthodox fathers,—

'That not only a signification of the Lord's Body is made in the sacrament, but that *with it is exhibited* to the pious and faithful the grace of Christ's Body, that is to say, the life and food of immortality, (as Cyprian says.) And so we eat and drink life, (with Augustine,) we perceive the Lord present in grace, (with Emissenus,) we receive the heavenly food that cometh down from above, (with Athanasius,) the nature and life-giving benediction of His Flesh in bread and wine, (with Cyril,) the virtue of Christ's Flesh, the life and grace which are the property of the only begotten Body, that is— as Cyril himself explains—*Life.* We confess with Basil, "a mystic advent of Christ,"—with Ambrose, "the grace of His true Nature, and the sacrament of His true Flesh;"—with Chrysostom, "grace flowing into the sacrifice," and the "grace of the Spirit,"—with Augustine, "the invisible verity, grace, and fellowship, of the members of Christ's Body."—lastly, with Bertram, that the Body of Christ in the sacrament is the Spirit or power of the Divine Word, which not only feeds but purifies the soul. This is altogether different from holding nothing but a figure of Christ's Body.'[1]

The *Diallacticon*, commonly ascribed to Bishop Ponet, but which Dean Goode shows to have been written by Sir Anthony Cook, tutor to Edward VI., has the following:—

'Now in this sacrament the fathers of old time have noted two things, for either of the which it may well be called and accounted the Body of Christ, but especially when it comprehendeth them both. For both because the bread is a figure of the true Body, it is justly called His Body, and much more because it hath *the lively force of the same joined thereto;* but, in especial, because it comprehendeth both.'[2]

Again:—

'We said there was another thing which the ancient fathers acknowledging in this sacrament would have it verily to be the Lord's Body, and that is the virtue of the Body itself, that is of force and giveth life, which virtue by grace and mystical blessing is joined with the bread and wine, and is called by sundry names, when the matter itself is all one. Of Augustine, 'an intelligible, invisible, and spiritual body'; of Hierom, 'divine and spiritual flesh'; of Irenæus, 'a heavenly thing'; of Ambrose, 'a spiritual food,' and 'Body of a Divine Spirit'; of other, some such like thing. And this also doth make, much the more, that the sacrament is most worthy to have the name of the true Body and Blood, seeing not only outwardly it showeth forth a figure and image of it, but also inwardly it draweth with it a hid and secret natural property of the same Body, that is to say, a virtue that giveth life: so that it cannot now be

---

[1] Reply to the three Articles at Oxford. Collier, Appx. No. lxxi.

[2] Goode, 778.

thought a vain figure, or the sign of a thing clean absent, but the very Body of the Lord, Divine indeed and spiritual, but present in grace, full of virtue, mighty in operation. And it happeneth often, that the names of the things themselves be given to their virtue and strength. We say leaven is in the whole lump, whereas a small quantity of leaven cannot spread so far abroad, but the strength and sharpness of the leaven. We say that the fire doth warm us, when the heat of the fire doth it, we being a good way off from the fire. Likewise that the sun is present, doth lighten, burneth, nourisheth, when indeed the heat of the sun doth it, and the sun himself cannot go out of his sphere. So is a king said to be in all his realm, because of the power of his dominion.'

Of unworthy reception, the Diallacticon teaches that the grace is withdrawn not from the sacrament but from the sinner.

'If we consider the sacrament in itself, the Divine virtue cannot be absent from the sign; but if we consider the way of living and disposition of the receiver, that which is in itself life and grace is neither the one nor the other to *him*, because the pravity of wicked men is incapable of receiving so great goodness. Sacraments, while they remain sacraments, retain their virtue; and there can be no separation, whether they who receive them be good or bad, worthy or unworthy.' But this only, 'so long as the sign serves for that use, and is applied to that end for which it is appointed by God's Word. For if we use it contrary to the institution of Christ, it either is no sacrament at all, or it ceases to be one. Therefore they sin not a little who make use of the symbols of bread and wine, not for the purpose which Christ intended, but consecrate them for pomp, which is not allowed by the Word of God, and yet put them off for a sacrament to the silly people. For though they be prepared with due rites and for lawful ends, yet when that use and their proper function ceases, they no longer retain the name or virtue of sacraments.''

---

¹ Waterland is not satisfied with this explanation, and blames the author for carrying much too far 'the notion of

Of the sacrifice the Diallacticon cites the words of S. Ambrose,

'The shadow in the Law, the image in the Gospels, the verity in Heaven,'[1] and after tracing them to Origen's comment on Psalm xxxviii., concludes that 'the sacrifices which are offered here are images of that Verity who has entered into the Heavens; and though these images have their verity also, it is different from the proper verity in heaven.'

Of equal or greater authority in this reign was Edward the Sixth's Catechism, the undoubted production of *Ponet*, who was the first bishop consecrated according to the Reformed Ordinal.[2]

---

inherent virtues lodged in the elements themselves,' and 'making the conjunction of grace and element absolute and physical.' But the justice of this censure may be questioned. The author clearly held the old orthodox opinion that God withdraws the grace from the lips of the unworthy. And when he speaks of good and bad 'receiving the Lord's Body alike,' he clearly meant the 'figure of the true body,' and not 'the lively force,' since this is the same with the 'virtue,' of which he expressly declares the wicked to be incapable. He supposes nothing to be *inherent* in the elements but their natural properties. Neither does he anywhere represent 'the conjunction of grace and element as absolute and physical.' His language may seem to lack 'caution' to the divinity of the last century, but fairly understood, it seems free from reproach.

[1] De Off. i. 48.

[2] The question lately raised on the private character of this prelate, is quite irrelevant to his value as a witness to the Church-teaching, of which he is admitted to have been an able and learned expositor. There are writers it seems at present, who think to dispose of the Protestant Reformation by calling its authors 'unredeemed villains.' Cranmer is 'a cowardly time-serving hypocrite, a perjured person and a traitor,' (Saturday Review, 25th July, 1868,) Edward VI. is

'The supper is a certain thankful remembrance of the death of Christ, forasmuch as the bread representeth His Body betrayed to be crucified for us; the wine standeth in the stead and place of His Blood plenteously shed for us. And even as by bread and wine our natural bodies are sustained and nourished, so by the Body, that is the Flesh and Blood of Christ, the soul is fed through faith, and quickened to the heavenly and godly life.'[1]

In a sermon preached before the king, Ponet warmly combats the opinion that Christ's Body can be in sundry places at one time, ridiculing the school distinction of its being in the sacrament *realiter* and *substantialiter*, but not *naturaliter*. Still he maintains that the Body of Christ, which sits at the Father's right hand, is really present at the ministration of the sacrament.

'Even as the sun, which is far off distant, is absent from mine eye, and yet is present to my sight, even so is Christ's Body absent from my mouth, and yet present to my belief. .... And when I receive this Holy Communion, *mea conversatio est in cœlis*, my conversation is in Heaven, where Christ's Body is even so present to my faith as the sun is present to my sight, and as the bread and wine be present to my mouth. So that if I have no faith, Christ is not present to me when I receive the sacrament of the Body and Blood of Christ.'[2]

---

a 'tiger cub,' though the authority of Parliament in the second year of that king is at other times the bulwark of our Catholic inheritance! These revilers seem to have forgotten Pope John X. and his paramours, with the more infamous Borgias. Yet the morals of a pope are of greater importance to an infallible papacy, than the personal character of any bishop, prince, or doctor, to the cause of Reformed religion.

[1] Goode, 733. [2] Ib. p. 787.

Bishop *Bilson* maintains, from John, vi. 51-54, that unworthy communicants

'neither eat the Flesh of Christ nor drink His Blood; not because their teeth or jaws fail them, but by reason they want faith, which is the right and proper instrument of spiritual eating.'[1]

He defines 'sacramental eating' to be the 'carnal and visible pressing with teeth the sacrament of Christ's Body and Blood; it is not the real eating of Christ Himself.' For this he cites S. Augustine's distinction between the *sacramentum* and the *res sacramenti.*

'Of the sacrament (he saith) It is received at the Lord's Table, of some to life, of some to destruction. *Res vero ipsa,* &c.—but the thing itself whereof that is a sacrament (is received) of all men to life, and of none to death, whosoever is partaker of it.' .... 'The signs which are called after consecration by the names of Christ's Body and Blood, do enter our mouths and pass our throats; the true Flesh and Blood of Christ do not, but are eaten at the Lord's Table only of the inward man by faithful devotion and affection, preparing the heart that Christ may lodge there, and dwell there where He delighteth.'

The language of the fathers, that 'our mouth receiveth the Body of Christ,' Bilson reconciles by referring to the well-known habit of calling the signs by the name of the things signified.

'For this cause the great Council of Nice[2] directed the whole Church to lift up their understanding from the bread and wine which they saw, and by faith to conceive the Lamb of God slain for the sins of men, and proposed and exhibited on the Lord's Table in those mysteries; .... which admonition the Church ever after observed, by crying upon

---

[1] Goode, 790.
[2] See the passage referred to in Sect. vii. *post.*

the people to 'lift up their hearts,' not to the sacraments which they saw, but from them to Him that lived and reigned in Heaven. Against them which defend that this sacrament doth only figure not offer,—signify not exhibit,—grace, the letter may well be forced to prove the Divine power and operation of the mystical elements. Against us which hold the visible signs in substance to be creatures, in signification mysteries, in operation and virtue the things themselves, whose names they bear, this illation concludeth nothing; .... together with the name go the virtues of Christ's Flesh and Blood, united in manner of a sacrament to the visible signs. Since the substance of the creatures is not changed, the signs could not justly bear the names of the things themselves except the virtue, power, and effect, of Christ's Flesh and Blood were adjoined to them, and united with them, after a secret and unspeakable manner, by the working of the Holy Ghost, in such sort that whosoever duly receiveth the sign is undoubtedly partaker of the grace..... And that spiritual force and grace, as Gregory saith, may very well be construed to be the *truth* of His Body and Blood in the mysteries.'[1]

The *Cadaver* of Bishop *Andrewes* has been already quoted;[2] but when Archbishop Wake remarks upon his words, that 'a presence of the crucified Body must be *either* figurative in the elements, *or* spiritual to the souls of the worthy receivers,' he hardly does justice to the Anglican teaching. The older divines, we see, regarded the consecrated elements as far more than 'figurative;' they were figures *with the virtue, force, and efficacy of the truth annexed to them.* Whether *per, in, cum,* or *sub,* Andrewes says is matter of opinion, not of faith.[3] What they held was that the thing signified is so really present that it is received together with the sign by all believing

[1] Goode, 800–802.   [2] *Ante,* p. 21.   [3] Adv. Bell. i. 11.

communicants. This is a *mystical* presence, and the same was intended by the old word 'antitypes.' Hence Andrewes prays that

> 'He that breathed, and He that was breathed, may both of them vouchsafe to breathe into these holy mysteries a Divine power and virtue, and make them to us the bread of life and the cup of salvation: God the Father also sending His blessing upon them, that they may be His blessed means of this thrice blessed effect.'[1]

Bishop *Lake*:—

> 'The elements of bread and wine were consecrated that they might be the Body and Blood of Christ. But how are His Body and Blood to be considered? Surely not as Christ is glorified, but as He was crucified. For it is that Body that was given, (as St. Paul speaketh, "was broken,") and the Blood is that blood which was shed.'[2] ... 'The Church of Rome, not distinguishing between Christ crucified and glorified, or rather not building their conclusion answerable to this undeniable principle,—the sacraments represent Christ crucified, not glorified,—are driven to coin so many new articles: 1. of real presence corporal; 2. of a metaphysical transubstantiation; 3. of an ill-applied concomitancy. All which easily vanish, if we consider Christ's purpose to represent Himself in the sacrament, not as He is now at the right hand of God, but as He was upon the cross. Not but it is the same Body and Blood which is in glory, but it must not be so considered as it is in glory. Which will necessarily enforce us to acknowledge, that the union between the thing earthly and the thing heavenly can be no more than sacramental, and that respective also to what was done on earth, not what is in heaven, was, I say, done *formaliter* on the cross, but is effective, working in heaven.'[3]

Archbishop *Laud*:—

> 'Protestants of all sorts maintain a true and Real Presence of Christ in the Eucharist,' and in this particular Calvin "comes no whit short" of Cranmer and Ridley.

---

[1] Sermon ix. Of the Holy Ghost.   [2] Goode, 836.   [3] Ib. 837.

'The Eucharist is a sacrament *Sanguinis effusi*, or blood shed and poured out. And Blood poured out, and so severed from the Body, goes not along with the Body *per concomitantiam*.

'My third instance shall be in the sacrifice which is offered up to God in that great and high mystery of our Redemption by the death of Christ. For as Christ offered up Himself once for all, a full and all-sufficient Sacrifice for the sin of the whole world, so did He institute and command a Memory of this Sacrifice in a sacrament, even till His coming again. For at and in the Eucharist we offer up to God three sacrifices. One by the priest only—that is, the commemorative Sacrifice of Christ's Death, represented in bread broken, and wine poured out. Another, by the priest and people jointly; and that is the sacrifice of praise and thanksgiving, for all the benefits and graces we receive by the precious Death of Christ. The third, by every particular man for himself only; and that is the sacrifice of every man's body and soul, to serve Him in both all the rest of his life, for this blessing thus bestowed on him.' In the note he cites Peter Lombard, that the thing done at God's Board is a sacrifice, and so is that also which was made upon the cross, but not after one manner of understanding. For this was the *thing indeed*, and that is the *Commemoration of the thing*. Such was the 'unbloody sacrifice' of the Fathers; and this Bishop Jewel disliketh not in his answer to Harding.'[1]

Bishop *Cosin* repeats the doctrine of his predecessors:[2]—The Real Presence of Christ in the Eucharist means His real reception into the soul of the communicant. There is no Presence to any but communicants, nor to them without faith.[3] He adopts the great Protestant canon, that no sacrament has the virtue of a sacrament beyond the use ordained by God: and among the 'abominable disputations' of the Romish schools, recited at the end of the tract, one is

---

[1] Fisher, s. xxxv. No. 7, pp. 2, 3.
[2] Hist. Trans. i. 1.   [3] Ibid. iv. 5.

whether the Body of Christ can be moved up and down at the same moment?—elevated (that is) by one priest, and set down by another.'[1] Again, the virtue of the Body is given with the bread, and of the Blood with the wine. When the outward part of the sacrament is said to be changed into the inward and divine, it is only because it represents it truly and efficaciously. And this, he affirms, was the faith of antiquity for a thousand years.[2]

In his 'Notes on the Book of Common Prayer,' Cosin thus comments on the kneeling at Communion:—

'True it is that the Body and Blood of Christ are sacramentally and really (not feignedly) present when the blessed bread and wine are taken by the faithful communicant; and as true it is also that they are not present but only when the hallowed elements are so taken, as in another work I have more at large declared. Therefore whosoever so receiveth them, at the time when he receiveth them, rightly doth he adore and reverence his Saviour, there together with the sacramental bread and wine, exhibiting His own Body and Blood unto him. Yet because the Body and Blood is neither sensibly present, (nor otherways at all present but only to those who are duly prepared to receive them, and in the very act of receiving them and the consecrated elements together, to which they are sacramentally united,) the adoration is then and there given to Christ Himself, neither is nor ought to be directed to any external sensible object, such as are the blessed elements.'

Bishop *Patrick* proves at length from the Fathers,

'That the Presence of Christ's Body in the Eucharist, which they speak of, is of His Body as crucified and slain

---

[1] Hist. Trans. vii. 35.   [2] Ibid. vi. 1.

and dead. Now this cannot agree to His Natural Body, which by our adversaries' confession is impossible and invulnerable, now it is glorified, and cannot admit any separation of parts, which crucifixion does suppose.' He cites as examples the famous passages of Chrysostom: 'Christ lies before us slain.' 'The sacrifice is brought forth, the Lord's Sheep is slain.' 'Thou seest the Lord slain and lying, and the Priest standing by the Sacrifice praying, and all the people purple-dyed in that precious Blood.'[1]

Of the Communion he says:

'If it be worthily received, it is the Body and Blood of Christ: if unworthily, it is but bare bread and wine. But yet this must be cautiously understood, for His Presence is with the Bread, though not *in* it. Though it be only *in* us, yet it comes with it *to* us if we will receive Him; because else we shall not know how unworthy persons are said to be guilty of His Body and Blood, if He be not present with His Body and Blood to work in men's souls.'[2]

Bishop *Bull* writes :—

'In the Holy Eucharist we set before God the bread and wine as figures or images of the precious Blood of Christ shed for us, and of His precious Body, (they are the very words of the Clementine Liturgy,) and plead to God the merit of *His Son's* sacrifice. . . . .
'The Eucharistic Sacrifice was believed in the ancient Church to be an ἀνάμνησις, or commemoration, by the symbols of bread and wine, of the Body and Blood of Christ once offered up to God on the cross for our redemption: it could not therefore be then thought an offering up to God of the very Body and Blood of Christ, substantially present under the appearances of bread and wine; for these two notions are inconsistent, and cannot stand together. . .
Some of the most ancient doctors of the Church, as Justin Martyr and Irenæus, seem to have had this notion, that by or upon the sacerdotal benediction, *the Spirit* of Christ, or a *divine virtue* from Christ, descends upon the elements, and accompanies them to all worthy communicants; and that

---

[1] Full View, &c. Gibson's Preserv. against Popery, p. 213.
[2] Mensa Mystica, i. 5.

therefore they are said to be, and are, the Body and Blood of Christ; the same Divinity, which is *hypostatically* united to the Body of Christ in heaven, being *virtually* united to the elements of bread and wine on earth, which also seems to be the meaning of all the ancient Liturgies.'

Even Bishop *Burnet* asserts in the consecrated elements a

'Real Presence of the Body and Blood of Christ, but not of His Body as it is now glorified in heaven, but of His Body as it was broken on the cross, when His Blood was shed and separated from it. . . . In this sense we acknowledge a Real Presence of Christ in the sacrament.'[1]

Burnet, however, like Ridley, disliked the word Real as applied to the mystical Presence, and would have confined it to the Gift to the faithful receiver, which all admit to be a Presence of the glorified Body by means of the Spirit.

One more extract must suffice.

'The natural Body of our Blessed Saviour comes under a twofold consideration in the Eucharist:—1. *As a body dead;* under which notion we are said to eat it in the sacrament, and to drink the *Blood as shed;* as appears by the words of the Institution, 'Take and eat; this is My Body, which is given or broken for you:' 'Drink ye all of this; for this is My Blood, which is shed for you:' in which words (as Mr. Bradford long ago observed) what God has joined we are not to put asunder. 2. *As a glorified Body;* in which condition it now sits at the right hand of God, and shall there continue till the restitution of all things, imparting grace and influence, and all the benefits purchased by the sacrifice of the dead Body, to those that (in the Holy Eucharist most especially) are through faith, and by the marvellous operation of the Holy Ghost, incorporated into Christ, and so united to Him, that they 'dwell in Christ, and Christ in them; they are one with Christ, and Christ

---

[1] Goode, 672.

with them; they are made members of His body, of His flesh, and of His bones:' and by partaking of the Spirit of Him, their Head, receive all the graces and benefits purchased for them by His bitter death and passion.

'Wherefore it is evident, that since the Body *broken* and the Blood *shed* neither do nor can now really exist, they neither can be really present, nor literally eaten or drank, nor can we really receive *them*, but only the benefits purchased by them. But the Body which now exists, whereof we partake, and to which we are united, is the glorified Body, which is therefore verily and indeed received, (as we shall see anon,) and by consequence said to be really present, notwithstanding its local absence; because a real participation and union must needs imply a real presence, though they do not necessarily require a local one."

These extracts are given at sufficient length to avoid injustice to the several writers: the Church, of course, is never limited by the expressions, or even the conceptions, of individual fathers and doctors. The force of the Anglican, as of Scriptural and patristic theology, lies in distinguishing between the four objects which the Council of Trent labours to confuse. All parties assert the Real Presence (1) of the Divine Person of God the Word; (2) of His true Humanity, Body and Soul now glorified in Heaven; (3) of His Body broken and Blood shed upon the cross; (4) of the Eucharistic bread and wine. But instead of shutting all up in the paten and the chalice, the Anglican divines hold that each is present in its proper manner;—the first by the Omnipresence of God ever working with His gifts, but not comprehended or contained in them;—the second by the hypostatic union of

[1] Sermon by Dean Aldrich, A.D. 1687.

God and Man in Christ, a 'presence (as Hooker phrases it) of true conjunction with Deity;'—the third by mystical power, 'a presence of force and efficacy throughout all generations of men;'—and. the fourth by the natural material presence of the elements in form and substance unchanged.

Each of these is a *real* Presence, in no degree the product of imagination or faith, but the genuine presence of an outward object, and the only presence (it may be reverently affirmed) which that object is capable of exhibiting to man. The province of faith lies in discerning and receiving each in the due sacramental order. First is the oral eating and drinking of the consecrated bread and wine, without which there is neither sacrament nor sacrifice, but a profane empty pageant. In so eating and drinking, the communicant partakes by faith of the Sacrifice of the cross; he spiritually eats the Flesh, and drinks the Blood, which Christ gave for the life of the world; and with this, the sacramental act is complete. But in so partaking of the Body of the Sacrifice, we receive the further gift of incorporation in the Body of the Resurrection. That glorified Humanity, which is bodily at the Right Hand of the Father, is the Instrument— the ὄργανον—of all spiritual life to man,—the true Bread of God which cometh down from heaven,— the life-giving Flesh,—the germ of our resurrection, and the food of immortality. Being cleansed by the sacrificed Body and Blood of the cross, we are incorporated with this new Head of Humanity on high, and so nourished to eternal life. 'We dwell in Christ, and Christ in us: we are one with Christ, and Christ wtih us.'[1] Hence, we are one with God the Word, and in Him with the Eternal Father.

Meantime, the glorified Body of Jesus Christ 'is in heaven and not here.' Its presence in the Eucharist is a presence of conjunction with the Omnipresent Deity. What is *here* is, first the *personal* Presence of the Son of God, drawing with it the Life-giving fellowship of His Humanity in heaven; and secondly, the *mystical* Presence of His sacrificed Body and Blood in the consecrated elements. The first is recognized by all Churches and Confessions as the main object of Eucharistic worship and participation: all acknowledge this Real Presence of the God-man; all too distinguish the spiritual act, which admits Him to the tabernacle of the heart, from the external reception of the sacrament. The Council of Trent itself confesses that the unworthy communicant receives sacramentally only, the worthy both sacramentally and spiritually, and even the believer who desires the sacrament without the opportunity of obtaining it, receives spiritually though not sacramentally. In this highest view of the Presence, then, all agree with Hooker that it is to be sought not in the sacrament, but in the faithful receiver of the sacrament.

[1] Exhortation in Communion Office

The controversy thickens round the mystical Presence in the consecrated elements: but holding fast by the words of Institution, the Body *broken* and the Blood *shed*, it is certain that these are present only in force and efficacy, since Christ is no longer dead in fact. The Sacrifice was finished on the cross, and the state of death passed away in the Resurrection, but the force and efficacy of that death remain with God and man for ever. Now, a thing is as really present in the place where it *operates*, as in the place where it simply *exists* in form and substance. Nay, the power is often the only certain presence; *i.e.* it is sure and cognizable when the substance it proceeds from is unknown and absent. Such a presence our Lord assigns to the Spirit, 'The wind bloweth where it listeth, and thou hearest the sound thereof, but canst not tell whence it cometh nor whither it goeth.' And to the question *how* His Flesh can be given us to eat, He expressly says, 'The words that I speak unto you, they are Spirit, and they are life.'

The Body and Blood of the cross, then, are now nowhere present, save in spirit, power, and efficacy; these our Lord so truly confers on the Eucharistic symbols, that the Body is not another thing united to the bread, or substituted under its form, but the bread is itself the Body, and the wine the Blood, as His own words expressly affirm. The 'divine thing' in the sacrament is neither a Divine Person nor a

Divine substance, but a Divine *quality* (so to speak) imparted to the bread and wine, whereby they are made the communion of the Body and Blood of the cross, and through these of the glorified Body in heaven. This is no rationalizing interpretation, like transubstantiation and the co-existent theory, invented to sustain the presupposed error of a corporal presence, but it is the closest and most literal following of the words, 'This is My Body broken, this is My Blood shed.' Moreover, it is the only reading, we contend, which harmonizes the *entire* Eucharistic doctrine of Holy Scripture and the Primitive Church.

The Protestant Reformation had an easy triumph in re-asserting the Spiritual Presence 'in the heart,' which the corporal error had obscured but not denied. It was equally unanimous in rejecting transubstantiation, but beyond this negative definition it was never successful in restoring the primitive agreement on the mystical presence in the elements.

While Luther held to the corporal error in one direction, the so-called Sacramentaries rushed to the opposite extreme, and denied any spiritual change or gift in the elements at all. They reasoned that no divine act on the material symbols was required, to make them the Lord's Body and Blood to the receiver, since that object was effected by his own faith; and that bread and wine were not fit subjects for the operation of the Holy Ghost. This rationalistic argument reduced consecration to a form, and made a present to the Church of Rome of all the ancient Liturgies and Fathers. For while it is true that these habitually call the sign by the name of the thing signified, yet this custom could never have become so fixed and universal, but for the belief that the sacrament is not only a figure, but 'much more, hath the lively force of the true Body joined thereto, and so comprehendeth both.'

The notion of 'bare signs' is earnestly repudiated in our Articles and Homilies. The liturgical witness against it is *consecration*, on which no episcopal Church ever wavered. If the faith of the receiver alone invests the element with sacramental grace, consecration must be either nugatory or misleading. But consecration meets us from the first. Our Lord Himself not only gave thanks to God over the bread and wine, but He distinctly blessed *them*, before delivering them to His disciples as His Body and Blood. The same condition precedent is repeated by the apostle, 'The cup of blessing *which we bless*, is it not the communion of the Blood of Christ?' *Symbols* the elements are before consecration; after it they are *Sacraments*—*i. e.* symbols with a power and efficacy annexed, which makes them, to the faithful receiver, verily and indeed the Body and Blood of Christ. To deny this is to part at once with Scripture and antiquity. Our Lord's blessing of the bread and wine is solemnly recited in all the Liturgies; all invoke the Holy Ghost to come down upon the elements, and make them His Body and Blood. The Fathers are unanimous in calling them so, as the effect of that prayer.

To the rationalistic argument, that the Holy Ghost disdains to act upon senseless matter, it is answer enough that our Lord and His apostle blessed the bread and the cup. We read that the Spirit moved on the face of the waters to create the world, and the Spirit was breathed into the lifeless clay to make the first man a living soul. Further, the very Flesh of the Second Man was 'conceived by the Holy Ghost.' God the Spirit prepared the tabernacle for God the Word to dwell in. And when 'there went virtue out of Him' to the bodies and souls of men, it commonly passed by some material medium. Such was the 'hem of His garment,' of which S. Augustine finely says, *Turba premit, fides tangit;* such was the clay applied to the sightless eyes, useless, it is true, without faith, yet not void of a Divine gift, since without it the miracle was not wrought. Such, too, were the handkerchiefs and aprons from the apostle's body;[1] —not indeed mechanically saturated with healing for whoever might intercept them, yet still channels, no less than pledges, of grace to the right receiver. Just so the ancient Liturgies invoked the Holy Ghost on the Eucharistic gifts,

[1] Acts, xix. 12.

believing, with Cyril of Jerusalem, that 'what the Holy Ghost touches is thereby sanctified.' They did not ask the glorified Manhood, or the Divine Person, of Christ to descend upon the elements, but the Holy Ghost, 'the Spirit which quickeneth.' Neither was the Spirit expected to unite Himself, or Christ, *hypostatically* to the bread and wine, but to endue them with the power and efficacy of the Crucified Flesh to the communicants.

No less is taught by our own Church in defining Sacraments to be 'not only badges and tokens, but rather certain sure witnesses and effectual signs of grace, and God's good will towards us, *by the which* He doth work invisibly in us, and doth not only quicken, but also strengthen and confirm our faith in Him.'[1] There would have been little occasion to restrain the name of *sacraments* so jealously to the two Institutions of Christ, if she had not understood the word to imply a spiritual virtue in the elements. Visible signs and inward grace are common to Confirmation and Holy Orders; the difference is, that in these latter the sign, not being ordained of Christ as generally necessary to salvation, cannot with equal confidence be alleged as that *by which* God works invisibly in us. The sign and the grace are present together, but the connexion between them is not declared 'certain,' as in Baptism and the Holy Eucharist.

[1] Article XXV.

With the same feeling our Church declares Water and the Name of the Holy Trinity,—not the sponsions, or even the prayers,—to be the 'essential parts of Baptism': and her doctrine is again expressed in the petition, 'sanctify this water to the mystical washing away of sin.' Now no one will suppose the sanctification of the sacramental bread to be less real than that of the sacramental water: on the contrary, consecration is not deemed so indispensable in Baptism as in the Eucharist. The fathers regard these two sacraments as each communicating Christ for its own purport: neither contains Him in substance, but each is endowed with a special gift, whereby His spiritual Presence is both pledged and conveyed to the fit receiver.

The reality of this gift does not depend on the faith of the receiver, any more than on the worthiness of the minister, but on the commission and authority of Christ.[1] It is not less really present because the unworthy communicant receives it not, any more than the sun is absent because a blind man cannot see it. Indeed, the judgment pronounced on those who 'discern not the Lord's Body' implies its Presence, though it is a spiritual not a corporal Presence.

Clear, however, as the distinction seems between a Divine Person and a Divine quality, it is to be regretted that many Protestants, and some, it may be feared, in our own Church, are still as

[1] Article XXVI.

unable to receive it as the Romanists themselves. The Romanist will have the living Person of Christ to be veiled under the forms of bread and wine,—in the face of his own prayer, that the bread and wine themselves may be made to those who receive them His crucified Body and Blood. With no less inconsistency, the ultra-Protestant can see nothing but an empty figure in that which Christ consecrated to the Real participation of His Body and Blood. Between these extremes the Church of England keeps the middle path of primitive truth. For Christ, she bids her children prepare the tabernacle which He loves, in the heart. To His one Sacrifice on the cross she refers all our propitiation. Yet with deepest reverence would she handle, and on her knees receive, the Holy Gifts, which are to us the Body and Blood of that all-reconciling Sacrifice. For these are not symbols only, but symbols which the Holy Ghost has touched, and to the faithful receiver verily and indeed what they represent.

Widely different was the doctrine maintained in Johnson's 'Unbloody Sacrifice,' and generally imputed to the Nonjurors. Though illustrated by a large array of patristic learning, that writer's views were unsound in a vital point; they are now seldom heard of, but it may help to complete the Anglican view if we point out the defect. Johnson insisted so much on consecration and a real sacrifice, that he was most unjustly accused of Popery. But the *oblata* with him were nothing but bread and wine, and not even symbols of the Body and Blood of the cross. So far from holding a corporal Presence, he characterized the adoration of the elements as horrible idolatry, and even denied a Real Presence altogether. His theory was, that our Blessed Lord constituted and offered in the paschal chamber a *symbolical* Body and Blood in bread and wine; and *this*, not the sacrifice of the cross, is the sacrifice both offered and partaken of in the Blessed Sacrament. 'That our Saviour commanded His disciples to eat that very Body of His, which was given or offered to God for them' on the cross, he treats as 'the gross error of transubstantiation,' or one of the 'other odd conceits of the Lutherans and Calvinists.' The sacrifice of the cross, he says,

'has now no being in the nature of things; for the Body and Blood of Christ, as they are represented in the Eucharist, separate from each other, are now nowhere in the universe. If Christ had never offered any but His Natural Body, then, it must be confessed, this argument would be of some weight. But now the sum and substance of the true doctrine of the Eucharist I take to be this: that what Christ offered to God and gave to His disciples to eat, was consecrated bread; and that the reason why He honoured it with the *title* of His Body was because He did, in offering the bread to God, in His own intention offer His Body as a sacrifice for the sins of men.'[1]

Agreeing with the Romanists that the thing *sacrificed* in the Eucharist is identical with the

[1] Unbloody Sacrifice, Part ii. Pref.

thing *partaken of*, he denied that this was really the Body of Christ, and so reduced communion itself to a merely figurative action. Instead of being a feast on the true Sacrifice of the cross, he made it only a feast on the symbolical sacrifice of the Supper. He says expressly,

'Unless the consecrated bread and wine be the sacrifice on which we feast, it is certain that both the sacrifice and the feast must be a mere airy notion.'[1]

At the same time, Johnson firmly held that Christ offered but one Sacrifice once for all.

'He began this oblation in the Eucharist, and continued it on the Cross. Nothing but His death could be a satisfaction for our sins, and this was actually accomplished on the Cross. And this death of His was never to be repeated; it was the effect of His personal oblation of Himself, which He began in the Eucharist; and since He was but once to offer, He was but once to die. It seems clear to me that the one personal oblation performed by our Saviour Himself is not to be confined to any one instant of time, but commenced with the Paschal solemnity, and was finished at His Ascension into Heaven, there to appear in the presence of God for us.'[2]

The peculiarity of his view is that it makes the Eucharist exhibit and communicate not the Body and Blood of the cross, but the bread and wine 'honoured with those titles' in the paschal chamber; and to this effect Johnson interprets these names throughout the fathers. It is true that he holds the bread and wine to be the Body and Blood of the cross 'in power and

[1] Unbloody Sacrifice, Part ii. Pref.
[2] Ibid. cap. ii. sect. i.

effect,' by virtue of the Institution; but they communicate *directly* of the Supper, and only *indirectly* of the Cross. In short, there is no *res sacramenti* in his system; and the result, in spite of his high Catholic pretensions, is something lower than Zwinglianism itself. He avows that his doctrine 'is not only inconsistent with transubstantiation, (and consubstantiation,) but with that Real Presence of the Body of Christ in the Eucharist, which is the common opinion of Protestants abroad.'[1]

Nothing certainly could be further than this view from the sacrifice of the Mass. Yet it was based on the same fundamental error, of supposing that nothing is *communicated* in the Holy Eucharist but that which is there *sacrificed*. The Romanists, holding a true participation of the Sacrifice of the cross, insist also on a true oblation of it. Johnson, perceiving the oblation to be mystical and symbolical, reduced the participation to the same character. The true doctrine of a *symbolical oblation*, and a *Real Communion*, escaped both.

[1] Unbloody Sacrifice. Preface to 2nd Part, ii. iii.

V.—THE NEW OBJECTIVE THEORY.

AFTER so many painful disputations, it was to be hoped that a new theory of Sacramental Presence would never again be attempted. The Church of England had especial reasons for accepting the exhortation of her most judicious divine, 'Let disputes and questions, enemies to piety, abatements of true devotion, hitherto in this cause but over patiently heard, let them take their rest.'[1] The Blessed Sacrament had risen to a degree of reverence among our people, not surpassed in any Church since the primitive ages. Its celebration was becoming daily more frequent and devout. The cavils of the Puritans were forgotten; the rationalistic explanations of the eighteenth century were almost everywhere superseded by higher and holier expositions of Catholic truth; and at no time since the Reformation was the Liturgy so loyally rendered, both in doctrine and ceremonial. At such a time it is peculiarly distressing that the hope of still higher unity, in this central bond of light and love, should be imperilled by new scholastic definitions.

What the 'Real *Objective* Presence' precisely means no one has distinctly explained; but as the word is not to be found in any of our elder

[1] Eccl. Pol. v. lxvii. 12.

divines, nor any equivalent to it in the fathers, it cannot escape the suspicion which justly attaches to every innovation on the terminology of the Church. We are not now to learn that new and unauthorized words imply new and unauthorized conceptions.

The new term is put forward in supersession of the recognized distinction of *corporal* and *spiritual*, and at first sight it is not clear to which of those antagonistic terms it is most closely allied. Its authors wish to mark more emphatically the *reality* of the sacramental Presence, but when interrogated whether it is a *corporal* or *spiritual* reality, their language is found ambiguous and inconclusive.

The term itself is a metaphysical one, imported into English theology within our own recollection. It was coined by the German philosophers to indicate an object existing independently of the observer, in opposition to an idea within his own mind, which they call a *subjective* impression. The metaphysicians, however, are themselves divided on the truth of this distribution. While one school conceives the mind may employ itself on objects wholly external to itself, another contends (with more probability) that the object of cognition is never matter *per se*, but matter *plus* the mind's own perception, or (as Professor Ferrier quaintly phrases it) not *thing* absolutely, but *thing mecum*.[1] In this view,

[1] Ferrier's Philosophical Remains.

then, a strictly *objective* presence is an impossible conception.[1]

However this may be, it is certainly a very novel and unskilful attempt, to subject the Divine Presence to this metaphysical distribution. God is present with all His works, and all things live and move in Him; yet He is neither contained in matter, nor subject to mind. When the soul seeks communion with its Maker, His Presence is not the offspring of imagination, but the Real Presence of a different and higher Personality. And when we contemplate Him in His own perfections, He is still none the less in ourselves. Hence the metaphysical ideas of objectivity and subjectivity are radically inapplicable to the sacramental Presence; the introduction of the words can only tend to substitute some vague indeterminate conception, in place of the recognized ideas connected with the old theological terms 'spiritual' and 'corporal.'[2] Such conceptions are always fluctuating; an inaccurate terminology is necessarily ambiguous, and ambiguous words easily exceed the arbitrary limits originally assigned to them.

[1] 'The unhappy disjunction of subjective from objective, of idea from appearance, of history from speculation, has brought our national mind into great confusion.'—*Baron Bunsen, Letter, June,* 1835. *Memoirs*, vol. i. p. 412.

[2] It is to be regretted, therefore, that an Oxford Divinity Professor should permit himself to defend a subjective presence *against* the objective. The novelty ought to be firmly resisted.

One of the first to write of the Objective Presence was Archdeacon Wilberforce, in his 'Doctrine of the Incarnation.' (1848.)

> 'When spiritual presence is spoken of, there are two notions which may suggest themselves. Such presence may either be supposed to result from the action of the mind, which receives an impression, or from the action of the being who produces it. The first would be a subjective and metaphorical, the second is an objective and real presence. .... A real presence is when there is some object external to ourselves which produces upon us those effects which result from its propinquity. And such presence may be said to be spiritual, as well as real, when the medium of communication by which this external object affects or is present with us, is not material contact but spiritual power.'[1]

Here the words 'objective' and 'subjective' are plainly superfluous. The doctrine maintained is simply the old Real and Spiritual Presence;—*real* because the effect of an object external to ourselves; and *spiritual*, because the medium of communication is 'not material contact, but spiritual power.' Such a Presence the archdeacon ascribes to the sacrament of Baptism, no less than to the Eucharist, and he follows Hooker in deriving it from our Lord's Human Nature *in heaven*, as the channel of mediation between God and man. This is the doctrine of all our old divines, and of the fathers before them; and there was no occasion for new metaphysical terms to express it.

Since then, however, the word 'spiritual' has been dropped, and 'objective' is joined with

[1] Doctrine of the Incarnation, p. 433.

Real, as if denoting some additional conception. Moreover, the 'Real Objective Presence' is not now predicated of both sacraments alike, but of the Eucharist only. And in fine we are told that Hooker was 'not a believer in the Real Presence,'[1] (meaning the Objective,) although the same writer, in the preface to his greatest work, some twenty years earlier, after doing justice to the 'limitations under which the doctrine of the Real Presence is to be received,' writes that 'whatever notion of the Real Presence does not in effect interfere with this foundation of the faith, that, the genuine philosophy of Hooker, no less than his sound theology, taught him to embrace with all his heart.'[2]

It is clear, then, that the meaning of the new term has undergone some considerable development within our own time: nor is this surprising, seeing it never had any scientific footing to stand upon. Such fluctuations may occur without the observation of the mind that submits to them; it was doubtless such an unconscious process that induced the mutilation of the really Catholic lines,

> 'O come to our Communion feast!
> There present in the heart,
> *Not* in the hand, the Eternal Priest
> Will His true Self impart.'

---

[1] Keble's Euch. Adoration.
[2] Eccl. Pol. Pref. lxxxi. Mr. Keble selects the reality and exclusiveness of sacramental grace as a point of superiority in Hooker over Jewel, yet Bishop Cosin considers Jewel to hold the Real Presence.

The posthumous substitution of 'as' for 'not,' in the third line, not only spoils the poetry and vigour of the whole stanza, but makes an expression which few intelligent Romanists would like to endorse. After this, it is no wonder that a later disciple should avow that 'Objective' not only means what used to be called 'corporal,' but includes the tenet of transubstantiation itself; it being quite a mistake to suppose there is any difference between the Anglican and Roman Churches on the Doctrine of the Real Presence![1]

The most authentic enunciation of the Objective theory is contained in a manifesto, styling itself a 'profession of faith,' lately addressed to the Archbishop of Canterbury, and circulated in the Appendix to the First Report of the Royal Commission on Ritual. This paper is signed by twenty-three clergymen anxious to purge themselves from the imputation of 'disloyalty to the Church of England.' It claims to state what they

'believe to be the mind of our Lord, as expressed in Holy Scripture, and as received by the Church of England in conformity with the teaching of the Catholic Church in those ages to which the Church of England directs us as "most pure and uncorrupt," and of the "old godly doctors," to whom she has in many ways referred us.' This 'profession of faith' is made known (the writers add) 'for the quieting of the minds of others, and for the satisfaction of our own consciences.'

This somewhat overweening language is not supported by a single citation or authority from

[1] Kiss of Peace.

antiquity, and by only a few dislocated extracts from our own formularies. No explanation is offered of the term 'Objective,' though certainly unknown to any church, father, or doctor, ancient or modern: on the dogma which it is meant to denote, we read as follows:

'We repudiate the opinion of "a Corporal Presence of Christ's natural Flesh and Blood," that is to say, of the Presence of His Body and Blood as they "are in Heaven;" and the conception of the mode of His Presence, which implies the physical change of the natural substances of the Bread and Wine, commonly called Transubstantiation. We believe that in the Holy Eucharist, by virtue of the consecration, through the power of the Holy Ghost, the Body and Blood of our Saviour Christ, "the inward part or thing signified," are present, really and truly, but spiritually and ineffably, under "the outward visible part or sign" or "form of Bread and Wine."'

This article, it will be observed, evades the point of the controversy, whether the Presence is by material contact or by spiritual power—*i. e.* whether it is corporal or spiritual. The corporal Presence here repudiated is one that was never affirmed: neither Romanists nor Lutherans believe that Christ's natural Flesh and Blood are present in the sacrament 'as they are in heaven.' On the contrary, they assert it to be in a manner altogether different, and peculiar to the Eucharist. They say that Christ is present in the matter of the sacrament, *i. e.* by material contact; and the Church of England says, in the rubric misquoted by the memorialists, that His Body and Blood 'are in heaven, *and not here*, it being against the truth of Christ's natural Body to be at the same time in more places than one.' This is certainly widely different from the repudiation in this manifesto.

Equally ineffective is the disclaimer of the *word* transubstantiation: for in the first place it might only substitute the Lutheran for the Tridentine 'conception;' and in the next, the disclaimer is so encumbered by the epithets 'physical' and 'commonly called,' as to leave it doubtful whether the Tridentine doctrine be excluded after all. Dr. Pusey has publicly stated that the words 'commonly called' were inserted by himself expressly to lessen the force of the protest against the Romish definition. By others it is argued that our Articles are not levelled at the true doctrine of that Church, but at 'certain carnal notions current in the sixteenth century which were very considerably rectified by the Council of Trent.'[1] One writer boldly asserts that there is *no difference* between the teaching of the Church of Rome and the Objective Presence of his own school.[2]

In presence of these statements, the carefully restricted 'repudiations' of this manifesto amount to little or nothing: we must proceed to its positive enunciations in order to know the extent of the new dogma.

Now, if the words Body and Blood of Christ mean in this paper—as they ought to mean—the

[1] Church and the World, p. 207.   [2] Kiss of Peace.

crucified Flesh of Christ, and not, as the Romanists and Lutherans teach, His glorified Person, it must follow that they are 'really and truly present' in mystery, not in substance—*i.e.* in spiritual power, not by material contact. This is truly Catholic and Anglican doctrine. But this interpretation seems to be shut out by the Romish expression, 'under the form of bread and wine.' It is true that in the Latin fathers *species* means substance, and not mere accidents, yet the presence of two substances under one form would imply 'material contact.' The phrase imports the Lutheran, if not the Tridentine, conception, and was probably on that account deliberately rejected from the Anglican formularies.[1] Cranmer accuses Gardiner of 'a plain untruth' in imputing the use of this phrase to the Church of England; and it is clear

[1] It is hardly ingenuous, after the mistake has been repeatedly exposed, to persist in fathering this expression on the 'Book of Homilies.' In his letter to the Bishop of London (1851) Dr. Pusey justifies his use of the phrase on the ground that 'they are the words used in the Homilies, "of the due receiving of the Blessed Body and Blood of Christ under the *form* of Bread and Wine."' He writes, 'I have meant them in the same sense in which the Homilies use them, and have used them *because* they were there used.' The truth is that these words are *not* used in any Homily, nor was there ever a Homily bearing the title here alleged. Such a Homily was *promised* in a notice appended to the First Book of Homilies,—a notice for which no better authority than the King's printer can be cited,—but the Homily itself appeared in the Second Book under the title of 'The Worthy Receiving of the Sacrament of the Body and Blood of Christ;' and by that title alone it is recognized in the Thirty-fifth Article.

that its removal from the title of the Homily was a designed repudiation of the words, as involving the Corporal Presence, which Cranmer was at first inclined to retain on the Lutheran explanation.[1] Bishop Andrewes censures the Latin equivalent as a novelty unknown in the time of Augustine.[2]

Neither is it in any way recognized (as the manifesto insinuates) by the use of the word 'form' in the Church of England Catechism. For, in the first place, this word is *not* there applied to the Eucharist, but only to Baptism, of which no one would say that the inward part or thing signified (a death unto sin, &c.) is really and truly present under the form of water. In the next place, the only presence asserted in the Catechism is the Real Presence to the faithful receiver. The words 'inward' and 'outward' refer not to the sacrament, but to the receiver. The 'outward visible sign or form' in baptism is outward (or objective) to the person baptized; the inward and spiritual grace is the gift received by him along with, but not enclosed in, the water. The same construction must of course belong to the 'outward and inward parts' of the other sacrament. The Catechism (like the fathers) speaks of these two sacraments in the same language. Each is the sign of an inward and spiritual grace

---

[1] The authorities are given at length in the late Dean of Ripon's industrious compilation, 'The Nature of Christ's Presence in the Eucharist,' (London, 1856,) pp. 40–47.

[2] Adv. Bell.

given to the fit receiver. The grace is given and received when the sacrament is given and received, 'semel et simul,' as Bishop Cosin says; but it is not therefore mechanically enclosed in the sign (like a jewel in a casket) in the one sacrament any more than the other. Bishop Andrewes remarks that *in, per, sub,* or *cum,* are matters of opinion, not of faith. What is Catholic is the Real Presence to the devout receiver: if the Objective Presence mean the Presence of Christ's Person, either in the material elements or 'under their forms,' irrespective of communion, it is neither Catholic nor true.

Archdeacon Wilberforce observes on Transubstantiation:

> 'First, that the consecrated elements, even if they undergo a material change, have no more tendency than without such change to produce the real ends which result from Sacraments; and secondly, that to rest on such a change is incompatible with a reference to our Lord's *ascended* Manhood, as that Head of the renewed race, with whom it is the purpose of Sacraments to unite us. . . . A spiritual efficacy indeed our Lord's Body has on all those with whom, *according to its proper law of action,* it is brought into connexion, *but would this action attend its material consumption?* Is there any relevance between union with the Flesh of the Son of Man and the carnal devouring Him? We are united to Adam by one means; to Christ by another. The first is by the law of paternity; the second by that of regeneration. Why should we increase our relation to Christ by this carnal banquet, any more than we should to Adam by the eating of his flesh? A spiritual effect of the Manhood of our Great Head *must proceed through spiritual action from His purified Humanity.*'[1]

---

[1] Incarnation, p. 428.

Now, that Humanity being beyond question in heaven, the argument here framed against transubstantiation is equally cogent against every form of material contact—*i. e.* every hypothesis which would lodge the thing signified in the matter of the sacramental elements. Such a Presence effects nothing towards the object in view, while it is inconsistent with the true action of our Lord's Manhood in heaven; to which our Church has added, as the result of a sad experience, 'it hath given occasion to many superstitions.'[1]

It is singular that a Paper, designed to repel the suspicion of disloyalty to the Church of England, should contain no allusion to *participation*, which is, after all, the main use of the sacrament, and in which *alone* the Anglican formularies assert the Real Presence. The Catechism affirms that 'the Body and Blood of Christ are verily and indeed *taken and received* by the faithful in the Lord's Supper; but it maintains a significant silence on the Presence in the elements by consecration, apart from reception, asserted by the Tridentine and Lutheran definitions. Hooker says, 'The bread and the cup are His Body and Blood, because they are causes instrumental upon the receipt whereof the participation of His Body and Blood ensueth.'[2] As far as was known to this great divine, there are but three expositions

[1] Art. XXVIII.   [2] Eccl. Pol. v. lxvii. 5.

made of 'this is My Body,'—the Lutheran, the Popish, and that of the Church of England, which Bishop Cosin thinks to be common to other Protestant Confessions. The former two Hooker describes as defining 'what the sacrament is *in itself and before participation;*' the last as asserting only 'what it is unto faithful receivers.' This last he affirms to

'have in it nothing but what all the rest do approve and acknowledge to be most true, nothing but that which the words of Christ are on all sides confessed to enforce, nothing but that which the Church of God hath always thought necessary, nothing but that which alone is sufficient for every Christian man to believe, concerning the use and force of this sacrament, finally nothing but that wherewith the writings of all antiquity are consonant, and all Christian confessions agreeable.'[1]

In the fathers it is certain that *all* which they teach of the Sacramental Presence has relation to the act of communion; and no passage can be produced from Scripture or any 'godly doctor of the most pure and uncorrupt ages' in which the Real Presence is asserted irrespective of participation. Yet this essential condition is wholly omitted from the late enunciation of the 'Objective' Presence. Is it probable that a *fourth* interpretation, unknown to Hooker, has been discovered? or must these writers be supposed to imply a condition which they have omitted to express? Either supposition is fatal to their pretensions to represent

[1] Ibid. lxviii. 12.

the true doctrine of antiquity and the Church of England. Writers who choose to speak where the Church is silent, and to keep silence where the Church has unequivocally pronounced, are not entitled to complain if they are suspected of disloyalty. It is their own fault if their Objective Presence is classed in the corporal rather than the spiritual category.[1]

The ambiguity thus cast over the first article of the new profession, will be found to envelope all the remainder.

The second article runs thus:—

'We repudiate the notion of any fresh Sacrifice, or any view of the Eucharistic Sacrificial Offering as of something apart from the one all-sufficient Sacrifice and Oblation on the Cross, which alone "is that perfect Redemption, Propitiation, and Satisfaction for all the sins of the whole world, both original and actual," and which alone is "meritorious."

'We believe that as in heaven Christ our great High Priest ever offers Himself before the Eternal Father, pleading by His Presence His sacrifice of Himself once offered on the Cross; so on earth, in the Holy Eucharist, that same Body, once for all sacrificed for us, and that same Blood, once for all shed for us, sacramentally present, are offered and pleaded before the Father by the Priest, as our Lord ordained to be done in remembrance of Himself when He instituted the Blessed Sacrament of His Body and Blood.'

---

[1] How *far* the Objective theory follows the Roman error is left in doubt by the ambiguity of the language; but that it already begins to waver on the *mystery of the cup* is seen in Mr. Keble's strange suggestion that it may be the symbol of our Lord's *Human Soul.* (*Euch. Adoration.*) Such a symbol would doubtless be a great help to the Corporal Presence; but it is necessarily *absent* from the sacrament, since the Soul was in Paradise when the Body was *broken* and the Blood *shed.*

Here, again, every one acquainted with the controversy with Rome must desire that a charge of 'disloyalty to the Church of England' had been met in language more frank and intelligible. The 'Eucharistic Sacrifice' means either the sacrifice of praise and thanksgiving made in the whole celebration, closing with participation; or the ritual act of oblation during the consecration of the sacrament. Which of these two is here intended by the 'Eucharistic sacrificial offering,' is not said, though far more important than anything actually stated in this Paper.

Supposing the ritual oblation to be intended, the article follows the Church of Rome, against the unanimous testimony of antiquity, in making it consist of the *consecrated* elements. In the primitive Church (as will be shown from the Liturgies) the Oblation introduced, and was completed in, the Consecration. The bread and wine were offered as symbols of the Body and Blood; and it was in order to *reception* that the Holy Ghost was invoked, to make them the Body and Blood in spiritual truth and efficacy.

This mistake at the outset cannot but excite some suspicion of what follows. The paragraph opens, as before, with repudiations, designed to parry the censure of the English formularies. But it is remarkable that they extend only to the *first half* of the Thirty-first Article, and cease at the very point where the Church directs them against the Tridentine tenet :—

'*Wherefore* the sacrifices of masses, in the which it was commonly said that the Priest did offer Christ for the quick and the dead, to have remission of pain or guilt, were blasphemous fables and dangerous deceits.'

In the *application*, then, of their repudiation, the memorialists decline—or at least omit—to follow their Church. The theory that the Article was not aimed at the doctrine of the Mass as defined at Trent, but at some popular and coarse misconceptions current at the time, is refuted by the *date*: the Tridentine decree was adopted on the 17th September 1562, and our Article was subscribed the 29th January *following*, obviously as the protest and denial of this Church.[1]

Not to dwell, however, upon this, the first difficulty is to know in what sense the Body of Christ is said to be 'offered before the Father by the priest.' This is not cleared by repudiations which repudiate nothing affirmed in the Tridentine decree, while the statements 'that the same Body and Blood are offered by the priest that were sacrificed on the cross,' and further that 'this is not a fresh sacrifice,' nor 'anything apart from the sacrifice of the cross,' seem to go the whole length of the Roman Mass. It is true that the words 'sacramentally present' are introduced, which, if interpreted '*figuratively* present,' would entirely change the meaning. But this interpretation seems inconsistent with the definition of the Objective Presence in the first

[1] By the English computation the year began in March.

article, and with the adoration declared in the third to be due to 'Christ in the sacrament.' Taken as a whole, the majority of readers would probably understand the doctrine as identical with the sacrifice of the Mass.

On the other hand, if the elements remain unchanged in the oblation, a *compound* sacrifice of the real Body and Blood, *along with* bread and wine, is a notion hitherto unheard of. In asserting the Corporal Presence, the Church of Rome gets rid of the elements, and the Lutherans suppress the oblation; but no one ever imagined a united sacrifice of Body and bread together. Again, it must be borne in mind that the English Liturgy contains in fact no oblation of the *consecrated* elements: *nothing* whatever is allowed to be done with them but to eat and drink them in Holy Communion. So that, without avowing the disloyalty which they come forward to disclaim, the writers of this paper could not possibly claim to offer what the priest is supposed to offer in the Mass.

When thus compelled to go in quest of another meaning, we find expressions which might do away with the sacrifice altogether. The Body and Blood are rightly said to have been 'once for all sacrificed on the cross;' hence they cannot be sacrificed again. Moreover, 'any fresh sacrifice' is expressly repudiated, and 'offering' is explained by 'pleading,' which *may* import nothing more than prayer. Further, this pleading is likened to that of Christ in heaven, where it is certain He does not 'offer

Himself often,' but pleads by His Presence, and the value of the Blood once shed upon the cross. According to this comparison, then, there might be no sacrifice at all in the Eucharist, but only a Presence and Remembrance. After steering right upon Scylla, these navigators suddenly threaten us with Charybdis.

The middle course has to be sought in yet a third interpretation. The words 'sacramentally present,' properly mean 'present in sacrament or figure;' and by pursuing this clue, we may arrive at the Memorial Sacrifice, really taught by the fathers and the great Anglican writers. But then this sacrifice, though certainly 'not apart from the cross,' *is* a 'fresh sacrifice' every time it is offered; and this the article denies. And again, it requires participation by all who make the oblation; and on this the article, like the Tridentine decree, is silent.

The great English divines, quoted not many years ago in Dr. Pusey's Letter to the Bishop of London, speak with no such uncertain sound:—

'We offer to Thy view and set before Thine eyes the *crucified* Body of Christ Thy Son, which is here present *in mystery and sacrament*, and the Blood which He once shed for our sakes, which we know to be that pure, holy, undefiled, and eternal Sacrifice, wherewith only Thou art pleased; desiring Thee to be merciful unto us for the merit and worthiness *thereof*, and so to look upon the same sacrifice, which *representatively* we offer to Thy view,' &c.— *Field.*

'Christ intercedes for us, and represents an eternal Sacrifice in the heavens on our behalf. . . . Now what Christ does in heaven He hath commanded us to do on earth, that is, to *represent His Death*, to *commemorate* His Sacrifice.'—*Jeremy Taylor*.

'The holy fathers very often say that the very Body of Christ (crucified) is offered and sacrificed in the Eucharist, ... not properly and really, but by a *commemoration* and *representation* of that which was once accomplished in that one Sacrifice of the Cross.'—*Bishop W. Forbes*.

'Whereas the Holy Eucharist is by itself a Sacrament, wherein God offers unto all men the blessings merited by the Oblation of His Son, it likewise becomes *by our remembrance* a *kind of sacrifice also*; whereby we present and expose before His eyes that same holy and precious Oblation once offered.'—*Dr. Brevint*.

'There is no new sacrifice, but the same which was once offered, and which is every day offered, to God by Christ in heaven, and continueth here still on earth, by a *mystical representation* of it in the Eucharist.'—*Bishop Overall*.

'It is not mental thinking or verbal speaking, there must be actually somewhat done to celebrate this memory. That done to the *holy symbols* that was done to Him, to His Body and His Blood, in the Passover:—break the one, pour out the other, to *represent* κλώμενον, how His sacred Body was broken, and ἐκχυνόμενον, how His precious Blood was shed.

'And in *Corpus fractum* and *Sanguis fusus* there is *immolatus*. This is it in the Eucharist that answereth to the sacrifice in the Passover—the Memorial to the figure. To them it was, *Hoc facite in mei præfigurationem*—"do this in prefiguration of Me." To us it is, "Do this in commemoration of Me." To them, *prænuntiare;* to us, *anuntiare*. There is the difference. By the same rules that theirs was, by the same may ours be, termed a sacrifice. In rigour of speech, neither of them : for, to speak after the exact manner of Divinity, there is but one only sacrifice, *veri nominis*, properly so called : that is Christ's death. And that sacrifice but once actually performed at His death, but ever before represented in figure from the beginning ; and ever since repeated, in memory, to the world's end. That only absolute ; all else relative to it, representative of it, operative by it. The Lamb, but once actually slain, in the fulness of time; but virtually was from the beginning, is, and shall be to the end of the world. That, the Centre, in which their lines and ours—their types and our antitypes—do meet. While yet this offering was not, the hope of it was kept alive, by the prefiguration of it, in theirs. And after it is past, the memory of it is still kept fresh in mind, by the *commemoration* of it, in ours. So it was the will of God; that so there might be with them a continual foreshowing, and with us a continual "showing forth the Lord's death, till He come again." Hence it is that what names theirs carried, ours do the like, and the Fathers make no scruple at it, no more need we. The Apostle (in the tenth chapter) compareth this of ours to the *immolata* of the heathen; and (to the Hebrews) *habemus aram*, matcheth it with the sacrifice of the Jews. And we know the rule of comparisons; they must be *ejusdem generis*.'—*Bishop Andrewes*, Sermon vii. on the Resurrection.

'If we take a sacrifice properly and formally, whether for the action of sacrificing (as it is this day taken by the Roman priests) [or for the thing sacrificed[1]] then truly, although by the Commemoration and Representation it be the same numerical sacrifice with that which was offered on the cross, yet the action itself, or the oblation which is now made by us in the Eucharist, agrees neither in species nor genus with the oblation or immolation which was on the cross. For there is no form or reason of the oblation given which can be univocally predicated of that: for upon the cross the Oblation was made by a true destruction and death of the Live Thing, without which no sacrifice, properly so called, can be; but in our Eucharist there is a sacrifice made by prayers, a *Commemoration*, and a *Representation*, which is not properly called a sacrifice. But nothing hinders but that the Eucharist may be accounted and called the Commemorative Sacrifice of the proper Sacrifice of the death of Christ, which our Lord Himself hath taught us when He said, "This do in remembrance of Me."'—*Bishop Cosin*, Notes in Nicholl's Book of Common Prayer.

'His Bloody Sacrifice upon the Cross is by this unbloody *commemoration represented*, called to remembrance and applied.'—*Bishop White*.

---

[1] The alternative is omitted in the Bishop's note.

'We acknowledge a *representation* of that Sacrifice to God the Father. We acknowledge an imputation of the benefit of it, and we maintain an application of its virtue.' (in the communion.)—*Archbishop Bramhall.*

'1. We do show forth the Lord's Death, and declare it unto men. 2. We do show it forth unto God, and *commemorate* before Him the great things He hath done for us. We keep it, as it were, in His memory, and plead before Him the sacrifice of His Son.'—*Bishop Patrick.*

'The mystery of this rite they took to be this: that as Christ, by presenting His Death and Satisfaction to His Father, continually intercedes for us in heaven, so the Church on earth semblably approaches the throne of grace by *representing* Christ unto His Father in these holy mysteries of His death and Passion.'—*Mede.*

These are the teachers whom the subscribers to this Paper would be thought to follow. One and all they regard the Eucharistic Sacrifice as a very different thing from the Sacrifice of the Cross, which it commemorates. *Representation* and *commemoration* are the ideas constantly repeated. These are the key-notes of the Catholic harmony—*identity* is the peculiar discord of Rome. Is it permissible, then, in a paper professing to represent the doctrine of the Church of England, to suppress the thoughts continually on her lips, and expatiate in the terms proper to her adversary? This is assuredly not the way to rebut suspicion, or 'quiet the minds of others.'

The third article enunciates the opinion of the writers on Eucharistic Adoration;—another phrase, like the Objective Presence, wholly unknown to Catholic antiquity. Beginning, as before, with an unmeaning repudiation, it disclaims 'all adoration of the Sacramental Bread and Wine, which would be idolatry,'—words logically importing that *some* adoration of them is not idolatry,—and further, 'all adoration of a corporal Presence of Christ's natural Flesh and Blood,' but with the same absurd limitation to a condition never asserted, 'that is to say, of His Body and Blood *as they are in heaven.*' The logical inference again is that a corporal Presence under some other conditions *is* the object of adoration in the Eucharist; and this is exactly the Tridentine doctrine.

If we take the repudiation in the most favourable sense, as disclaiming any adoration whatever of the sacramental bread and wine, the question remains, what the writers mean by adoration? At the close of their paper they justify certain ritual acts practised by some of their number, (admitted to be 'beyond what had become common in our churches,') as parts of 'a worship in harmony with the principles and law' here imputed to the Church of England.

Now one of the most questioned of such practices, is the priest kneeling down before each element, immediately after pronouncing the words of Institution, and then elevating it for a similar act of homage on the part of the people. There is no rubric in the existing Liturgy to authorize this practice, and in the First Book of Edward VI. the showing the sacrament to the people was expressly forbidden. Those who adopt it, rely on the rules or usage in force in England before the Reformation, of which the Roman Missal is regarded as the authorized exponent; now in that Missal they are expressly termed the 'adoration of the sacred host.'[1] Is it maintained that an act so characterized by the Church which invented and authorized it, is not the same act when copied, without authority, in another Church? or are we to fall back on the mental reservation of the Lutherans that, although the act is the same, the *intention* is different?

Suppose that in the primitive Church one accused of adoring an idol, had replied that he did indeed cast the incense into the fire upon the altar, but that in his own mind he directed his adoration to Christ, would the fathers have held him guiltless of idolatry? This very case was in fact often before the early Church. The educated heathen pleaded then—as the Brahmans plead still—that they worshipped not the image, but God in the image. Yet this was ever counted as idolatry. Indeed it is the act rather than the intention, which is regarded in the second Commandment. The worship of another God is forbidden by the first: what the second prohibits is the bowing down to a material object as embodying the true God. Hence the Israelites

---

[1] In point of fact, the Sarum rubric simply directed elevation and exhibition of the Sacrament, which are accordingly the acts forbidden in the First Book of Edward VI. The Roman Missal has plainly *hostiam consecratam genuflexus adorat*.

were guilty of this sin, notwithstanding that they professed to adore Jehovah, and proclaimed before the golden calf, 'These be thy gods which brought thee up out of the land of Egypt.'

The Church of Rome, it is well known, offers the same explanation of its image-worship—that not the image, but the saint it represents, is the object of adoration. Yet this practice is stigmatized as 'most horrible idolatry' in the same Homily which contains the famous reference to 'the usage of the primitive Church, which was most pure and uncorrupt,' and to the 'judgments of the most ancient, learned, and godly doctors of the Church.'[1]

Hooker takes a similar view of the adoration of the Cross.

'Forasmuch as the Church of Rome hath hitherto practised and doth profess the same adoration to the sign of the cross, and neither less nor other than is due unto Christ Himself, howsoever they varnish and qualify their sentence, pretending that the cross, which to outward sense presenteth visibly itself alone, is not by them apprehended alone, but hath in their secret surmise or conceit a reference to the Person of our Lord Jesus Christ, so that the honour which they jointly do to both respecteth principally His Person, and the cross but only for His Person's sake— the people not accustomed to trouble their wits with so nice and subtile differences in the exercise of religion are apparently no less ensnared by adoring the cross, than the Jews by burning incense to the brazen serpent. . . . . . Howbeit, seeing that we have *by over true experience* been taught how often, especially in these cases, the light even of common understanding faileth, surely their usual adoration of the cross is not hereby freed. For in actions of this kind we are more to respect what the greatest part of men is com-

---

[1] First part of the Sermon against Peril of Idolatry.

monly prone to conceive, than what some few men's wits may devise in construction of their own particular meanings. Plain it is that a false opinion of some personal divine excellency to be in those things which either nature or art hath framed, causeth always religious adoration. And as plain, that the like adoration applied unto things sensible argueth to vulgar capacities, yea leaveth imprinted in them, the very same opinion of Deity from whence all idolatrous worship groweth.'[1]

With regard to the Eucharist, the tenet of transubstantiation seems to have been elaborated mainly to escape the charge of idolatry in adoring the host. The Roman divines are careful to explain, that they do not worship one object in union with another which is not worshipped, but that, while the substance of the bread and wine is annihilated, the visible species are included in the adoration, as one *compositum* with the Body and Blood of Christ. They perceive the impossibility of adoring Christ in the Sacrament without adoring the Sacrament at the same time. This delusion with respect to the nature of the object, perhaps withheld the Church of England from formally extending the charge of idolatry to the adoration of the host: but Rome herself would admit the charge if she could be convinced that the host were composed of two substances—bread and Body.

What the Church of England holds is shown by the prohibition of elevation in the First Book of Edward VI.,—by the direction to say the prayer of consecration *standing* throughout, omitting the acts of adoration previously prac-

[1] Eccl. Pol. v. lxv. 15.

tised,—and by the anxiety evinced in the Declaration at the end of the Office, lest the kneeling at reception should be 'misconstrued and depraved.' The words which the present writers have distorted, when read in their natural construction, plainly exclude any other act of homage but that of kneeling at reception; and of this it is declared that 'no adoration is intended, or ought to be done, (neither in intent or deed,) either unto the sacramental bread or wine there bodily received, or unto *any* corporal Presence of Christ's 'natural Flesh and Blood.' The first, because it is idolatry; the second, because they 'are in heaven, and *not here*.' These words are so generally felt to be opposed to the modern 'Eucharistic adoration,' that its advocates have long stigmatized them as 'the Black Rubric.'[1]

To be consistent, the writers of this paper should have censured the 'more than common ritual' which they rather justify, and have explained what sort of adoration—apart from those practices—they ascribe to the primitive Church and our own. They say that 'Christ Himself, really

[1] It is hardly necessary to note the gloss on the Twenty-eighth Article offered by one of the witnesses before the Ritual Commission, who disposed of the prohibitions at the close as a merely historical statement of 'Christ's ordinance;'—the Sacrament was not to be reserved, carried about, lifted up or worshipped by *Christ's ordinance, non constat*, that it is not to be so treated by some other authority! This ingenious critic could hardly have studied the Latin original. 'Sacramentum eucharistiæ ex institutione Christi non servabatur circumferebatur elevabatur nec adorabatur.'

and truly, spiritually and ineffably, present in the Sacrament, is therein to be adored.' Certainly no statement in these words, or to the same effect, is to be found in Scripture, the fathers, the ancient liturgies, or our own. At best the proposition can be only an *inference* from the doctrine of the Presence. And it is conceivable that some who have made the strongest statements of the Presence, might reject the adoration. Surely some distinct recognition of the worship itself ought to be produced, before it is affirmed to be 'the mind of our Lord, (!) as *expressed* in Holy Scripture, and received in the Church of England.'

When it is known, on the contrary, that not a word of 'Eucharistic adoration' exists for a thousand years after Christ, thoughtful men will be inclined to test the sacramental Presence by the proved absence of adoration, rather than graft the adoration on a particular interpretation of the Presence. That Christ is to be adored wherever He is, is a truism which no Christian disputes; but when it is said that He is to be adored in the sacrament, the question returns upon us whether 'sacrament' means the visible symbols of His Body and Blood, or the whole rite in which He is undoubtedly present to the faithful communicant? In the latter sense we all adore Him; in the other it has yet to be shown that Christ is *therein* with such a Presence as to be the object of special worship. Certainly Body and Blood are not co-extensive terms with Christ Himself.

Hooker observes that it is only 'some *personal divine excellency*' that warrants adoration; and S. Augustine explains how the Person of the Son of God, being incarnate in His glorified Body, includes the Humanity in the adoration properly due to Himself. His Human Nature, however exalted in heaven, is still created, and therefore in itself not an object of worship. It becomes so by hypostatic union with God the Word. Now the Word is not hypostatically united to the sacramental bread and wine. The Body wherein He is tabernacled is 'in heaven, and not here;' consequently to that Body in heaven, not to any other spot in created space, the adoration of Christ is to be directed.

The fathers, like our own Church, insist on Christ's Body being necessarily circumscribed within a certain place, and the impossibility of its being in two places at once. To say that His Human Nature is in the paten and the chalice, is to assign it another place than heaven: or to say that Christ Himself is there to be adored, is to assign Him another temple than His glorified Body. All attempts to escape this dilemma result in affirming and contradicting with the same breath.

'Local, not local,' says Bishop Bilson, 'corporal, not corporal, be plain contradictions, and by no means incident to the natural Flesh of Christ. One it must needs be; both it cannot be, though you sweat out your hearts with wrangling.'

It is the natural Flesh of Christ which is hypostatically united to the Divinity, and thereby exalted to be the object of Christian worship. If Eucharistic adoration mean that this is to be worshipped in heaven,—*cadit quæstio*,—we need neither an uncommon ritual, nor a new profession of faith, to teach this elementary truth of Christianity. But if we are asked to worship Christ as contained in the consecrated elements, the Scriptures, the Fathers, and our own Church, unanimously forbid it.

When the Romanist in Bishop Bilson's dialogue, complaining of misconception, says,

'We adore Christ, the Son of the Living God, and Second Person in the Trinity, in those mysteries, as S. Ambrose saith, or as we speak more usually, under those forms of Bread and Wine;'

the Catholic answers:—

'I mistake you not. I know you adore that which is locally and really enclosed within the compass of your host and chalice, supposing it in matter and substance to be the glorious Body of Christ: but your foundation we say is false, and therefore your building must needs be ruinous. Christ is present in the mysteries not by the material substance of His Body, closed within the forms of bread and wine, but by a divine and spiritual virtue and efficiency;— not mixing His substance with the elements, but entering the hearts of the faithful, and nourishing them with His Spirit and Grace to eternal life, the elements abiding in their proper and former essence and substance.'

Bishop Andrewes, though often cited for this adoration, carefully distinguishes the 'veneration' due to the symbols from the divine adoration belonging to Christ.[1] He affirms that 'No

[1] Answer to Perron's Reply.

Christian man will ever refuse to do what Augustine says, that is, to adore the Flesh of Christ;'[1] but he protests against the Romish interpolation *sous les especes,* 'under the forms' of Bread and Wine, as a thing unheard of till long after Augustine. Further, he censures Bellarmine's expression of adoring 'Christ in the Sacrament'— the very language of the paper before us—as 'a shameful stumble on the threshold :'—

'Truly' (he says) 'Christ Himself, the *res sacramenti,* both in and with the sacrament, out of and without the sacrament,—*ubi, ubi est,*—is to be adored. And we also, with Ambrose, "adore the Flesh of Christ in the mysteries," (*i.e.* plainly in the sacramental action.) Yet not that thing, (*id,*) but Him, (*eum,*) who above (not *upon*) the altar is worshipped.'[2]

The meaning of this great divine cannot be doubted: for when distinguishing (as we saw before) between the glorified and the crucified Body, he says :—

'We are in this action not only *carried up to Christ,* (*sursum corda,*) but we are also carried back to Christ in the act of His Offering.'

The *sursum corda* plainly denotes the *place* of the Object of adoration.

According to Jeremy Taylor,

'We may not worship Christ's Human Nature present in the Sacrament without peril of idolatry, because His Human Nature is *not there,* and to worship it would be to worship a *Non ens,* which is the Apostle's definition of idolatry.'

---

[1] Answer to Perron's Reply.
[2] Resp. ad Bell. No conclusion can be drawn from the genuflexions with which Andrewes approached the altar, when the sacrament was not upon it.

Johnson, in his 'Unbloody Sacrifice,' censures the author of the *Diallacticon* for saying, 'to him who adores and receives it, it is the Body; not to him who adores and receives it not.' Taking this to sanction the adoration of the host, Johnson observes with truth,

'That the ancients never supposed the Divine Nature either of Christ or the Holy Ghost to be hypostatically united to the bread and wine, so as to entitle them to the worship due to the Manhood of Jesus.'

But Johnson probably misunderstood the passage. The elevation of the sacrament was at that time expressly forbidden in the English rubric, and the arm of authority was then too strong to be trifled with. The author moreover insists on the Protestant canon that there is 'no Presence out of the right use of the sacrament;' hence there is no reason to suppose he intended any other adoration but that of Christ in heaven.

On the whole, the teaching of this self-confident 'profession of faith' must be pronounced *eclectic* rather than *catholic*. So far as the ambiguity of the language admits of grasping the meaning, it seeks to combine the *Lutheran Presence* with the *Tridentine Sacrifice*. The subscribers may have 'delivered their own consciences,' but they have done little to 'quiet the minds of others.' No Church, ancient or modern, no Council, no single father, is adequately represented in this Paper. Its very existence would have been impossible in the ages when private judgment was regulated by catholic teaching.¹ As for the mind of our blessed Lord, as expressed in Holy Scripture, we propose to consider it at large in the next section.

VI.—THE TEACHING OF HOLY SCRIPTURE.

FROM these barren polemics it is inexpressibly refreshing to turn at last to the mind of our Blessed Lord, as really expressed in Holy Scripture by Himself and His inspired apostle, S. Paul. Brief as the passages are, the whole Catholic doctrine may be as certainly collected from them now, as it was by the primitive Church, which received no other teaching. Unfortunately the fullest and most didactic piece of the whole has been altogether diverted from the subject by the forced interpretations of the sixteenth century. The early Church never doubted the Eucharistic application of the discourse in John vi.: it was

¹ It is hardly necessary to observe on the violation of all Catholic *discipline*, involved in a body of priests obtruding their uninvited opinions in a 'round robin' on the Archbishop of the province. If their own bishops were among the number of those who mistrusted the 'loyalty' of the subscribers, the propriety of so replying to those who are set over them in the Lord is still more questionable.

questioned by Luther and Calvin, from an apprehension that the value it would ascribe to the sacrament might be detrimental to their views of the great doctrine of justification by faith. Cardinal Cajetan endorsed the objection from the other side, in order to exclude the irrefutable argument for communion in both kinds. And in this the Cardinal showed himself wiser than the majority of his communion, who still adhere to the earlier tradition.

The Church of England intimates her agreement with the general voice, when she unhesitatingly adopts the words of this discourse in the Exhortation at the Communion.[1] The objection that the sacrament was not instituted when these words were spoken, is surely of little weight; since neither was the sacrament of baptism instituted when it was said, 'Except a man be born of water and the Spirit, he cannot enter into the kingdom of heaven.' In both cases the purport and necessity of the sacrament were shadowed out before the institution of the positive rite, even as the institution itself preceded the descent of the Spirit which gave it spiritual power.

If the discourse be allowed to speak for itself, it will be found full to most of the points in question. Originating in the miracle of the loaves, and the

---

[1] The Eucharistic expressions, 'eat the Flesh of Christ and drink His Blood' are clearly taken from this discourse, since S. John is the only evangelist who uses the proper sacrificial word 'flesh' ($\sigma\grave{\alpha}\rho\xi$) of the Body of Christ.

subsequent invidious allusion to the manna of the desert, its main subject is the True Bread from heaven, of which both the elder and the later marvel were but prophetic types. Our Lord first takes this title to Himself, (verses 35–50,) and then indicates the particular method of *sacrifice*, by which He was about to make Himself the food of immortality to man. 'The bread which I will give is My Flesh, which I will give for the life of the world.'[1] To the question, 'How can this Man give us His Flesh to eat?' He replies, by a stronger and more literal assertion of its necessity: 'Verily, verily I say unto you, Except ye eat the Flesh of the Son of Man, and drink His Blood, ye have no life in you. Whoso eateth my Flesh, and drinketh my Blood, hath eternal life; and I will raise him up at the last day. For my Flesh is meat indeed, and my Blood is drink indeed. He that eateth my Flesh, and drinketh my Blood, dwelleth in Me, and I in him.' Then in the next two verses He returns to the type of the manna, and the more general figure of the Bread of Life.[2]

Plainly, then, the main subject of the discourse

---

[1] Compare this 'give' with the 'given' of Luke xxii. 19.

[2] A deeply interesting fact has been brought to light in the series of photographs just published by the *Palestine Exploration Fund:* No. 55 exhibits the ruins of the good Centurion's synagogue at Capernaum, *the* synagogue (as it was proudly called, Luke vii. 5.) in which probably this discourse was delivered: and among the devices carved on the lintel is actually the *pot of manna.*

is the revelation of the Incarnate God as the bread of spiritual life to man; and if bread were the only figure introduced, it might be thought that we eat this bread by coming to Christ in faith, without any special liturgical act. But bread is not the only figure. Our Lord insists even more dogmatically on the necessity of partaking of His redeeming Sacrifice, and that not in general language, but in the strongest literal terms. We must *eat the Flesh*, and *drink the Blood*, of that most precious Sacrifice. Now, remembering that sacrificial offerings under the law were actually eaten and drunk, the natural interpretation is that some corresponding manducation was to be established under the Gospel. And when these very acts of eating and drinking are found in the Eucharist,—confessedly the communion of the Lord's Body and Blood,—it must be a very resolute prejudice that refuses to recognise the allusion.

One expression it is impossible to understand of anything else. If it could be allowed that flesh and bread are the same thing,—if it could be supposed that eating Christ's Flesh is only another expression for eating the Bread of Heaven, and means nothing more than believing in Him,—a supposition sufficiently violent,—what is to be done with the further figure of 'drinking His Blood?' To drink water is a scriptural metaphor for imbibing the doctrine of salvation, but to drink *blood* is a thought utterly abhorrent to the language and ritual of the Old Testament.

Rivers of blood were shed under the law: without it there was no remission of sins; but none was ever *drunk*. It was all sacredly reserved to God, and the prohibition extended from the altar to the usages of private life. 'For it is the blood that maketh atonement for the soul.'[1] Nowhere in all the Scripture is there a hint of drinking it, either literally or metaphorically, save in this discourse at Capernaum, and again in the words of the same Speaker, 'Drink ye all of it, for this is my Blood of the New Testament, which is shed for many for the remission of sins.' Expressions so plainly related are not to be dismissed as mere verbal coincidences, to suit the needs of a modern controversy.

The words of Institution supply a direct answer to the question, 'How can this man give us His Flesh to eat?' and our Church is sustained by Catholic consent in holding that they were so intended. Bengel explains the relation with his usual *acumen*, when he remarks that Jesus 'framed His words with such perfect knowledge that they should, then and always, properly express the spiritual fruition of Himself, but that after the institution of the Supper they should further refer to that august mystery. For the very thing proposed in this discourse He afterwards conferred upon the Holy Supper; and this sacrament is so momentous that it may well be thought, that as Jesus foretold the treason of Judas in the 71st verse, and His own death in the 51st,

[1] Lev. vii. 17.

so He also foretold the Holy Supper, which He most certainly cogitated within Himself while He was speaking, a year before the Institution, that His disciples might remember He had told them of it. This whole discourse has regard to the Passion, and with it to the Holy Supper. Hence the separate mention of Flesh and Blood throughout. For in the Passion the Blood was drawn out of the Body and the Lamb was slain.'[1]

Taking, then, the discourse at Capernaum as a foreshadowing of the Holy Eucharist, it is important to observe the distinction it draws between the living communion with Christ, and the Sacramental *means* by which it is effected. He Himself is the True Bread of Life; whence communion with Him implies the Real Presence of His Living Person, God and Man. But this Presence is accessible only to the communicant seeking Him by faith. The special means of approaching Him is through the sacrifice of His Flesh given for the life of the world on the Cross. This sacrifice, therefore, is also present in the Holy Eucharist; but inasmuch as in act it was finished on the cross, it is present in the sacrament only by commemoration and power. Further, we are to eat the Flesh of this Sacrifice, and drink its Blood;—two distinct acts, having each a proper virtue; and for this purpose the Eucharistic Bread *is* the Body, and the Cup *is* the Blood. Hence neither element alone con-

---

[1] Alford's Gr. Test. in John vi. 51.

tains, or exhibits, 'whole Christ,' but each its own part of the Sacrifice of the cross. Together they exhibit, in a mystery, the true *Oblata* of that most precious Sacrifice: exhibited apart in two elements they signify the Death of Christ; but when eaten and drunk in faith, they impart communion with Christ Living, the True Bread of God who cometh down from heaven.

This distribution is expressly taught in the 56th verse, where the sacramental acts, and their spiritual result, are distinctly enumerated. 'He that eateth my Flesh, and drinketh my Blood, dwelleth in Me, and I in him;'—the Flesh in the bread, the Blood in the cup, but 'whole Christ' in the communicant who abides in Him by faith. There is the same threefold distribution in the prayer of humble access, retained from primitive antiquity in the English Liturgy, 'that our sinful bodies may be made clean by His Body, and our souls washed through His most precious Blood, and that we may evermore dwell *in Him*, and He *in us*.'

This unforced and consistent exposition thoroughly harmonizes with the Anglican doctrine, while it is impossible to reconcile our Lord's words with any view, which either places whole Christ in the bread apart from the cup, or displays Him in the elements without eating and drinking, or dreams that He is received in them without a living faith in the communicant. These positions are, all and each, absolutely contradictory to the words of Christ, in this chapter.

The imputation of Nestorianism to this distinguishing between the dead Body of the Sacrifice, represented in the sacrament, and the Living Person of the High Priest who offered it, implies a strange ignorance of the doctrine of the Incarnation. When the evangelist says the 'Word was made Flesh,' he does not mean that Christ's Person was *identified* with His Humanity, but that He assumed man's flesh into His Divine Person as the instrument—ὄργανον, the great fathers call it—of His mediation with man.[1] His Flesh is not the Life, but *Life-giving*, because given by Him for the life of the world. The Flesh is what He gives to God in sacrifice, and to man in communion, whence the Eucharistic elements also were called 'gifts.' But Christ is the *Giver*, 'who through the eternal Spirit offered Himself without spot to God,' and 'after He had so offered one sacrifice for sins, for ever sat down on the right hand of God.'[2] It is not Nestorianism to distinguish Christ's Person from His Flesh, whether living or dead; but it savours of the worse heresy of the Eutychians to

---

[1] 'He did not become other than Himself on taking the flesh, but being the same He was *robed* in it, (alluding to the high priest.) .... The Word, being Creator, was afterwards made High Priest by clothing Himself with a generated created Body, which He could offer on our behalf.'—*Athanasius, Cont. Ar. Orat.* ii. 8. 'In Him dwelleth all the fulness of the Godhead bodily;'—which is as much as to say that being God He had His own Body, and using this as an instrument (ὀργάνῳ) was made man for us.'—*Ibid. Orat.* iii. 31.

[2] Heb. ix. 14; x. 12.

confound His Humanity with His Divine Person, and so remove His Presence from the tabernacle which He has chosen for Himself in man's immortal consciousness, to material elements of bread and wine.

If we must still demand, with the murmuring Jews, *how* can He give us His Flesh to eat? two gleams of light are seen to flash across the mystery in *vv.* 62 and 63. First, the Son of Man will have ascended up where He was before: His Body will be in heaven, beyond the sphere of any such literal eating as they stumbled at. Secondly, 'it is the Spirit that quickeneth: the Flesh profiteth nothing.' It will not be the dead matter of the Oblation, but the Spirit of the risen Christ, that will enable them to partake of the Sacrifice, and share His undying Life.

Proceeding now from this preliminary discourse to the Institution itself, we find it introduced at the close of the *paschal feast*, as an analogous rite—an antitype—to be observed in the evangelical Church. The Passover was emphatically 'the Lord's Sacrifice,'[1] inaugurated in Egypt by the death of the first-born, and continued as 'an ordinance for ever,' till the True Lamb came to effect the true deliverance from the house of bondage. This annual commemoration consisted (1) of the sacrifice[2] and manducation of a lamb;

---

[1] Exodus, xxiii. 18.

[2] Luke, xxii. 7. 'When the passover must be sacrificed.' (θύεσθαι.)

of which the master of the feast said in distributing it, 'This is the sacrifice of the Lord's Passover, which our fathers ate in the land of Egypt—let him that hath need come and eat the passover, for this passover is our saviour and refuge.'[1] (2) Of unleavened bread eaten with the lamb; of which it was said, 'This is the bread of affliction which our fathers did eat in the land of affliction.' (3) Of successive cups of wine; which, though not mentioned in the Pentateuch, were plainly a part of the paschal Supper as celebrated by our Lord and His disciples.[2] Both the bread and the wine were introduced with a grace or 'blessing' from the person presiding. The analogy between this rite and the evangelical commemoration is confirmed by S. Paul, when he says, 'Christ our Passover is sacrificed for us, therefore let us keep the feast,'[3] and is an important element in every scriptural exposition of the Eucharistic symbolism.

The Institution itself is recorded in three independent narratives, illustrated by a fourth, which S. Luke would appear to have derived from S. Paul. The apostle's own is the fullest,

[1] Exodus, xii. 27. The other words are found in the Mishnah, which, though not reliable in every detail, may be so far safely taken as authoritative.

[2] The Mishna prescribes four cups (at least) of red wine mixed with water. Two are mentioned by S. Luke, the last of which (after supper) seems to be that which our Lord blessed and distributed as His Blood.

[3] 1 Cor. v. 7, 8.

and most generally followed in the Liturgies, as coming from the Risen Lord, after the atoning Sacrifice had been 'finished,' and the Sacrament was to exhibit it in His Church till He come.

He took bread, He gave thanks over it, He blessed it, He brake it, and gave to His disciples, saying, 'Take, eat, this is my Body.' So far the four accounts are almost verbally the same. S. Luke supplies the important addition, 'which is given for you.' This he appears to have obtained from S. Paul, whose words in our translation are, 'which is *broken* for you;' but the best MSS. read simply τὸ ὑπὲρ ὑμῶν,—'broken' being supplied from the foregoing word 'brake.' The ancient Liturgies all express the word so supplied, with the further addition, (taken from the blessing of the cup,) 'for the remission of sins,' showing the reference to the *sacrificed* Body. The Roman Canon alone characteristically stops with S. Matthew and S. Mark at the words, 'This is my Body.'

With regard to the cup, the variations are greater, but without inconsistency. The two former evangelists mention the giving thanks, but not the 'blessing.' This is implied, however, in St. Paul's narrative, '*after the same manner also He took the cup*,' and confirmed by his words, 'The cup of blessing *which we bless.*' The words at the delivery of the cup as reported by S. Matthew, 'Drink ye all of it,' are not in the other accounts; but S. Mark says, 'they all drank of it;' and the fact is implied both by S. Luke and S. Paul. The two former evangelists proceed, 'For this is my Blood, which is shed for many;' where S. Matthew adds, 'for the remission of sins.' In S. Paul the words are, 'This cup is the New Testament in my Blood,' to which S. Luke adds, 'which is shed for you.' Finally, this evangelist subjoins the command, 'This do in remembrance of Me,' which S. Paul more particularly applies to both elements, saying after the delivery of the bread, 'This do in remembrance of Me;' and after the cup, 'This do ye, as oft as ye drink it, in remembrance of Me.'

It is remarkable that neither account contains the word 'wine.' In the evangelists, our Lord speaks of the contents of the cup as the 'fruit of the vine;' but S. Paul mentions only 'the cup.' This is the common expression in the Liturgies and fathers, though they also specify the contents as 'wine and water,' the 'mixture,' and sometimes 'wine.'

The words and actions of our blessed Lord were harmonized and made technical, so to speak, in the earliest Liturgies. S. Paul appears to imply that this much was done by the apostles themselves, and that the Institution was specially revealed to himself for the purpose. Certainly such a recital is found in every Liturgy, and must therefore have originated in apostolic times.[1]

[1] See the remarks of Deans Stanley and Alford *in loc.*

In Scripture, then, the Institution consists of three principal and indispensable acts—*consecration, distribution,* and *participation.*

The first is contained in the taking, giving thanks over, and blessing the elements, accompanied by the acts of breaking the bread, and (apparently) pouring out the cup.

The second is the delivery of each gift to all present, with the words, 'This is my Body,' &c.

The third is the entire consumption of both gifts by eating and drinking.

This is what Christ commanded to be done in remembrance of Him, and whatever be the liturgical order followed in the doing, it is plainly no Institution of His from which either of these acts is omitted. In fact, as already pointed out, the several acts did not follow, one after another, in the original Institution, but were so intertwined and contemporaneous, that neither could be completed without the rest. The cup was not consecrated till the bread had been consumed, and the consecrated gifts never existed *together* save in the receiver.

With respect to the object of the celebration, it was, first, 'for the remembrance of the Sacrifice of the death of Christ,' or in S. Paul's words, to 'show the Lord's Death till He come.' Secondly, according to the same apostle, for the 'communion of His Body and Blood' offered in that Sacrifice; and thirdly, for the sacrifice of ourselves, as one with Christ and Christ with us; for 'in being all partakers of one bread, 'we being many are one bread, one Body.'¹

This is *all* we learn from the Inspired Scripture; and it is manifest that, throughout, the sacramental elements remain unchanged in substance. The Romanists themselves admit that transubstantiation cannot be proved from Scripture; and not a few of their divines plainly indicate a misgiving that Scripture is *against* it. At the same time, the Eucharistic Gifts are distinctly the Body and Blood of Christ, *i. e.* His Body broken and His Blood shed; and the receiving of them is the Communion of His Body and Blood—an expression which grammatically means, not the union of two substances, but a power in the one of communicating the other to the receiver.

It has often been wished that we knew the words in which the Lord blessed or consecrated the elements. It is very improbable that He confined His prayer to the ordinary thanksgiving of a Jewish Passover; for that supper, we read, was ended, when the Eucharist was given to inaugurate the 'New Testament in His Blood.' These words point to the action of Moses when he took the blood of the sacrifice and sprinkled it on the people, and said, 'Behold the blood of the covenant which the Lord hath made with you concerning all these words.'² In initiating a New Covenant in His own Blood, the Lord's thanks-

---

¹ 1 Cor. x. 17. ² Exodus, xxiv. 8.

giving and blessing would naturally indicate the character of the Sacrifice He was about to offer, and its relation to the Memorial now established. Many have lamented the want of these benedictory words; but perhaps it has not been sufficiently observed that S. John does in fact supply a solemn prayer of thanksgiving and blessing, uttered at the very time of the Eucharistic Institution.[1] What, if in this prayer the evangelist, who contributes nothing else to the Eucharistic narrative, should have supplied a portion of the consecratory Benediction?

A *consecration* it undoubtedly is; and one link of connexion with the Eucharist is supplied in the words, 'lifted up His eyes to heaven;' for this sentence, though not occurring in either of the narratives of the Supper, was always religiously preserved in the ancient Liturgies. In this prayer, which throughout is eminently priestly, our Lord consecrates Himself to His Heavenly Father on behalf of His Church,[2] speaking of the work which was given Him to do as already 'finished;' and challenging the glory due to Him in return. He prays for those whom He had kept in the Father's Name, while He was in the world, that God would keep them through the same, when He Himself should

---

[1] S. Matthew tells us that 'when they had sung a hymn, they went out into the Mount of Olives;' and S. John, that 'when Jesus had spoken these words, He went forth with His disciples unto the brook Cedron.'

[2] John xvii. 19.

have returned to Him. They are to be kept in communion with Himself, and through Him with the Father, 'that they may be one, even as we are one. I in them and Thou in Me, that they may be made perfect in one.' Such were certainly some of the utterances of our great High Priest just before, or after, the delivery of the bread and wine as His Body and Blood; and they speak of that communion with Him which the sacrament was designed to impart.

He has closed the Old Testament with the last Passover, and now stands before God to initiate the New Testament with the Blood of the great Sacrifice, regarded as already 'finished.' He is going out to the Agony, and the Betrayal, and the Passion. It is a night to be much remembered unto the Lord of all the children of the spiritual Israel. Christ our Passover is sacrificed; for, though a few hours must intervene before the consummation, it is now that He 'lays down His life *of Himself.*' On the cross the Sacrifice will be bound, and pierced and slain, by the hands of wicked men. It is in the chamber of the Passover that He spontaneously devotes Himself 'to do the will of God.' There He says of Himself, as Agent, 'I have finished the work that Thou gavest Me to do,' though it was not till the next day that He could say of the work passively, 'It is finished.'

The hour then is come; the Mediator of the New Covenant is passing from the paschal sacrifice to its fulfilment in the kingdom of God. And first He initiates a sacrificial Memorial of the impending Sacrifice of Himself. His actions and His words are all sacrificial. The solemn benediction and devotion, the Body broken, the Blood shed for the remission of sins, no Jew could have understood of anything but sacrifice. Especially significant is the word 'remembrance,' —εἰς τὴν ἐμὴν ἀνάμνησιν. The 'remembrance,' or 'memorial,' was the technical name of that part of the meat-offering, or peace-offering, which represented the whole before God. The continuous central sacrifice of the law was the *holocaust*, renewed morning and evening on the altar, and slowly burning through the intervening hours. Every other offering derived its value from this national act of homage and acceptance, and there were various provisions to bring them into relation with it. Of the meat-offering of fine flour a handful was cast into the altar fire, to be consumed along with the holocaust, and this was called the 'Memorial.'[1] It was held to communicate the virtue of the burnt sacrifice to the entire meat-offering, so that the remnant was eaten by the priests in the holy place as a 'thing most holy of the offerings of the Lord made by fire.'

In like manner, of the 'peace-offerings,' (or sacrifices of *salvation*,) a choice morsel was burnt with the holocaust as 'the food of the Lord,' and

[1] Lev. ii. 1, 2.

the remainder being divided between the priests and the people, they were accounted to eat with God as guests at His table, reconciled by the sacrifice.

The shew-bread was made a burnt-offering (though no part of it was ever burnt) by fumigating it with the incense of the altar. And this incense again is called a '*memorial.*'[1]

The same word is used of the sin-offering by the apostle when he says, 'There is a *remembrance* again made of sins every year.'[2] The allusion is not to the recollection remaining in the sinner's mind and conscience, but to the sacrificial act of the high priest in sprinkling the mercy-seat with the blood of the sacrifice.[3] This was the atonement, or reconciliation, of the Holy Place; and the annual bringing in of this memorial or 'remembrance' of the sin-offering, argued the reconciliation to be imperfect. 'It is not possible that the blood of bulls and goats should take away sins,' *i. e.* efface them altogether from before God. Hence the superiority of the Blood of Christ, that entering but '*once* into the holy place, He has obtained eternal redemption for us.'

Under the law, then, a Memorial, or Remembrance was, (1) A representative oblation, bringing the thing which it represented to the presence of God upon the altar and the mercy-seat; (2) A liturgical medium, by which the value of the central Sacrifice was derived into sacred food,

[1] Lev. xxiv. 7.   [2] Heb. x. 3.   [3] Lev. xvi. 14, 15.

which the worshippers partook of as from the altar of God. Now these are precisely the two uses ascribed in Holy Scripture to the Eucharist. 1. It shows the Lord's death till He come; and 2. It is the communion of the Lord's Body and Blood to those who eat and drink at His table. These conceptions flowed so naturally out of the Levitical liturgy, that the apostles no sooner understood the Sacrifice of the cross, than they saw at once the relation borne to it by the Holy Eucharist. We read of no further question or instruction. S. Paul had only to learn the fact of the Institution—revealed to him as part of the credentials of an apostle—and he asks, as of a thing admitting no room for doubt, 'Is it not the communion of the Lord's Body?'

One feature, however, of the Christian rite, it has been observed, was altogether new—the mystery of the Cup. Under the law there was no *participation* of the blood of any sacrifice. It was sprinkled about the altar, or poured out at its base; all that was not consumed in the fire being drained away into the cavities below, where the earth opened her mouth to receive it. Its 'remembrance' was brought before God on the mercy-seat, but no communion in it was vouchsafed to people or priest. Consequently it was a new thing when our Lord spoke of drinking His Blood, and gave it a place in the Holy Eucharist. The cup is the New Testament in the Blood of Christ. The blood of the first Testament was sprinkled externally on the people and the Book; the Blood of the second is to be received into our souls as a new and spiritual life. It is exhibited in wine, the great restorer of the blood and life of man. 'Drink ye all of it, for this is my Blood, shed for the remission of sins.'

To this novel feature the apostle makes especial reference in Heb. xiii. 10, 11: 'We have an altar, whereof they have no right to eat which serve the tabernacle. For the bodies of those beasts, whose blood is brought into the sanctuary by the high priest for sin, are buried without the camp.' The law is laid down in Lev. vi. 30: 'And no sin-offering, whereof any of the blood is brought into the tabernacle of the congregation to reconcile withal in the holy place, shall be eaten: it shall be burnt in the fire.' The spiritual abrogation of this restriction completed the Christian Sacrifice. The Jew, in eating of his peace-offering, communicated through the memorial with the great Burnt Sacrifice accepted of God on behalf of the people; but communion in the *Sin-offering* he had none. Under the Gospel, Christ is not only the Holocaust Lamb, but the Sin-offering for all mankind; and accordingly His new Peace-offering, the Eucharist, represents and communicates Him in both capacities. This is a new Passover; a translation into a better covenant, secured by an inexhaustible Sacrifice, and imparting personal reception both of its Body and Blood.

Two things, then, and two only, are revealed as the mind of our Blessed Lord in Holy Scripture, with regard to the Eucharist. (1) It is the Memorial of Christ's Sacrifice on the cross; and (2) It is the Communion of His Body and Blood, then given for the life of the world. Rightly receiving this sacrament, we dwell in Christ and Christ in us. Eating and drinking it unworthily, we are 'guilty of the Body and Blood of the Lord; we eat and drink damnation, not discerning the Lord's Body.' These expressions imply that while there is no sacrificial Presence to such as do not apprehend it by faith, it is a profane affront to the Sacrifice of our salvation, to receive its *media* without realizing their spiritual use. The tenet that Christ's Body is received by such persons to condemnation, is merely a logical inference from the Corporal Presence of the Schoolmen. It cannot be extracted from the apostle's words by any sound critical exegesis, and it is directly opposed to the Saviour's declaration, 'Whoso eateth my Flesh, and drinketh my Blood, hath eternal life, and I will raise him up at the last day.' *Commemoration* and *Communion* are the twin objects of the Eucharist as revealed in Holy Scripture, and no others, it will be found, are contemplated in the Canons and Liturgies which come next under review.

VII.—THE CANONS AND LITURGIES.

In inquiring into the doctrine of the Catholic Church before the separation of East and West, it must be borne in mind that there was then no formulated system of divinity, such as grew out of the controversies of later periods. Holy Scripture was the rule of faith, and the Creeds were the Confessions, of Catholic antiquity. The only other authentic standards were the Canons and Liturgies; both intended as rules of discipline rather than of doctrine, yet indirectly affording clear evidence of the faith on which all Christian discipline depends.

Canons are not required till some error or question supervenes; and as little difference existed about the Eucharist, the Canons relating to it are few, though significant. One of the earliest forbids anything to be offered on the altar besides the Lord's ordinance for the sacrifice, save only the first-fruits of corn and wine.[1] The African Church allowed milk and honey on a particular day, probably for use in the baptism of infants.[2] The Eucharistic elements are

---

[1] Ap. Can. iii. The *oil* and *incense* are interpolations of later date; see Johnson's Vade-mecum, ii. 4.

[2] Conc. Cart. can. xl.

THE HOLY EUCHARIST. 135

described as bread and wine,[1] or wine mixed with water.[2]

The faithful—*i.e.* all admitted to communion— are forbidden to leave the church without communicating.[3] A clergyman present at the oblation and not receiving, is commanded to give his reason for such a scandalous reflection on the celebration.[4]

Deacons were not to give the Body to priests, but receive in their order after them, and assist in the ministration. Bishops and priests alone may offer, and they not in private houses.[5]

Penitents were excluded for various periods, according to their sin, before being 'perfected,' or restored to communion.[6] No one, however, at the point of death was to be refused the *viaticum*.[7]

These are the provisions of universal obligation down to the middle of the fifth century; throughout this period the terms *sacrifice* and *oblation* are used both of the whole rite and of the material symbols. The elements after consecration are called the Body and Blood of Christ, and the Holy Table the altar.[8] The phrase

---

[1] Ap. Can. iii. [2] Conc. Cart. Can. xl.; Ancyr. Can. ii.
[3] Ap. Can. ix. Ant. ii. [4] Ap. Can. viii.
[5] Nic. Can. xviii.; Ancyr. ii.; Arles, x., xv.; Laod. lviii.
[6] Nic. Can. xii.; Ancyr. iv.; Laod. ii.
[7] Nic. Can. xiii.
[8] Ancyr. Can. i., ii.; Neo-Cæs. ix., xiii.; Nic. xi., xiii., xviii.; Gangr. iv.

'Divine or Holy Table' is sometimes used metaphorically for the whole rite, as 'sacrament' is among ourselves. Thus in the Acts of the First General Council the heading 'of the Divine Table and the mystery there present of the Body and Blood of Christ,' may be interpreted either of the *banquet* or the *altar*. The Council says:—

'Also in (or on) the Divine Table let us not meanly fix our intent on the bread exhibited and the cup, but, lifting up the mind in faith, let us understand in that Holy Table the Lamb of God who taketh away the sin of the world *unsacrificially sacrificed* ($\dot{\alpha}\theta\acute{v}\tau\omega\varsigma\ \theta\nu\acute{o}\mu\epsilon\nu o\nu$) by the priests, and, really receiving His precious Body and Blood, believe them to be symbols of our resurrection. Therefore also we receive, not much but a little, that we may know it to be taken not for satiety, but for sanctification.'[1]

The Quinisext Canons, which the Greeks account œcumenical, (A.D. 683,) sanction the appellation, 'unbloody sacrifice.'[2] They prohibit, as an innovation of the Armenians contrary to the ancient Liturgies, the use of wine unmixed with water,[3] and command both elements to be received separately in the hand, not together in a spoon or other receptacle.[4]

These canons bring us to the close of the seventh century: down to this time there is no allusion to reservation, except for the sick, nor

[1] Act. Con. Nic. ii. 30, p. 427; apud Act. Concil. Paris, 1715.
[2] Conc. Trull. Can. xxviii.
[3] Ibid. xxxii. Still the Armenian usage may have been really ancient and even primitive.
[4] Ibid. ci.

to the elevation or adoration of the elements. Johnson[1] cites a canon as directing the administration of a sacrament consecrated at a previous celebration, and then reserved; but this is a forced and unnatural construction of the words. The true reading is simply that no country priest should either offer or consecrate in the city church if the bishop or his clergy were present; but if called upon in their absence to offer, he should also consecrate and give the communion.[2] Neither is any reservation implied in Dionysius's well-known story of the sacrament being conveyed to Serapion by the hands of a lad.[3] The priest may have consecrated it for the purpose, or sent it from a public celebration at the time. The transmission from the Holy Table to the sick or the absent was merely an enlargement of the communion, and would by no means interfere with the entire distribution of the consecrated gifts at every celebration. Indeed, the frequency of the celebration would exclude any need of reservation.

An attempt has been made to found a precedent for non-communicating attendance on the

[1] Clergyman's Vade-mecum, part ii. p. 79.
[2] Conc. Neo-Cæs. Can. xiii. 'Vicani autem presbyteri in urbis Dominico non possunt offerre præsente episcopo vel urbis presbyteris; neque panem dare in oratione neque calicem. Sin autem absit, et solus ad precationem vocatus fuerit, det.' On the distinction between *orationem* and *precatio*, see S. Augustine, *post*, p. 175.
[3] Eus. Eccl. Hist. vi. 44.

canons which require the people to remain for the Communion, but do not specify actual reception.[1] No such direction however was needed; the words of Institution plainly command reception, and the Liturgies contemplate no exception. Moreover, the words of the Antiochian Canon—'qui egreditur et aversatur *communionem*'—incontestably prove that actual communion was the object in view.

The same writer[2] finds an example of the practice which he contends for, in the case of certain penitents *(consistentes)* who were required to 'participate in the prayers without the oblation or communion.'[3] But then where would be the difference between these penitents and the laymen in full communion, for whom the same melancholy privilege is claimed? It is plain that the 'prayers' in which the penitent participated were those which *preceded* the Communion Office;[4] and we find in the Liturgies a direction for their retiring before the sacramental celebration began.

The testimony of S. Chrysostom is explicit upon both points. When some at Constantinople

---

[1] Archdeacon Wilberforce on Euch. p. 464. [2] Ibid. 469.
[3] Nic. Conc. can. xi., xii.
[4] Archdeacon Wilberforce observes that the ministration of the Holy Eucharist appears to have been the only public ritual '*coeval with the Church*.' But these canons were not 'coeval with the Church,' and Justin Martyr distinctly mentions the 'prayers' and the kiss of peace *before* the bread and wine were brought forth. See Sect. ix. *post*.

attempted to remain during the celebration without receiving, he rebuked them as follows:—

'Thou hearest the minister standing and crying, "All you that are in penitence (under penance) depart." Whosoever does not receive is in penitence: if thou art one of those in penitence, thou must not receive, for not to receive is to be of those in penitence. To what purpose, then, does he say "depart all ye that cannot join in the service,"[1] when thou impudently stayest? But thou art not of those, (in penitence,) but of those permitted to receive: and dost thou nothing care? dost thou deem this Thing nothing?'

In the next paragraph he remarks that the man in the parable, who had not on a wedding garment, was expelled, not merely from the feast, but from the *house* in which it was celebrated.

'He did not say, why didst thou sit down? but, why camest thou in? And the same He now says to all of us who stand impudently and without shame: for every one who receives not the mysteries stands impudently and without shame..... Tell me if anyone invited to a feast should wash his hands, sit down, and make ready for the banquet, and then not partake of it, would he not insult his host? *Would it not be better for such an one not to have been present?* In that state, then, thou art now present: thou hast sung the hymn, thou hast professed thyself to be among those worthy (to receive) in not departing with the unworthy; how canst thou stay, and not partake of the banquet? I am unworthy, he says,—then thou art unworthy of the communion in the prayers.[2] For not only by the gifts,[3] but by the hymns also, the Spirit is descend-

---

[1] οἱ μὴ δυνάμενοι διωθῆναι—literally 'who are not able to *pray*,' showing that no one was admitted to the *eucharistical* prayers who was excluded from the sacrament.

[2] τῆς κοινωνίας ἐκείνης τῆς ἐν ταῖς εὐχαῖς—another proof that 'communion in prayers without the oblation' did not include the prayers of oblation and consecration.

[3] διὰ προκειμένων.

ing all around. Of these sights the eyes and ears (of the unworthy) are also unworthy.'

After referring to the command in Exodus, xix. 12, he proceeds:—

'When He is present, depart: thou hast no more license to stay than the catechumen. Not that it is by any means the same thing, never to have attained to the mysteries, and, after attaining to stumble at and despise them, and render thyself unworthy of this Thing.'

This last sentence completes the dilemma. By their own confession these persons were unworthy to receive; by the rule of the Church, and the nature of the rite, they could not be present and not receive; and if they retired with the penitents and catechumens, they would fall under the penalty of the canon and be excommunicate. The preacher could suggest but one way out of the dilemma. 'We exhort you (he concludes) not to absent yourselves, but to become worthy both of attending and communicating.'[1]

[1] καὶ τῆς παρουσίας καὶ τοῦ παρόδου ἀξίους—Chrys. Hom. iii. in Ephes. Ben. Ed. xi. 23. My late lamented friend, Archd. Wilberforce, omits the most decisive parts of this homily, to argue from other sources that Chrysostom *could not* mean what he most unequivocally says. Doubtless this rigid discipline could not long be maintained. The canon for constant attendance must either have been relaxed, or non-communicating attendance connived at. The former alternative seems to be indicated in the canons which reduce the minimum of lay reception to three times a year. The latter is found *as a penance* in the decrees of Pope Siricius, (A.D. 385.) but it seems to have become a common practice in France at the date of the Council of Agde. (A. D. 506.)

THE HOLY EUCHARIST. 141

Such are the Synodical provisions of the undivided Church. Of the *Liturgies* referred to in the Trullan Canon, the remains are more numerous, but less authentic. No one now believes the legend attributed to Proclus,[1] (*d.* 445.) that the Apostles dictated a Liturgy to Clement, which was written down by James the Lord's brother, and re-edited first by S. Basil and from him by S. Chrysostom. The so-called Clementine Liturgy first appears in the Apostolical Constitutions, which were certainly not collected by Clement of Rome, and cannot be traced higher than about A.D. 400. Basil (*d.* 379.) probably did revise and adapt the Liturgy of the Church of Jerusalem, which carried the name of S. James; but it is obvious that he could not suppose it to be the actual composition of an apostle, or he would not have presumed to alter it. Neither would Chrysostom (*d.* 407.) have proceeded to a further recension if he had been aware of any really Apostolic Liturgy.[2]

Whatever traditions may have been handed down in different churches, there was clearly no Liturgy possessing Apostolic authority, and probably no written Liturgy at all, prior to the First General Council. That the apostles did indeed celebrate the Holy Eucharist with fixed

---

[1] Theod. Dial. ii.

[2] Renaudot (Liturg. Orient i.) thinks that none were reduced to writing before the time of Basil, except the Clementine, which he allows to be an Ante-Nicene composition.

rites, seems to be indicated by S. Paul,[1] and is almost certain from Jewish associations, and from their recorded application to Christ for a form of prayer. These rites would of course descend to their converts; but according to the best authorities, they were continued by oral tradition, without being reduced to writing, till the Church obtained legal establishment under Constantine. Then the traditional forms and written fragments were collected and arranged in Liturgies, which received the names of the founders of the respective churches.

Hence the Liturgies of S. James, S. Mark, and S. Peter. The first was in existence in the time of Basil, and is confirmed by the annotations of Cyril. (A.D. 350.) The second is supposed to have been in use at Alexandria before A.D. 451, from its similarity to that of the Coptic Monophysites, who separated from the orthodox in that year. S. Peter's, or the Liturgy of the Church of Rome, is a comparatively recent compilation, of which nothing can be traced higher than the Sacramentary of Gregory the Great, though some unknown portion of it may have been compiled by Gelasius. (A.D. 492.) From these Liturgies, and from other similar sources, a variety of Offices were composed, at different times and in different places, of which as many

[1] 1 Cor. xi. 23-25, where Stanley observes 'an appearance of fixed order, especially in the opening words, which indicates that this had already become a familiar formula.' This remark is approved by Alford.

as a hundred are said to be still extant, whole or in part.

This variety is conclusive evidence that no one Liturgy was ever securely traced to Apostolic authority, or held binding on the whole Church. Still we might reasonably expect to find the substance, at least, of the Ante-Nicene traditions in the earliest Liturgies, if we now possessed them as used in the fourth and fifth centuries. Here, however, is the weak point of the evidence. The oldest MS. now extant is one of the Liturgies of Basil and Chrysostom, dated by Montfaucon A. D. 691. Of S. Mark's there is one of the tenth or eleventh century. These MSS. are no more the Liturgies of the fourth century, than Chrysostom's was the Liturgy of Basil, or Basil's of S. James.[1] They come to us with the interpolations and adaptations of at least three centuries. They represent the age not of the Four General Councils, but of the Sixth, when the Constantinopolitan rite had, in some respects, already varied from S. Chrysostom's.[2]

These deductions do not altogether destroy the credit of the Liturgies, as evidence to the early worship of the Church Catholic. They apply only to the interpolated details, each of which must be judged by its character, and consistency

[1] Moreover, Archdeacon Freeman has adduced strong reasons for suspecting some important departures from the Apostolic age, even prior to the Fourth Century. *Principles of Divine Service*, ii. 3.

[2] Trull. Can. 32.

with contemporaneous theology. No feature can be pronounced ancient which is found in only a few Liturgies; but it may be safely inferred that where they all agree, they retain the substance of the original deposit.

Now this agreement is strikingly close in the *oblation* and *consecration* of the Eucharist. This will be seen by comparing the principal forms with the Clementine Liturgy, which, though nominally later than Basil, has many pretensions to be considered the purest type. The Apostolical Constitutions, though proved by internal evidence to be posterior to the death of Theodosius, (A. D. 395.[1]) undoubtedly contain genuine relics of the Ante-Nicene churches; and this character has been amply vindicated for the Clementine Liturgy by Bingham and Brett. The objection that it was a private composition, never used as the written Liturgy of any church, is greatly in its favour for our present purpose, since it has thereby escaped the emendations of successive bishops, and probably remains as it was first taken down for private use. It differs from that of S. James chiefly in greater simplicity, both of language and ritual,—another presumption in favour of its retaining the earlier type. The learned Dr. Grabe conceived it to be the most authentic monument of the Ante-Nicene worship; and Dr. Brett believes, with Johnson, that 'if we had the very form in which the apostles

[1] Pearson's Vind. Ignat.—Grabe's Spic. Patr. i. 284.

ministered the Holy Communion, it would be found in all essential points the same.'[1]

This Liturgy commences with a warning to the catechumens, hearers, unbelievers, and all who were not in communion,[2] to depart, and only those who were in charity and without hypocrisy, to come and present their offerings.[3] A rubric follows, directing the bishop to put on his 'shining garment,' which Dr. Brett admits to be probably a white linen vestment: but all rubrics are confessed to be interpolations of later date, and must be left out of the comparison.

Having placed the gifts upon the altar, the bishop commences the *anaphora*, or oblatory portion of the service, with the apostolic salutation. (2 Cor. xiii. 14.) Then follows the *sursum corda*, retained in our Communion Service; then the *vere dignum*; and then a long Thanksgiving for the works of God in creation, providence, and revelation, recounting His mercies to the elect from Adam downwards. This Eucharistical act closes with the *Seraphic Hymn*, 'Holy, holy,' &c.

The Thanksgiving is then renewed for the special mercies of the Incarnation, concluding with

---

[1] Brett's Liturgies.—Johnson's Unbloody Sacrifice.
[2] See Chrysostom's interpretation, p. 139. *ante.*
[3] These were the first-fruits and other contributions of the people, of which the canon allowed only bread and wine to be brought to the altar, the remainder being sent to the Bishop's house. From the offerings so presented on the altar, the celebrant selected the portion to be consecrated for the sacrament.

a recital of the *Institution* of the Eucharist. This is followed by the *Oblation* and *Benediction*, which will presently be produced in full. Then come the *Intercessions* for the whole Church, living and dead. Then a prayer of humble access; and then the exclamation, 'Holy things for holy persons.'

After this the Bishop receives; and then, according to the rubric, the presbyters, deacons, subdeacons, readers, singers, and ascetics; next the women, the deaconesses, virgins, widows; then the children; and finally, 'all the people, in order, with fear and reverence, without tumult or noise.' In giving the Oblation the Bishop says, 'The Body of Christ,' and the receiver answers, 'Amen.' The Deacon, with the cup, says, 'The Blood of Christ, the Cup of Life,' and the receiver says, '*Amen.*'

Such, according to the Clementine Liturgy, was the Eucharistic Office of the Ante-Nicene Churches. It contains six elements:—

1. The Thanksgiving, closing with the Seraphic hymn;
2. The Commemoration, ending with the words of Institution;
3. The Oblation of the elements;
4. The Benediction, or Consecration;
5. The Intercessions; and
6. The Communion in both kinds by all present.

These elements, and these only, uniformly recur in all the other Liturgies; often in the same words, and always to the same sense. The order of the several parts is for the most part the same; but in the Alexandrian and Ethiopic Liturgies the Intercessions begin the service, immediately on the gifts being set upon the altar, as in the present English Liturgy. In the others they intervene between the Benediction and the Communion, as in the Clementine model. A still greater departure from primitive usage is charged upon *all* these Liturgies by Archdeacon Freeman, who maintains that in the First Century the Invocation *preceded* the words of Institution.

The nature of the Eucharistic Sacrifice, as offered in these Liturgies, will appear from the expressions used in the three principal parts,— the *Institution*, the *Oblation*, and the *Benediction*, or *Consecration:* these therefore shall now be produced at length.[1]

The Clementine runs thus :—

'Having therefore in remembrance all that He endured for our sakes, we give thanks to Thee, O God Almighty, not as we ought, but as we are able,[2] and fulfil His Institution. For in the same night that He was betrayed, having taken bread into His holy and immaculate hands, and looking up[3] to Thee, His God and Father, and breaking it, He gave it to His disciples, saying, This is the Mystery of the New Testament; take of it, eat, this is my Body, which is broken for many for the remission of sins. Likewise also having mingled the cup of wine and water, and blessed it, He gave it to them, saying, Drink ye all of it; this is my

---

[1] Dr. Brett's Collection, London, 1720. The originals are in the Appendix to Johnson's Unbloody Sacrifice. (1714.) See also Renaudot and the other Liturgists.

[2] Compare Justin Martyr, *post*, Sect. ix.

[3] Not in the Gospel accounts of the Supper, but in Luke ix. 16, and in John xvii. 1.

Blood, which is shed for many for the remission of sins. Do this in remembrance of Me: for as often as ye eat of this Bread, and drink of this Cup, ye do show forth my death till I come.'[1]

'Wherefore having in remembrance His Passion, Death, and Resurrection from the Dead, His Ascension into Heaven, and His future second appearance (when He shall come with glory and power) to judge the quick and the dead, and to render to every man according to his works, we offer to Thee our King and God, according to His Institution, this Bread and this Cup; giving thanks to Thee through Him that Thou hast thought us worthy to stand before Thee, and to minister (ἱερατεύειν[2]) unto Thee. And we beseech Thee that Thou wilt look graciously on these gifts now lying before Thee, O Thou self-sufficient God, and accept them to the honour of Thy Christ.

'And send down Thy Holy Spirit, the Witness of the sufferings of the Lord Jesus, on this Sacrifice, (θυσίαν,) that He may exhibit (make[3]) this bread the Body of Thy Christ, and this cup the Blood of Thy Christ; that all who shall partake of it may be confirmed in godliness, may receive remission of sins, may be delivered from the devil and his wiles, may be filled with the Holy Ghost, may be made worthy of Thy Christ, and may obtain everlasting Life, Thou, O Lord Almighty, being reconciled to them.'

S. James's Liturgy, or that of the Jerusalem patriarchate, reads thus, omitting *rubrics* as of later date:—

'And when the hour was come[4] that He who had no sin was to suffer a voluntary and life-giving death upon the

---

[1] It is remarkable that these words of S. Paul are attributed in the Liturgies to the original Institution, showing how inseparable in the tradition of the Church the *receiving* was from the *sacrifice*.

[2] The word applied to Aaron's ministry in the Septuagint, Exod. xxviii. 1, 3, 4, xxix. 1, and frequently. 'Sacrifice' is usually expressed by θύω, or θυσιάζω.

[3] ἀποφήνῃ, from ἀποφαίνω, ostendo, efficio, reddo, &c.

[4] Compare John xvii. 1.

cross for us sinners, in the same night that He was offered,
or rather offered up Himself, for the life and salvation of
the world, having taken bread into His holy, immaculate,
pure, and immortal hands, looking up to heaven, and presenting it to Thee, His God and Father, He gave thanks,
sanctified, and brake it, and gave it to His disciples and
apostles, saying, Take, eat, this is my Body, which is
broken and given for you for the remission of sins. (Amen.)
Likewise, after supper, having taken the cup and mixed it
of wine and water, and looking up to heaven and presenting
it to Thee His God and Father, He gave thanks, sanctified
and blessed it, and filled it with the Holy Ghost, and gave
it to His disciples, saying, Drink ye all of this; this is my
Blood of the New Testament, which is shed and given for
you and for many for the remission of sins. (Amen.) Do
this in remembrance of Me: for as often as ye eat this bread
and drink this cup ye do shew forth the death of the Son of
Man, and confess His resurrection until His coming again.

' Wherefore having in remembrance His life-giving passion,
salutary cross, death, burial, and resurrection on the third
day from the dead, His ascension into heaven, and sitting at
the right hand of Thee His God and Father, and His
second bright and terrible appearance, when He shall come
with glory to judge the living and the dead, and shall
render to every man according to his works; we sinners
offer to Thee, O Lord, this tremendous and unbloody sacrifice,¹ beseeching Thee not to deal with us after our sins, nor
reward us according to our iniquities; but according to
Thy clemency and ineffable love to mankind, overlook and
blot out the handwriting that is against us Thy servants,
and grant us Thine heavenly and eternal rewards, such as
eye has not seen, nor ear heard, nor have entered into the
heart of man, even such as Thou hast prepared for them
that love Thee; and reject not this people for me and my
sins, O Lord, for this people and Thy Church make their
supplications before Thee.

' Have mercy upon us, O God the Almighty, have mercy
upon us, O God our Saviour, according to Thy great mercy,
and send down upon us and upon these gifts which are here
set before Thee Thy all-holy Spirit; even the Lord and

---

¹ ἀναίμακτον θυσίαν. Cyril's Catechism has the words ἀναίμακτον λατρείαν.

Giver of life, who with Thee, O God the Father, and with Thine only-begotten Son, liveth and reigneth a consubstantial and co-eternal Person;[1] who spake by the Law, by the Prophets, and by the New Testament, descended in the form of a dove upon our Lord Jesus Christ in the river Jordan, and rested upon Him, and came down in the shape of fiery tongues upon Thy Apostles, when they were assembled on the day of Pentecost in the upper room of holy and glorious Sion: Send down, O Lord, this Thy most holy Spirit upon us, and upon these holy gifts here set before Thee; that by His holy, good, and glorious Presence He may sanctify and make this bread the holy Body of Thy Christ. (Amen.) And this cup the precious Blood of Thy Christ. (Amen.) That all who are partakers thereof may obtain remission of their sins and eternal life, may be sanctified in soul and body, and bring forth the fruit of good works, for the confirmation of Thy Holy Catholic and Apostolic Church, which Thou hast founded upon the rock of faith, that the gates of hell may not prevail against it; delivering it from all heresy and scandal, and from the workers of iniquity, and preserving it to the consummation of the world.'

S. Basil's Liturgy, as retained on the great festivals in the patriarchate of Constantinople, is in these words:—

'For when He was just going to His voluntary, glorious, and life-giving death, in the same night wherein He gave up Himself for the life of the world, taking bread into His holy and immaculate hands, and presenting it to Thee, His God and Father, He gave thanks, blessed, sanctified, and brake it. He gave it to His holy disciples and apostles, saying, Take, eat, this is my Body, which is broken for you, for the remission of sins. (Amen.) In like manner, taking, mixing, giving thanks, blessing, sanctifying the cup of the fruit of the vine, He gave it to His holy disciples and apostles, saying, Drink ye all of this: this is my Blood of the New Testament, which is shed for you and for many, for the remission of sins. (Amen.) Do this in remem-

---

[1] Evidently inserted after the Second General Council. (A.D. 881.)

brance of Me: for as often as ye eat this bread and drink this cup, ye show forth My death and confess My resurrection.

'Having therefore in remembrance, O Lord, His saving Passion, His life-giving cross, His lying in the grave for three days, His resurrection from the dead, His ascension into heaven, His session at the right hand of Thee His God and Father, and His glorious and terrible second appearance; through all, and in all, we offer to Thee Thine own out of Thine own. We sinners, O most holy Lord, Thy unworthy servants, to whom Thou hast vouchsafed the honour to minister unto Thee, not upon account of our own righteousness, (for we have done nothing praiseworthy,) but according to Thy mercies and compassions, which Thou hast liberally bestowed upon us, approach Thy holy altar.

'And laying before Thee the antitypes¹ of the holy Body and Blood of Thy Christ, we pray and beseech Thee, O Thou Holy of Holies, of Thy gracious goodness to send down Thine Holy Spirit upon us, and upon these gifts here lying before Thee, to bless, to sanctify, and to perfect them. (ἀναδεῖξαι.) Make this bread the precious Body of our Lord, our God and Saviour Jesus Christ. (Amen.) And this cup the precious Blood of our Lord, our God and Saviour Jesus Christ. (Amen.) Changing them by Thy Holy Spirit.² (Amen, Amen, Amen.) Unite us all who partake of this Bread.' &c.

---

¹ ἀντίτυπα. This word is translated 'figures' in Heb. ix. 24, and 'like figure' in 1 Peter iii. 21. In both places the meaning is something more than a bare type. The holy places made with hands were in some degree *inhabited* by the Presence in the heavens. And Baptism is the actual instrument of the salvation of which the preservation of Noah was a type. A *type* is the sign of a thing not present, but *antitype* is as nearly as possible equivalent to our word 'sacrament,'—not only 'the sign of a sacred thing,' but the sign of that thing *given unto us;*—'a means whereby we receive the same, and a pledge to assure us thereof.'

² So this clause is usually translated. The Romanists insist that the aorist participle, μεταβαλών, refers the 'change' back to the words of Institution. But besides that the aorist cannot be so pressed against the plain meaning of the petition,

The ordinary Liturgy of Constantinople, attributed to S. John Chrysostom, gives the clauses in these words:—

'In the same night wherein He was delivered up, or rather He delivered up Himself, to suffer death for the life of the world, having taken bread into His holy, spotless, and undefiled hands, He gave thanks, and blessed it; He sanctified and brake it, and gave it to His disciples and apostles, saying, Take, eat, this is my Body, which is broken for you for the remission of sins. (Amen.) Likewise the cup after supper, saying, Drink ye all of this, this is my Blood of the New Testament, which is shed for you, and for many, for the remission of sins. (Amen.)

'Having therefore in remembrance this command of our Saviour, and all those things which He did for us,— His cross, His burial, His resurrection on the third day, His ascension into heaven, His sitting down at Thy right hand, and His second coming in great glory,—through all and in all things we offer to Thee Thine own, out of Thine own. We offer to Thee this reasonable and unbloody worship; (λατρείαν.)

'And we call upon Thee, we pray and beseech Thee, send down Thine holy Spirit upon us, and upon these gifts lying before Thee: Make this bread the precious Body of Thy Christ; (Amen.) and what is in this cup, the precious Blood of Thy Christ; (Amen.) changing them by Thy holy Spirit,' (Amen, Amen, Amen.) that it may be to those who partake of it, to cleanness of soul, to remission of sins, to communion of the Holy Ghost, to fulness of the kingdom of heaven, to confidence in Thee, and not to judgement or condemnation.'

The Alexandrine Liturgy, which probably re-

---

no physical 'change' is implied in the verb. It is the same which is rendered 'partake' in the next clause, and means no more than communicating the Spirit to the element, which is still 'bread' in the reception. Moreover, it is admitted by Goar that this clause is an interpolation, not in the ancient copies.

¹ See the preceding note on Basil.

presents an independent tradition consecrated by the name of the founder S. Mark, differs from the foregoing in beginning the *Anaphora* with a brief thanksgiving, and then proceeding at once to the Intercessions. The Thanksgiving contains the clause :—

'Wherefore giving thanks through Him and Thee, together with Him and the Holy Ghost, we offer this reasonable and unbloody worship, (λατρείαν,) which is offered to Thee by all nations, from the rising to the setting of the sun, from the north unto the south. For Thy name is great among all nations; and in every place, incense, sacrifice, and oblations are offered to it.'[1]

These expressions in this place have apparently exercised some effect on the Offices of the Church of Rome, which always cherished a closer intercourse with Alexandria than with the rival sees of Antioch and Constantinople. Nevertheless, they can hardly be allowed (as suggested in a recent admirable pamphlet[2]) to constitute the sacrificial oblation of the elements. The word λατρεία here means the whole rite, or act of worship, and this clause is a preliminary thanksgiving, introductory to the intercessions, as in 1 Tim. ii. 1. The proper Eucharistic Oblation follows in the usual place after the Seraphic Hymn, and is expressed in these words :—

'For our Lord Himself, our God and supreme King Jesus Christ, in the same night wherein He delivered Himself for our sins, and was about to suffer death for mankind, sitting down to supper with His disciples, having taken

---

[1] Compare Mal. i. 11.   [2] By the Rev. W. Milton.

bread in His holy, spotless, and undefiled hands, and looking up to Thee His Father, but our God, and the God of all, He gave thanks, He blessed, He sanctified, and brake it, and gave it to them, saying, Take, eat; for this is my Body, which is broken, and given for the remission of sins. (Amen.) In like manner, having taken the cup after supper, and mixed it of wine and water, looking up to heaven, to Thee His Father, but our God and the God of all, He gave thanks, He blessed, He filled it with the Holy Ghost, and gave it to His holy and blessed disciples, saying, Drink ye all of this; for this is my Blood of the New Testament, which is shed and given for you, and for many, for the remission of sins. (Amen.) Do this in remembrance of Me: for as often as ye shall eat this bread, and drink this cup, ye show forth my death, and confess my resurrection and ascension, till my coming again.

'Showing forth, therefore, O Lord Almighty, Heavenly King, the death of Thine only-begotten Son, our Lord, our God and Saviour Jesus Christ, and confessing His blessed resurrection from the dead on the third day, His ascension into heaven, and His session at the right hand of Thee His God and Father; and also looking for His second terrible and dreadful appearance, when He shall come in righteousness to judge both the quick and the dead, and to render to every man according to his works: We, O Lord God, have set before Thee Thine own, out of Thy gifts.

'And we pray and beseech Thee, O Thou lover of mankind, send down from Thy holy heaven, the habitation of Thy dwelling, from Thine infinite bosom, the Paraclete, the Spirit of truth, the Holy One, the Lord, the Giver of life, who spake in the Law, in the Prophets, and in the Apostles; who is everywhere, and fills all things, sanctifying whom He pleases,—not ministerially but according to His own will,—simple in nature but various in operation; the fountain of all divine graces; consubstantial with Thee, proceeding from Thee, and sitting with Thee in the throne of Thy kingdom, together with Thy Son our Lord, our God and Saviour Jesus Christ. Send down Thine Holy Spirit upon us, and upon these loaves and these cups, that the Almighty God may sanctify (τελειώσῃ) and consecrate them, and may make the bread the Body, (Amen.) and the cup the Blood, of the New Testament of our Lord Himself, our God, our Saviour and supreme King Jesus Christ; that they may be to us who partake of them, the means of faith, sobriety, health, temperance, sanctification; the renewing of our soul, our body, and spirit; the communion of the blessedness of eternal life and immortality; the glorifying of Thy holy Name, and the remission of our sins; that as well in this as in all things else, Thy holy, honourable, and glorious Name may, together with Christ and the Holy Ghost, be hallowed, praised, and glorified. (*Response*) As it was and is.'

These extracts are corrected from Dr. Brett's translations, omitting rubrics and interjectory anthems, interpolated at uncertain times. His collection includes another Alexandrian Liturgy by St. Basil, the Ethiopian use taken from S. Mark's, with the Nestorian and Monophysite Liturgies of Chaldea and Syria, all to the same effect. Other forms have been collected by Mr. Palmer and Dr. Neale, incontestably confirming the universal agreement of the Eastern Church in the points now under review. In all of them the consecration of the elements into Christ's Body and Blood is effected, not by repeating the words of Institution, as in the modern Roman Liturgy, but by the Benediction, or Invocation of the Holy Ghost, which follows them. Consequently the Oblation is always of the *unconsecrated* elements, designated by the words of Institution to be the memorials of the Passion, but not yet invested with the character of His Body and Blood. They are offered as the bread and the cup (so named in the oblation) to commemorate His Sacrifice, and to be sanctified as the means of communicating it to the receivers. Then the Holy

Ghost is invoked to descend upon these symbols, and make them the true Body and Blood *for the purpose of Communion.* This petition is what effects the Consecration, and imparts the spiritual virtue.[1] After this, nothing is offered but prayer and thanksgiving, with the living sacrifice of the bodies and souls of the communicants.

Hence it appears that the 'unbloody oblation' of the undivided Church was not in any sense a sacrifice of Christ, or of His Body and Blood, but of their *symbols*, to be made His Body and Blood in the Consecration. This has always been the doctrine of the Eastern Churches: it was laid down with great clearness in the Seventh General Council at Constantinople. (A. D. 754.)

'The true image of Christ—which He, our High Priest and God, who took our nature wholly upon Him, did at the time of His voluntary Passion deliver to His priests as a most emphatic type and memorial of Himself.'

Then follows a recital of the Institution as in the Liturgies, after which the Decree proceeds:

'See in this, the image of His life-giving Body.' And further on: 'He commanded chosen materials—that is, the substance of bread—to be offered as His image. As, therefore, the natural Body of Christ is holy, being deified,[2] so it is evident that His Body by adoption,—that is His image,—is holy, as being through a certain sanctification deified[3] by grace. This, therefore, (as we have said,)

---

[1] In the still earlier times when, according to Archdeacon Freeman, the Invocation preceded the Institution, the consecration would be due to the entire action of the Invocation and the Institution, accompanied by the manual handling of the elements. This detracts nothing from the argument in the text.

[2] θεωθέν, aor.   [3] θεουμένη, pres.

our Master Christ plainly intended; that as He deified the Flesh which He took on Him by the natural necessary holiness of the union itself, so it was His good pleasure that the bread of the Eucharist, as the true image of His natural Flesh, being sanctified by the descent of the Holy Ghost, should become a divine Body, by changing that which was common into holy, through the mediation of the priest who makes the oblation.'[1]

The image-worshippers of the Second Nicene Council,[2] in condemning this passage, asserted that none of the fathers had ever styled the unbloody sacrifice an 'image,' though they admitted the use of the word 'antitypes.' The Council of Frankfort also censured the word 'image,' understanding it to mean a 'prefiguration,' or '*typical* memorial, as in the transient shadows of the law,' whereas Christ has given us 'the sacrament of His Body and Blood.' They meant that a sacrament is the sign of a *present* grace, not a foreshadowed one; and this of course is true. Nevertheless both 'image' and 'type,' as well as 'antitype,' are unquestionably found in the fathers.

The Greek doctrine of consecration must have been originally the same with that of the Latin Church, since it formed no part of the first differences, and no complaint is heard on either side till long after the schism. The first dispute on this point was at the Council of Florence, (A.D. 1439,) long after the reception of transub-

---

[1] Johnson's App. 51. Mendham, 854.
[2] The pseudo Seventh General, A.D. 787.

stantiation in the West. The Latin divines then succeeded in obtaining some explanation from the Greeks, but the pope was so little satisfied with it, that he refused to have it inserted in the Acts, and it was promptly disallowed, with all the rest of the proceedings, at Constantinople. The Greek bishops who had agreed to it were driven from their sees, and the single dissident, Mark of Ephesus, was loaded with commendations. This bishop afterwards wrote a treatise, to prove that the Divine gifts are not consecrated by the Lord's words only, but by the subsequent prayer and benediction of the priest. He insists that

> 'No apostle or doctor of the Church ever consecrated the Eucharistic gifts with our Lord's words only, but that all of them with one consent, first indeed by way of narrative recited those words, putting us in mind of what was then done, and so qualifying the oblation for the change, but then after that added the prayer and blessing of the priest, to change what were already the gifts into the very prototype, the Lord's Body in energy.'[1]

Here we have the true account of the 'virtual' theory, which has been thought to be imperfectly apprehended by Calvin. The words of Institution make the elements symbols or *antitypes* of the crucified Body and outshed Blood; the Benediction advances them into the *prototype*—i.e. the reality of the symbols. But as the Body and Blood no longer exist in that state of crucifixion, the symbols

---

[1] ἐνεργείᾳ μεταποιῶν ἤδη τὰ δῶρα πρὸς αὐτὸ τὸ πρωτότυπον ἐκεῖνο σῶμα τὸ δεσποτικόν. Arcud. de Conc. Ecc. Occ. and Orient. iii. 28. Brett's Diss. p. 147.

are made so in *energy*—*i.e.* in power and effect to the communicant. There is no conversion or union to the *glorified* Body, nor is *that* the thing signified. Both parties clearly saw the effect of this doctrine of consecration on the nature of the Oblation; perhaps it was this difference in the Eucharistic Sacrifice, as much as the Double Procession, which induced the uncompromising Mark of Ephesus to pronounce the Latin dogmas *heretical.*

On the Participation of the sacrifice the Liturgies, though less express, are still sufficiently clear. The Communion was manifestly received by all who were present at the celebration, and in both kinds. This is shown by the dismissal of the catechumens, unbelievers, and non-communicants before the commencement of the Anaphora,—by the invitations addressed to the faithful,—and by the words employed in the distribution, independently of rubrics where they exist. In S. Chrysostom's Liturgy, after the communion of the clergy, the Deacon goes to the chancel door, and showing the elements to the people says, 'Draw near in the faith and fear of God.' To the same effect probably is the exclamation in all the Liturgies, 'Holy things to holy persons,' though some have imagined it to indicate a mysterious administration to the Holy Trinity.[1] In S. James's Liturgy there is a thanksgiving after the reception: S. Mark's preserves the words

---

[1] Rev. W. Milton's recent publication.

of distribution, 'The holy Body—the precious Blood—of our Lord, our God and Saviour.'

It may be observed, that the Eastern practice was to *stand* throughout the prayers on the Lord's Day, consequently there can be no doubt the sacrament was received in the same posture. But the head and body were bowed in profound reverence: the Liturgies contain several allusions to this practice, but have no trace of any other kind of 'adoration.'

All the Liturgies speak of the chalice as containing wine mixed with water, but without the mystical explanations suggested by some of the fathers; it is simply recited as part of the original Institution.[1] The later forms contain another mixture *after* consecration, which is perhaps the most daring innovation on Ante-Nicene usage. The priest puts a piece of the consecrated bread into the chalice, saying, in S. James's Liturgy,

'The union of the most holy Body and precious Blood of our Lord God and Saviour Jesus Christ. The union is made, sanctified, and completed, in the Name of the Father Son and Holy Ghost.'

In S. Chrysostom's Liturgy the words are,—

'The fullness of faith is of the Holy Ghost.'

And there is a further order to put some *warm* water into the cup, saying,

'The fervency of faith is of the Holy Ghost.'

Consequently the warm water was then supposed

[1] Such an explanation, however, occurs in the Syriac Version of S. James, which is probably older than the Greek.

to denote the descent of the Holy Ghost; the explanation, given at the Council of Florence, referring it to the water that issued with the blood from the side of the Crucified One, was of later growth.

These innovations speak trumpet-tongued of interpolation. The 'Union' is supposed to be as old as the fifth century, because it is found in the Nestorian Churches, which separated from the orthodox communion at that time. But this was just one of those dramatic rites that would find favour on both sides the pale, when the endeavour had begun to localize in material elements the objects presented in the mysteries to faith. It may have been intended to symbolize the revivification of the Lord's Body in the tomb, and if so it was the first step in the grand error which substituted the *risen* Christ in place of His sacrificed Body and Blood. It was followed by a practice, still retained throughout the Greek Church, of communicating the two kinds together from the chalice or a spoon. This practice was expressly forbidden by the Council in Trullo; and in Cyril's Fifth Catechism (A. D. 350) there are precise directions to the communicant, how to receive each element separately. The silence of that early 'Companion to the Altar' is conclusive proof that no Union was then practised in the Liturgy of Jerusalem.

Before we quit the Eastern Liturgies, some notice must be taken of the prayers which they contain for the dead. These have been manifestly subjected to continuous amplification, and were altogether absent from the very ancient Syriac Liturgy of S. James, where the departed were mentioned only with *thanksgiving;* the supplications afterwards inserted being inconsistent with the original expressions. The Clementine Liturgy immediately after the Consecration, proceeds :

'We further pray unto Thee, O Lord, for Thy holy Church, spread from the one end of the world unto the other, which Thou hast purchased by the precious Blood of Thy Christ.' After specifying the episcopate, the priests, deacons, and whole clergy, the king, with all in authority, and the army, it proceeds, 'Further, we offer unto Thee for all the Saints who have pleased Thee from the beginning of the world, the patriarchs, prophets, righteous men, apostles, martyrs, confessors, bishops, priests, deacons, sub-deacons, readers, singers, virgins, widows, laymen, and all whose names Thou knowest.'

It was probably at this part that the persons entered in the *diptychs* were enumerated by name. The word 'offer,' following close on the oblation and consecration of the sacrament, might at first sight countenance the notion that the consecrated elements were offered on their behalf, as in the modern sacrifice of the Mass. But on looking further we perceive that this word 'offer' is so interchanged throughout with words of simple petition, as to prove that no other offering but prayer is intended. The commendations are presented in this way:—

'We *pray* for the Holy Church,' &c. 'We *call upon Thee* for my unworthiness who am now offering,' &c. 'We *call upon Thee* for the king,' &c. 'We *offer* to Thee for all the saints,' &c. 'We *further offer* for this people, the virgins, widows, wives, and children,' &c. 'We *pray* unto Thee for this city, the sick, captives, exiles, prisoners,' &c. 'We *beseech* Thee for those who hate us, and for all that are without,' &c. 'We *pray* unto Thee for the catechumens, the possessed, and the penitents,' &c. 'We *offer* unto Thee for seasonable weather and the fruits of the earth,' &c.; and finally, 'We *pray* for the absent upon just cause,' &c.

Now certainly no reason can be assigned for offering *sacrifice* for the people, virgins, widows, and for seasonable weather, and *prayer* only for the bishops and clergy, the king, the city, the catechumens, penitents, and absentees. The 'offering' is plainly that of prayer and supplication throughout, though undoubtedly prayer and supplication were deemed most effectual at the sacramental remembrance of the Lord's death, since by His mediation all our addresses are presented to the throne of grace. This conclusion is confirmed by the African canon, which directs the dead to be commended in prayer alone when the Eucharist cannot be celebrated.[1]

[1] 'The sacraments of the altar are to be celebrated fasting, except on the single anniversary of the Lord's Supper. But if there be a commendation of the dead, whether bishops or others, in the evening let it be celebrated with prayers alone if the officiating ministers have dined.'—*Conc. Cart. can.* xliv. These 'commendations' were plainly at the hour of the death, otherwise there could be no necessity for celebrating them in the evening. The dying person would receive the *viaticum* from a morning consecration, but there was a further service for the repose of the soul immediately after its departure. The direction to omit the sacrament, for the reason here assigned, shows that prayer was the primary object of the

In the Liturgy of S. James the commendations are mostly introduced with the word 'remember.' Those for the departed run thus:—

'Remember, O God, the God of the spirits of all flesh, the faithful whom we have commemorated, or whom we have not mentioned, from just Abel unto this day. Make them to rest in the region of the living in Thy kingdom, in the delights of Paradise, in the bosom of Abraham, Isaac, and Jacob, our holy fathers, where there is no sorrow, grief, or lamentation, and where the light of Thy countenance continually shines upon them.'

This amplification of the Ante-Nicene form is still wholly free from any idea of releasing souls out of *purgatory*. So, too, the prayer in S. Mark's Liturgy:—

'Give rest, O Lord our God, to the souls of our fathers

---

office. This canon is remarkable as proving that 'the Lord's Supper' was not then the proper appellation of the Eucharist, (A.D. 418,) but of an annual love-feast held on the anniversary of the Institution—'the same night in which He was betrayed.' The Eucharist appears to have been generally celebrated with such a common meal in the earliest ages; and it has been thought that the phrase 'Lord's Supper' in 1 Cor. xi. 20 indicates the whole feast rather than the Eucharistic celebration itself. Maldonatus (on Matt. xxvi. 26) is very severe on the 'ignorance of Lutherans and Calvinists' in retaining this appellation after the 'supper' has disappeared; but it was a common usage with the fathers, and is followed in the Catechism of the Council of Trent. The *Agape*, or love-feast, must have been discontinued when the Eucharist was celebrated early in the morning, which Cyprian attests to be the universal practice of his Church. (A.D. 253.) The single exception allowed at Carthage on Maunday Thursday was prohibited by the Council in Trullo, (can. xxix.) as peculiar to that Church, a profanation of Lent, and contrary to apostolical tradition.

and brethren who are departed in the faith of Christ. Be mindful of our forefathers from the beginning of the world, patriarchs, prophets,' &c.[1]

In this Liturgy it will be remembered that the Intercessions *precede* the oblation and consecration of the elements, confirming the conclusion that no material sacrifice was offered for the departed.

S. Chrysostom's comes the nearest of any to the modern Mass, by proceeding after the consecration:

'We offer, moreover, this reasonable worship (λατρείαν) for those who are departed from us in faith; our forefathers, fathers, patriarchs, prophets, apostles, &c., and all other Thy saints, for the sake of whose prayers, O God, look upon us, and be mindful of those who rest in hope of a resurrection to eternal life; for the rest and forgiveness of the soul of Thy servant, N—. Give it rest, O God, in a pleasant place, where there is no sorrow or mourning, but where it may rejoice in the light of Thy countenance.'

Still there is no trace of *purgatory*. The idea is to regard the departed saints, like sick or absent brethren, as present and communicating in spirit;[2] accordingly, prayer is made for their particular necessities, as for those of the living. They are supposed to rest in hope, and even to intercede for the Church on earth. Such prayers are only a florid amplification of the apostle's aspiration for his departed friend: 'The Lord grant unto him that he may find mercy of the Lord in that day.'[3]

---

[1] The *Ave Maria* introduced into these two Liturgies is manifestly a late interpolation.
[2] 1 Cor. v. 8.   [3] 2 Tim. i. 18.

It is in connection with these intercessions for the dead, that we find the only mention in these Liturgies of the use of *incense*. It occurs, not in the prayers themselves, but in some rubrics inserted into the Liturgies of S. Mark and Chrysostom, which direct it to be burnt during the recital: the date of these rubrics is probably not earlier than the tenth century. Dodwell has clearly proved that incense in the divine Offices was unknown to the early Church. Bishop Andrewes thought it was first introduced 'in damp and unwholesome places.' The probability is that it was first copied into the Egyptian Liturgies, from the temple services of that country. Tertullian says it was much used in embalming the dead,[1] which may account for a portion being burnt during the prayers offered for their repose.

When the Eucharistic oblation came to be called Victim and Holocaust, and even to be pierced and 'immolated,' the same extravagant love of allegory and drama would revert to the 'sweet savour' indispensable to the animal sacrifices of the temple; but no *historical* connection can be traced with the Jewish Liturgy. The early fathers held that *prayer* is the incense which purifies the Christian sacrifice, and bears it, as on angels' wings, to the heavenly altar.

[1] Apol. 42.

VIII.—THE WESTERN LITURGIES.

THE liturgical remains of the West are inferior both in age and authenticity to those of the East. The Greek Liturgy which bears the name of S. Peter is only a translation of the Roman Canon, which at the Council of Trent was accused of departing from the ancient rite, especially in the matter of communion in one kind. The Dominican who made this charge affirmed that his own Order still retained the Office used at Rome three hundred years before; and a very different rite was even then observed at Milan.[1] Other Latin Liturgies were referred to at the same time, some of which are still extant, and are found to follow the Greek use in consecration. The Mozarabic rite which prevailed in Spain and Africa, the Gothic and Gallican Offices used in France and Britain, the two Missals attributed to S. Ambrose, with some others, all consecrate by the invocation of the Holy Ghost. So also the old African, which was perhaps the first Latin Liturgy.

'Grant, O Lord, that the Holy Ghost, the Comforter, the co-eternal and co-efficient worker of Thy benediction, may descend on these sacrifices, that this oblation which we offer unto Thee from Thy fruitful earth we may receive sanctified by Thee.'[2]

---

[1] Fra Paolo, ii. 250.   [2] Gothic Missal. Pfaff, 388.

'Almighty God, we beseech Thee let Thy Holy Word descend upon these which we offer unto Thee. Let the priceless Spirit of Thy glory descend, let the gift of Thine ancient bounty descend, that our oblation may be made a spiritual Host, accepted in the odour of sweetness,' &c.[1]

'We place upon Thy altar these holocausts of bread and wine, imploring that the Holy and undivided Trinity may sanctify these hosts.'[2]

'Send Thy Spirit from Thy holy heavens to sanctify the offerings.'[3]

'Let that invisible form and incomprehensible Majesty of Thy Holy Spirit, O Lord, descend as of old He descended upon the sacrifices of the Fathers, that He may also make these our oblations Thy Body and Blood.'[4]

The language of the Roman Church in the time of Clement, and probably of Justin Martyr, was Greek; and the same may be supposed of the churches in the south of France in the time of Irenæus. Such churches would doubtless use one of the Greek Liturgies, and from them the first Latin Offices may have been translated.

The original of the present Roman Liturgy is attributed both to Pope Gelasius (A. D. 492) and to Gregory the Great; there is no foundation for the conjecture which connects it with S. Leo, (420.) Gregory attributes the prayer of Consecration to an unknown 'scholastic' who probably translated from the Greek, and so many further alterations were subsequently introduced, that in

---

[1] Miss. Gall. in Miss. S. Germani. Pfaff.
[2] Miss. Mozarab. in die nat. Dom. Ibid. 384.
[3] Ibid. Dom. 1 Quad. Ibid. 384.
[4] Amb. in princ. Miss. Fer. vi. Ibid. 385.

the time of Charlemagne, Alcuin could only distinguish the authors by conjecture. Du Pin acknowledges it to be 'quite certain that the present editions do not give the Sacramentary of Gregory in its purity, but with many corruptions.'[1]

As it now stands, the Ordinary of the Mass begins with a preparatory Psalm and Confession: then come the Introit, Kyrie Eleison, and the Gloria in Excelsis, followed by the Nicene Creed. The elements are then presented for the Eucharist, each with a separate prayer, by the priest, here assuming the ancient privilege of the people. In like manner he presents the incense, with which the altar is occasionally fumigated. Then, after the twenty-fifth Psalm, an oblation of the elements is made by the priest, in memory of the Passion, Resurrection, and Ascension of our Lord Jesus Christ, and, as the present Office adds,

'In honour of the blessed Mary ever Virgin, of blessed John the Baptist, the holy Apostles Peter and Paul, and of all the saints, that it may be available to their honour and to our salvation, and that they may vouchsafe to intercede for us.'

This incongruous addition has been interpolated since the date of the so-called Liturgy of S. Peter, where the prayer of prothesis is simply,

'Look upon us and upon this Bread and Cup, and make it Thy unspotted Body and precious Blood, to the communion of our souls and bodies.'

---

[1] Bib. Cen. vi. Brett, 333.

The Preface, the Vere dignum, and the Ter Sanctus, complete the 'Ordinary' of the Mass.

Then follows the *Canon*, in these words:—

'We therefore most humbly pray and beseech Thee, most merciful Father, through Jesus Christ Thy Son our Lord, that Thou wouldest vouchsafe to accept and bless these gifts, these presents, these holy unspotted sacrifices, which in the first place we offer Thee for Thy holy Catholic Church, to which vouchsafe to grant peace, as also to preserve, unite, and govern it throughout the world; together with Thy servant N. our Pope, N. our Bishop, as also all orthodox believers and professors of the catholic and apostolic faith.

The Commemoration for the Living:

Be mindful, O Lord, of Thy servants, men and women, N. and N., and of all here present, whose faith and devotion are known unto Thee, for whom we offer, or who offer up to Thee, this sacrifice of praise for themselves, their families, and friends, for the redemption of their souls, for the health and salvation they hope for, and for which they now pay their vows to Thee, the eternal, living, and true God.

Infra actionem:

Communicating with, and honouring, in the first place, the memory of the ever glorious Virgin Mary, mother of our Lord and God Jesus Christ; as also of the blessed apostles and martyrs, Peter and Paul, &c., and of all Thy saints, through whose merits and prayers grant that we may be always defended by the help of Thy protection. Through the same Christ our Lord.'

Spreading his hands over the oblation, he says:

'We therefore beseech Thee, O Lord, graciously to accept this oblation of our servitude, as also of Thy whole family; [and to dispose our days in Thy peace, to preserve us from eternal damnation, and rank us in the number of Thine elect.]¹ Through Jesus Christ our Lord. Which oblation do Thou, O God, vouchsafe in all respects to bless,

---

¹ Introduced by Gregory the Great, A.D. 592. *Wendover.*

approve, ratify, and accept; that it may be made to us the Body and Blood of Thy most beloved Son, Jesus Christ our Lord. Who the day before He suffered took bread into His holy and venerable hands, and with eyes lifted up towards Heaven, to Thee, Almighty God, His Father, giving thanks to Thee, He blessed, brake, and gave to His disciples, saying, Take and eat ye all of this :

Holding the host with both hands, between his forefingers and thumbs, he pronounces the words of Consecration distinctly, secretly, and reverently.

FOR THIS IS MY BODY.

Having pronounced the Words of Consecration, he immediately kneels down and adores the consecrated Host: rises, shows it to the people, lays it again upon the Corporal, adores it again, and does not disjoin his thumbs and forefingers, except when the Host is to be handled, till the time of washing his fingers. Then uncovering the cup, he says:

'In like manner after He had supped, taking also this excellent chalice into His holy and venerable hands, giving Thee also thanks, He blessed, and gave it to His disciples, saying, Take and drink ye all of this :

He pronounces the words of consecration secretly over the Cup, holding it a little elevated.

FOR THIS IS THE CHALICE OF MY BLOOD OF THE NEW AND ETERNAL TESTAMENT, THE MYSTERY OF FAITH: WHICH SHALL BE SHED FOR YOU, AND FOR MANY, UNTO THE REMISSION OF SINS.

Having pronounced the words of Consecration, he sets down the Cup upon the Corporal, and saying secretly,

'As often as ye do these things, ye shall do them in remembrance of Me.'[1]

---

[1] It is remarkable that the Roman Church, which alone attaches such tremendous power to the words of Institution, should be more incorrect than any other in reciting them. She cuts short the blessing the bread with the five words of St Matthew, omitting the important additions of S. Luke and S. Paul. At the same time she enlarges the blessing of the cup with words and phrases not in either evangelist or apostle, while she removes the emphatic *Bibito ex eo omnes* from the Consecration.

He kneels down and adores it, rises, shows it to the people, sets it down, covers it, and adores it again; then disjoining his hands, he says:

'Wherefore, O Lord, we Thy servants, as also Thy holy people, calling to mind the blessed Passion of the same Christ, Thy Son our Lord, His resurrection from the dead and admirable ascension into heaven, offer unto Thy most excellent Majesty, of Thy gifts bestowed upon us, a pure Host, a holy Host, an unspotted Host, the holy bread of eternal life, and chalice of everlasting salvation. Upon which vouchsafe to look with a propitious and serene countenance, and to accept them, as Thou wert graciously pleased to accept the gifts of Thy just servant Abel, and the sacrifice of our patriarch Abraham, and that which Thy high-priest Melchisedek offered to Thee, a holy sacrifice and unspotted victim.

'We most humbly beseech Thee, Almighty God, to command these things to be carried by the hands of Thy holy angels to Thy altar on high, in the sight of Thy divine Majesty; that as many as shall partake of the most sacred Body and Blood of Thy Son at this altar, may be filled with every heavenly grace and blessing. Through the same Christ our Lord.'

Next follows the Commemoration for the dead, in which is a further elevation of the elements; and then the Lord's Prayer. Then, a peculiar form of the mixture, or union, of the Body and Blood, the *Agnus Dei*, the *Pax*, and after some prayers, the Communion of the priest in both kinds;[1] after which 'the Holy Communion is administered, if *there be any person to receive.*'

In comparing this Office with the Eastern Liturgies, the fact which first strikes us is that

[1] In the Missal as printed at Rome, 1647, (Brett,) the priest is directed to 'take all the Blood with the small piece (of bread) put into it;' but in the 'Missal for the Laity,' as published in England, he receives both kinds *separately*.

the Canon of the Mass nowhere pretends to offer that sacrifice of Christ, or of His Body and Blood, which is enunciated in the Tridentine Decree. Neither is there one word in it, from beginning to end, which expresses or implies the tenet of transubstantiation. In fact, corrupt as the Missal undoubtedly is, it is easier to reconcile its teaching with our own Twenty-eighth and Thirty-first Articles, than with the decrees of the Council of Trent.

The leading peculiarity of the Roman Canon is the double oblation of the elements, before and after Consecration. If the first be held to represent the sacrificial oblation of the Eastern Church, to which it bears a strong resemblance, the other must be a corrupt addition of later times.[1] In neither, however, are the *Oblata* designated as Christ, or as His Body and Blood. They are plainly bread and wine.

The modern Church of Rome regards the second oblation as the true Sacrifice; and in that case the first is only an amplification of the prayer of prothesis found in the Alexandrine Liturgy. It is observable, however, that it is the first oblation *alone* which mentions the Body and Blood of Christ, and the petition to make the bread and wine the Body and Blood *to us (ut fiat nobis)* plainly refers to their *reception* in the Communion. Moreover, this petition, uttered before consecra-

---

[1] This view is supported in Mr. Milton's excellent little treatise, lately published.

tion, cannot to the Romanists themselves imply the sacramental conversion which they call transubstantiation. In the second oblation the thing offered is 'the Host,' which, though by the Council of Trent identified with Christ Himself, undoubtedly means in the Canon nothing but bread. The epithets ascribed to it are all taken from the Greek, and the prayer that God would command these things to be carried by the hands of His holy angels to the altar on high, is clearly inapplicable to the Body of Christ, which is always in heaven. The same petition, in fact, occurs in the Clementine Liturgy, only in place of the angelic ministry it runs, 'by the mediation of Thy Christ'—a conclusive proof that the *oblatum* is not Christ Himself.

Assuming, then, the second oblation of the Roman Canon to be the sacrificial one, the Office will be found to be adapted from the Greek type, *omitting the Invocation of the Holy Ghost*. This will become apparent to anyone who will insert the Invocation, from one of those Liturgies, between the oblation and the petition for the gifts to be carried to the heavenly altar. With this addition, the Institution, Oblation, and Benediction would come in their usual Greek order. On the omission of this important feature from the Latin version, Gregory himself seems to have supplied some explanation. Referring to a tradition, extant in his time, that the apostles consecrated by the Lord's Prayer alone, he expresses his desire to restore their usage, in preference to the unauthorized departure of after times. His words are important:

> 'Orationem vero Dominicam idcirco mox post precem dicimus, quia mos apostolorum fuit ut ad ipsam solummodo Orationem oblationis hostiam consecrarent. Et valde mihi inconveniens visum est ut precem, quam Scholasticus composuerat, super oblationem diceremus, et ipsam orationem, quam Redemptor noster composuit, super ejus Corpus et Sanguinem taceremus.'[1]

The Roman divines would have us understand that Gregory attributed the consecration to the Lord's Prayer, *coupled with the words of Institution;* but, though these words were never omitted, it is plain that Gregory placed the *consecration* in the Lord's Prayer alone, *solummodo*. To say the Lord's Prayer *after* consecration was what all the Greek Liturgies did,[2] and, as Augustine remarks,[3] the Latin also. The change introduced by Gregory was to say it for the consecration itself,—*super oblationem*,—in place of the form composed by the *scholasticus*—*i. e.* in place of the Invocation which he found in his Latin version from the Greek. This conclusion is confirmed by another passage in Augustine, quoted by Mr. Milton, which tells us that the

---

[1] Ep. vii. 64.

[2] Except, however, the *Clementine*, the oldest of all, which is conclusive against an apostolical tradition.

[3] 'Totam petitionem, qua illud quod est in Domini mensa benedicitur et sanctificatur, fere omnis Ecclesia Oratione concludit.'—*Ep. ad Paul.*

prayers of the oblation were called *precationes*, while those of the consecration, by which the gifts were blessed and sanctified for Communion, were termed *orationes*. Gregory's *precem* was the same with Augustine's *precationes*, and what he did was to substitute the Dominica *oratio* for the *orationes* of human composition which previously formed the benediction.

This observation is important, as showing that all which now intervenes between the oblation and the Lord's Prayer, including the Commemoration for the Dead, is a later interpolation. Further, it is admitted by the Romanists themselves that this character pertains to all that *follows* the Lord's Prayer, which in Gregory's own Sacramentary was the conclusion of the Canon.[1] As he left it, the communion followed immediately on the consecration, as in Scripture and the present English Liturgy.

With these corrections the Roman Canon would become a somewhat poor and tumid version of the Greek Liturgies. As it stands, it is singularly *perplexed*, both in structure and expression; enunciating, in fact, neither the primitive nor the Tridentine sacrifice. The elements are never said to *be* the Body and Blood, either in type,

[1] Brett's Dissert. p. 280, where is a citation from the Antididagma of the Cologne Chapter against the reforms of their Archbishop Herman, showing that the Canon formerly ended with the Lord's Prayer, and the remainder was an *embolismum seu excrescentiam*. Note also Augustine's 'concludit' in the previous note.

antitype, or substance. There is only a petition to make them so '*unto us*,' and that *before* the words of Institution by which the conversion is supposed to be effected. Nowhere in the Canon of the Mass is there any oblation of Christ, or of His Body and Blood.[1] It requires the dogma of consecration by the words of Institution (which Gregory the Great did not hold) to produce an oblation of consecrated things at all. Even then the further dogma of transubstantiation must be interpolated, before there is any glimpse of 'a sacrifice of the Body and Blood of Christ under the forms of bread and wine.' On this prodigious miracle the Canon of the Mass is profoundly silent.

Remembering that this Office was originally taken from the Greek, its peculiar structure may perhaps be accounted for by the liberty of thought necessarily exercised in a translation. The Latin compiler found the recital of the words of Institution fixed, invariable, and apostolical; the Invocation was subject to alteration by authority of the Church. The first retained the Saviour's own words; the other was the composition of men. Moreover, it was the words of Institution which gave the symbolical character to the elements, and so far constituted the sacrament, or visible sign, of the unseen realities to be imparted to the receiver. Hence

---

[1] It is observable that Gregory, like the fathers, applied these designations to the *unconsecrated* elements.

Augustine's words, 'Accedit verbum ad elementum et fit sacramentum.'[1] In this symbolical character the gifts were offered to God. The further blessing had respect to the *communion* more than the *sacrifice*. The Spirit whom the Greeks invoked on the elements was to find His true tabernacle in the worthy communicant. The consummation of the rite lay in the communion of Christ with His ransomed people, through their participation of the Sacrifice accepted of His Father. To this end it would be apparent that His original words, 'This is my Body,' 'This is my Blood,' were of perpetual efficacy, and that in repeating them over the elements with thanksgiving and prayer, it could not be *essential* to add a form of benediction, neither delivered in Holy Scripture, nor received by invariable tradition. Hence Gregory chose to replace the Invocation by the Lord's Prayer, in which the petition, 'Give us this day our daily bread,' was often applied to the Eucharist.

Even among the strenuous adherents of the Greek use we find the sacramental virtue attributed at one time to the words of Institution, and at another to the Invocation. Gregory Nazianzen[2] and Epiphanius[3] assert the former,

---

[1] In Joh. lxxx. 15. De Catacl. c. iii. It should be borne in mind that this often-repeated dogma is by Augustine enunciated of *Baptism*, not of the Eucharist.

[2] Greg. Naz. Orat. ii. de Pasch.   [3] Epiph. in Ancorat.

Ephrem Syrus[1] and Theophilus[2] the latter; while Gregory Nyssen,[3] Chrysostom,[4] and the Sermons attributed to Eusebius Emissenus,[5] are cited on both sides. The practical conclusion is that *both* were included in the true idea of consecration. In his sermon on the treason of Judas, Chrysostom finely says,

'It is not man who makes the gifts to become the Body and Blood of Christ, but the same who was crucified, even Christ. He stands here (referring to the paschal supper) alone fulfilling the part of priest. It is He who offers the prayer and pronounces the words, "this is my Body;" but the grace and power which works the whole is of God. And as that voice which said, "increase and multiply, and replenish the earth," was spoken indeed once, but works through all time, by empowering our nature to produce offspring, so also the same voice once uttered by that Divine Tongue, "this is my Body," works as the power of the Word on every table, in all His churches, to this day and till His future appearing, to perfect the sacrifice.'[6]

The original consecration, that is, resides in the words and promise of Christ; the recital is to apply them to the particular sacrament, which is thus perfected, or consecrated to communicate the spiritual grace. A similar argument was used by two of the Greek prelates at the Council of Florence:

'Even as that divine precept once spoken by God, "let the earth bring forth grass, and the herb yielding seed,

---

[1] Ephrem Syr. περὶ ἱερωσύνης.   [2] Theophil. Alex. Ep. i.
[3] Greg. Nyss. Orat. in Bapt. Xti. Compare Orat. Cat. ii. 37.
[4] Chrys. De Sac. vi. Compare Hom. i. in Matt. and Hom. ii. in 2 Tim.
[5] Serm. v. de Pasch. Compare Serm. de Corp. et Sang. Dom.
[6] Pfaff, 390.

according to its kind," works from the beginning until now, and will work to the end; and yet we believe that, while it is the Divine precept which empowers the earth to produce and bear fruit, there is need also of the husbandman's energy, for we always see it co-working in the earth to the produce;—so also we say of the Holy Sacrifice, that it is those words (of the original Institution) which sanctify it; but there are conjoined moreover the prayers and invocations of the priest to perfect the consecration, like the care of the husbandman to the fruit of the earth. In thus saying, we Greeks do not rely on ourselves, but look to the tenor of what is written in the sacred liturgies. Much more ought not the Latins to consider only their own prejudices."[1]

This is precisely the view taken in our own Baptismal Office of the consecration of the water. First we recite the Lord's baptism in the river Jordan, as sanctifying the whole element of water to the mystical washing away of sin; and then we pray for the sanctification of that particular water to the same use, that 'the child now to be baptized therein may receive the fullness of grace.'

These considerations go to justify the early Western view of consecration by the words of Institution, coupled with prayer, independently of the special benediction customary in the East.[2] A widely different notion arose in the

[1] Syropulus, Hist. Conc. Flor. i. 1.

[2] Archdeacon Freeman is undoubtedly right in attributing consecration, in the primitive idea, to the entire Eucharistic prayer and action. This would render the *order* of its several parts of less moment than it afterwards became, when the Greeks restrained the consecration to the Invocation, and the Latins to the Institution. It is by no means improbable that the words of Institution *always* stood in the West at the close of the Consecratory prayer, and thence arose the notion that their pronunciation alone effected the consecration.

dark age that descended on the West, after it fell under the barbarian yoke. The mere pronunciation of the mystic words by a priest was then thought to fix the Divine Presence in the material element, irrespectively of prayer, or after use in communion. The gifts exhibited in the sacrament were mistaken for the Person of the Giver. It was no longer the *crucified* Body and *outshed* Blood, to be received in a mystery, but the *glorified* Christ in bodily presence, that filled the paten and the chalice. The gifts which He bestowed in two separate elements, to symbolize His Body and Blood sundered in death, were daringly brought together, first in actual mixture, then by the school dogma of concomitancy and the suppression of the cup. 'Whole Christ' was now lodged in the bread; that inward and spiritual Presence of the living Redeemer, which He taught us to expect as the result of feeding on His sacramental Body and Blood, was transferred, from its proper tabernacle in the soul, to the material symbols of His Death. This so confounded the sacramental mystery, that the schoolmen, who had wrought the mischief, were driven to the further invention of transubstantiation, as the only logical loop-hole from despair. And so He whom, S. Peter taught, 'the heaven of heavens must receive until the times of the restitution of all things,' was feigned to be brought down at the bidding of every priest, not to feed the hungry soul, but to be lifted up, or put down, upon altars without communicants; to be gazed at, or shut up in pyxes; to be carried about in processions without His will or consent; to be exposed for adoration by those who worship they know not what; to be made a hostage for the observance of unjust contracts; to lend His life-giving Blood to the pen of the diplomatist, or even—*horribile dictu*—to the infernal malice of the poisoner!

These awful profanations, with other consequences revolting alike to decency, morality, and religion, were the offspring of the deplorable superstition, which converted the sacrament of our Lord's crucified Body and Blood into the reality of His glorified Person.

IX.—THE FATHERS.

IN this section, the testimony of the Catholic Liturgies is to be corroborated from the remains of the contemporaneous Fathers. These are sometimes referred to as infallible oracles, whose lightest word is to silence all dispute. Others discard them as private individuals, of no greater weight than modern theologians. Controversialists have had recourse to them, as children rush to a heap of stones, in quest of a missile to throw at an opponent's head. They pelt one another with Fathers, but never dream of accepting their authority against themselves. The Romanist overrules all by the authority of the Papal See, the ultra-Protestant by his own interpretation of Holy Scripture; each finds enough to sustain his own predetermined view, but neither can deprive his adversary of the same advantage.

It is evident, then, that no great question can, or ought to be, decided by a mere *Catena* of Fathers. It is easy to construct one on any side by omitting all that makes against it. Every Father is not always in agreement with every other, nor every one invariably consistent with himself. They expressed their conscientious convictions of the truth as revealed in Holy Scripture, and taught by the Catholic Church; but not being inspired, they are no infallible guides on either point. Knowing, many of them, no other language but their own, their expositions of Scripture must be corrected by the better criticism of later times. Their great value is as *witnesses* to the interpretation and teaching of the Church in their own day. This is a matter of fact on which they could not be mistaken; and to know how the Scriptures were understood in the earliest ages, is our surest guide to the original and genuine interpretation. This evidence, however, manifestly depends on the *consent* and *antiquity* of the witnesses adduced.

One or two writers will not establish a Church doctrine in the third or fourth century, any more than in the sixteenth or seventeenth. Nor is it possible to set up Catholic consent, on evidence of the sixth or seventh centuries, when the propositions are unknown to the second and third.

When the Church of England appeals 'to the old godly doctors of the most uncorrupt ages,' she waives neither the supremacy of Scripture, nor her own authority as witness and keeper of Holy Writ. She does not propound the Fathers as an authority to her children, much less erect them into a court of appeal from her own sentence. She only challenges a comparison of her own action with that of the primitive churches, showing that in all the great questions at issue between Rome and herself, the Fathers are on her side, more than her adversary's. She cites them to prove that in the primitive churches Holy Scripture was the supreme rule of faith, that the several churches interpreted it with equal and independent authority, that each decreed its own rites and ceremonies, and that the Catholic agreement subsisting between all is retained, in all things necessary or important, in our own doctrine and discipline. This is all that is requisite to establish her claim as a living branch of the Holy Catholic Church: and that claim once established, her voice, and *hers only*, is the voice of the Church to her loyal children. For a churchman to bring up the Fathers again, is as irrelevant as for the dissenter to press us with his view of the Scripture. It is arguing over again on private judgment, the evidence already heard and decided upon by the Church.

In the present day we have the advantage of better and more authentic texts, than were open to the Divines of the sixteenth and seventeenth centuries; but there is little to be added to the evidence collected in such works as Jewell's Apology, or Bishop Patrick's 'Full View of the Doctrines and Practices of the Ancient Church.'[1] It has of course not convinced, and never will convince, the Tridentines: neither will they ever be able to refute it. If the mine of antiquity is to be worked again, it would be but fair to specify the mistake or new evidence relied upon, instead of involving the unwary in a cloud of 'godly doctors' from whom nothing is distinctly produced.

One reason which makes the testimony of the Fathers less conclusive than might be supposed, is that they wrote before much controversy had arisen on the Eucharistic doctrine. This is doubtless the condition most favourable to piety and devotion: but it fails to promote exactness of thought or language. Men do not begin to weigh their expressions, or even to analyze their conceptions, till they feel the danger of being misunderstood. A problem of any kind can hardly be thought out without the stimulus of

[1] Gibson's Preservative against Popery. Tit. vii. c. 4.

collision with other views; as for the mysteries of religion, few can even now express their belief with verbal accuracy, after ages of controversy and definition. Men of exact habits of thought constantly complain of want of clearness in the discourses of well educated preachers. Why should we expect more from the Fathers, whose circumstances would suggest so much less? Their testimony is sufficient if we do not press them beyond their knowledge; it fails only when we try to wrest it to support conclusions which they never thought of.

In the following citations much of course is lost by translation; the liturgical references in particular are far clearer in the original language, where the very words of the Liturgies constantly recur, to determine the sacrificial meaning of the author.

Clement of Rome, treating of the conduct of Divine Service, probably in the life-time of the Apostles, says:

'We ought to do all which the Lord has prescribed in due order. He has enjoined the oblations and the liturgies to be celebrated' at the appointed times, not thoughtlessly and irregularly, but at fixed hours and seasons. How, and by whom He will have them celebrated, He has Himself appointed by His sovereign pleasure; that all things being done holily in His good pleasure may be acceptable to His will. They therefore who make their oblations at the prescribed times are accepted and blessed, for following the law of the Lord they do not err.'[2]

---

[1] προσφοράς, λειτουργίας, ἐπιτελεῖσθαι, are all liturgical terms.
[2] 1st Ep. Cor. cap. xl.

Here we have not only proof of the use of a Liturgy in the Apostolic age, but the Christian Liturgy is paralleled with the Jewish. The author goes on to adduce the several offices assigned in the Levitical Liturgy to the high priest, the priests, and the levites, 'while the layman was bound by the lay regulations.'

'Even so every one of you, brethren, must give thanks *(make your eucharist)*[1] in his own order, abiding in good conscience, not transgressing the prescribed rule of his ministry *(the canon of his liturgy)*[2] in all gravity.' 'Not everywhere (he continues) are the daily sacrifices offered, whether of peace-offerings[3] or sin-offerings and trespass-offerings, but in Jerusalem alone. And even there they are not offered in any place, but in front of the Sanctuary upon the altar, the offering being first examined by the high priest and the aforesaid ministers. They, therefore, who offer anything contrary to His will, incur the pain of death.'

After observing that the greater the knowledge vouchsafed to Christians, the greater also is the responsibility, Clement comes to the object of his argument, which was to reinstate the ministers ejected at Corinth.

The apostles (he says) were sent by Christ, and Christ from God, in an orderly way. They in like manner appointed bishops and deacons according to the Scripture.[4] Referring to the contentions for the priesthood against Aaron, he says, 'The Apostles foresaw a similar strife for the right to the episcopate, and gave instructions to continue the succession; consequently those appointed by them or other rulers with consent of the Church could not be justly

---

[1] εὐχαριστεῖτε. [2] τὸν ὡρισμένον τῆς λειτουργίας αὐτοῦ κανόνα.
[3] θυσῶν, not the usual word, but used apparently in this sense in Lev. xxii. 29.
[4] Citing Isaiah, lx. 17, Sept.

dismissed without cause. For our sin (he concludes) will not be small if we cast out of the episcopate those who have blamelessly and holily presented the gifts."[1]

Throughout this argument Clement insists on the parallel between the high priest, priests, levites, and people of the then existing temple at Jerusalem, and the apostles, bishops, deacons, and laity of the Christian Church. The correspondence is laid in the *offerings* presented by each. The Jewish sacrifices are paralleled by the Christian oblations, the presenting of which is the special office of the bishops and deacons. He uses the same Greek words that we find in the Liturgies, thereby confirming the existence of a very similar Liturgy in the apostles' age. In fact, it was probably these very references which gave rise to the belief that Clement was the author of the Liturgy found in the Constitutions; since it has no historical connexion with the church over which he presided.

It will be observed that Clement attributes these oblations and liturgies to the ordinance of Christ: the same thing is said in the Liturgy which bears his name, and by many of the fathers. The text commonly adduced in support of this belief is Matt. v. 23, 24, which is interpreted of the first-fruits and other contributions for the support of the clergy. These included the sacramental elements, which the celebrant usually selected from the bread and wine, the only offerings

[1] Cap. xliii., xliv.

allowed to be placed on the altar. The priestly oblation of those elements in the Eucharistic rite is in the Liturgies attributed to the Institution of Christ, and in this they are corroborated by Clement, who was a fellow-labourer with the Apostles.

Ignatius, another contemporary of the Apostles, says:

'If anyone be not within (a partaker of) the altar, he is deprived of the bread of God.'[1] He exhorts the churches to cherish the unity of which the Eucharist was the seal, 'breaking one and the same bread, the medicine of immortality,'[2] 'Take heed to have but one Eucharist, for there is one Flesh of our Lord Jesus Christ, and one cup in the unity of His Blood, one altar, as there is one bishop together with the presbytery and the deacons my fellow servants.'[3] He complains of those who abstain from the Eucharist and prayer, as not 'confessing the Eucharist to be the Flesh of our Saviour Jesus Christ, which (flesh) suffered for our sins, which the Father graciously raised up. They who speak against this Gift of God, will die in their contradiction; it were better to love it, that they may rise again.'[4]

Justin Martyr (A.D. 114) is the first to describe the Eucharistic celebration at length.

'Having ended the prayers, we salute one another with a kiss.[5] There is then brought to the president[6] of the brethren bread and a cup of wine mixed with water; and he taking them, gives praise and glory to the Father of the universe, through the Name of the Son and of the Holy

---

[1] Eph. cap. v.   [2] Eph. 20.   [3] Philad. 4.   [4] Smyrn. vii.

[5] It was probably after this salutation that the *consistentes* of the Nicene Canon were to withdraw. See *ante*, p. 188.

[6] τῷ προιστῶτι, *antistes*, prelate.

Ghost, and offers thanks at great length¹ for our being counted worthy to receive these things at his hands. And when he has concluded the prayers and the thanksgiving, all the people present express their assent by saying *Amen*. This word *Amen* answers in the Hebrew language to γίνοιτο. (so be it.) And when the president has given thanks, and all the people have expressed their assent, those who are called by us deacons give to each of those present to partake of the bread and wine and water, over which the thanksgiving was pronounced, and to those who are absent they carry away a portion.² And this food is called among us Εὐχαριστία, (the Eucharist,) of which no one is allowed to partake but the man who believes that the things which we teach are true, and who has been washed with the washing that is ordained for the remission of sins and regeneration, and who is so living as Christ enjoined. For not as common bread and common drink do we receive these: but in like manner as Jesus Christ our Saviour, having been made flesh by the Word of God, had both flesh and blood for our salvation, so likewise have we been taught that the food which is blessed by the prayer of the Word delivered by Him, and from which our blood and flesh by transmutation are nourished,³ is the Flesh and Blood of that Jesus Who was made flesh. For the Apostles, in the memoirs composed by them which are called Gospels, delivered unto us that Jesus thus commanded them; that He having taken bread, and given thanks, said, " This do ye in remembrance of Me, this is My Body;" and that after the same manner having taken the cup and given thanks, He said, " This is My Blood;" and gave it to them alone to partake of.'⁴

In another place Justin has the words: 'It is written, Cleave to the holy, for those that cleave to them will be made holy.' This citation not being

¹ See the *long* prayer in the Clementine Liturgy. In cap. lxvii., Justin says he offers prayers and thanksgivings 'as he is able,' which very expression is found in this prayer—'not as we ought, but as we are able.'

² No 'reservation' for *future* use is implied.

³ Compare Irenæus, *post*.

⁴ Apol. i. (ad. Anton. Pium.) cap. lxv. lxvi.

found in the Bible, may perhaps refer to the Liturgical *exclamation,* 'Holy things for the holy!'

To Trypho, Justin alleges the offering of fine flour for the leper,[1] to be

'A type of the bread of the Eucharist, the celebration of which our Lord Jesus Christ prescribed in remembrance of the suffering He endured on behalf of the souls to be purified from sin, in order that we may at the same time thank God for having created the world with all things therein for the sake of man.'[2] To this rite he refers the prophecy of Malachi, affirming, (as in S. Mark's Liturgy,) that the bread and cup of the Eucharist are the pure sacrifice by which the Gentiles glorify His Name, while the Jews profane it. He quotes the prophets at some length against the Judaical notion of a value in the external services, repeating that God needs nothing, but has appointed all for the benefit of man. Having cited the fiftieth Psalm in the Septuagint Version, he dwells on the concluding verse. 'The sacrifice of praise shall glorify Me, and there is the way in which I shall shew him the salvation of God.'[3] This text was often applied to the Eucharistic sacrifice, probably because 'salvation' ($\sigma\omega\tau\eta\rho\iota o\nu$) is the name which the Septuagint gives both to the peace-offerings and the meat-offering of fine flour.[4] Justin argues that Christians are the true high-priestly race of God, because we know that God accepts sacrifice only through His Priests,[5] and He adduces Mal. i. 10-12 as anticipating the sacrifices which Jesus Christ enjoined us to offer; *i.e.* the Eucharist of the bread and the cup which are offered by all Christians throughout the world; and God bears witness that they are acceptable to Him.[6] At the same time he insists that prayer and thanksgiving are the only perfect and acceptable sacrifice, and maintains that 'these are truly offered by Christians only.' The material oblation is the visible exhibition of this inward spiritual sacrifice.

Irenæus (A.D. 182-8) refers to the Eucharist in

---

[1] Lev. ii. [2] Dial. Tryph. Cap. xli. [3] Cap. xxii.
[4] Exodus, xx. 24; Lev. ii. 1. [5] Cap. cxvi. [6] Cap. cxvii.

contending against the Gnostics, who denied the reality of our Lord's Human Nature, and attributed the creation of the world to a Demiurge in rebellion against the Supreme Being. He argues that Christ's Flesh was real from its being really partaken of in the Eucharist, and that He was also the true Lord and Creator of the world, because the elements which communicate His Body and Blood are parts of this earthly creation. The point of the argument is, that the consecrated elements are real bread and wine, taken into our flesh by natural assimilation. Like Justin he often repeats of the sacrifice the teaching of Scripture, that God needs nothing, citing the usual texts from the Psalms and the Prophets. After thus insisting on Hosea vi. 6,—urged against the Jews by Christ Himself,—he proceeds:

'Our Lord, counselling His disciples to offer to God the first-fruits of His creatures,'[1] (not as though He needed them, but that they themselves might not be unfruitful and

---

[1] It was the custom in the primitive Church to offer the actual first-fruits of the harvest, the vintage, and other produce, for the support of the clergy. These, with other contributions to the same use, were brought to the church to be dedicated and blessed before they were distributed: and no such offerings might be sold by the presbyters. (Con. Anc. Can. xv.) The third Apostolic canon directs that of these offerings nothing shall be brought *to the altar* 'beyond the ordinance of the Lord for the sacrifice, neither honey nor milk, nor made liquors instead of wine, nor birds, nor animals, nor pulse.' An exception is allowed for ears of new corn and grapes, at the proper season, to which an interpolation of after times adds, 'oil for the lamps and incense,' supposed to have

ungrateful,) took bread, which is one of these creatures, and gave thanks, saying, This is My Body: in like manner He confessed the Cup, which is of the same creation that we are, to be His Blood, and so taught the New Oblation of the New Testament, which the Church receiving from the apostles offers throughout the world to that God who supplies our aliment, as the first-fruits of her gifts under the New Testament; concerning which in the Twelve Prophets Malachi thus foreshewed, (Mal. i. 10, 11.) most evidently signifying by these words how the former people should indeed cease to offer to God, but that still in every place sacrifice should be offered to Him, and that a pure one, saying His Name shall be glorified among the Gentiles.' The incense (he adds) is explained by S. John in the Apocalypse to be the prayers of the saints.' [1]

Again:

'It behoves us to offer to God the first-fruits of His creation: ..... not offering in general *(genus)* is rejected, for there were oblations then, and there are oblations now, sacrifices among the people and sacrifices in the Church;—but the kind only *(species)* is changed, because that now it is offered not by servants but by sons,'[2] (or 'not by slaves but by the free.')

Referring to Phil. iv. 18,—a text applied to the Eucharist in all the Liturgies,—he contends that

the Church, and the Church alone, 'offers this pure sacrifice to the Creator in offering of His creatures with thanksgiving.

---

been used in embalming the dead. All other lay offerings were to be carried to the Bishop's house, the bishops and priests were to enjoy their Primitiæ, but not present them on the altar. (Nic. Can. iii., iv.; Carth. xxvii.) It would appear that from the Bread and Wine brought to the altar the celebrant selected a portion for the Eucharistic Oblation, and this Irenæus here designates by the name of *Primitiæ,* (whether strictly so or not,) as being the choice or most precious fruits of nature, and therefore fittest to be symbols of His Body and Blood, Who is 'the first-fruits of them that slept.'

[1] Adv. Hær. IV. xvii. 5, 6.   [2] Ibid. xviii. 1, 2.

The Jews do not offer so, because their hands are full of blood, and they have not received the Word by which the oblation is made.'¹ Neither do the heretics offer rightly, because they acknowledge another Demiurge, so accounting the bread and the cup which are the Lord's Body and Blood, the property of another Maker. 'How can they confess the bread over which thanks are given to be the Body of their Lord, and the cup His Blood, while they say He is not the very Son of the Maker of the world, that is, His Word by whom the tree is made fruitful, and the fountains flow, who gives first the blade, then the ear, after that the full corn in the ear?... But our judgment is conformable to the Eucharist, and the Eucharist in turn confirms our judgment. For we offer unto Him His own, fitly affirming the communion and unity of flesh and spirit; for as the bread which is of the earth, receiving the Invocation of God, is now no longer common bread, but Eucharist, consisting of two things, an earthly and a celestial; so our bodies receiving the Eucharist are no longer corruptible, (*i.e.* bound under corruption) but have hope of the resurrection to eternal life.'²

These passages plainly refer to the Eucharistic Liturgy; to the oblatory words, 'of Thine own we offer unto Thee,' and the Invocation³ by which the offering was made the Body and Blood. In like manner, when contending in another place for the resurrection of the body, Irenæus asks how it can be denied that our flesh is capable of the gift of eternal life,

'when the mixed cup and made bread receive the Word of God, and the Eucharist becomes Christ's Body, [and

---

¹ The words of Institution and Consecration.

² Adv. Hær. IV. xviii. 4, 5.

³ It has been suggested that ἐκκλησιν, in the Greek fragment, should read ἐπίκλησιν, and *vocationem* in the Latin translation *invocationem;* but the emendation is needless, since the meaning is the same without it, and Irenæus uses the same word elsewhere.

Blood,] and by these the substance of our flesh is nourished and increased?"[1]

The learned Lutheran divine, C. M. Pfaff, published a fragment of Irenæus from a collection of *anecdota* in the Royal Library at Turin,[2] which, if genuine, contains as direct a testimony to the ante-Nicene Liturgy as could be supplied. After quoting the standing texts, Mal. i. 10, Rev. viii. 3, Rom. xii. 1, and Heb. xiii. 15, (which last it should be remembered is taken from Hosea, xiv. 2,) the author proceeds,

'These oblations are not after the law, of which the Lord hath taken away the handwriting blotting it out, but after the Spirit; for it is necessary to worship God in spirit and in truth. Wherefore the oblation of the Eucharist is not carnal, but spiritual, and for this reason pure; for we offer to God the bread and the cup of blessing, giving Him thanks, (εὐχαριστοῦντες) that He has commanded the earth to bring forth these fruits for our nourishment; and then having completed the oblation, we invoke the Holy Spirit that He would make[3] this sacrifice and this bread the Body of Christ, that they who receive these antitypes may obtain forgiveness of sins and eternal life. They therefore who celebrate these offerings in the memorial of the Lord, (ἐν τῇ ἀναμνήσει) do not conform to the dogmas of the Jews, but ministering spiritually shall be called the children of wisdom.'

Whether this fragment be genuine or not, Irenæus certainly held the Eucharistic Sacrifice to contain two oblations, the *mincha* of bread and

[1] Adv. Hær. V. ii. 3.

[2] S. Irenæi Fragmenta Anecdota Lugd. Bat. 1743.

[3] ἀποφήνῃ, the same peculiar word as in the Clementine Liturgy, (Ap. Const. viii. 12.) from ἀποφαίνω, ostendo, declaro, efficio, reddo. Pfaff's note, p. 126.

wine, and the *incense* of prayer; both deriving their acceptance from the Sacrifice of the Cross, commemorated and spiritually partaken of in the Eucharist; and this is therefore a spiritual Sacrifice.

It has been objected to the Eucharistic Sacrifice that the primitive Christians never disclaimed the reproach of the heathen, that they had neither altars nor sacrifices. The truth is, that the Christian Sacrifice was *not* such a rite as their persecutors designated by the name, and it would have been a disingenuous artifice to take advantage of the word in a different meaning. The Jewish and Gentile sacrifices were offered as meritorious and propitiatory *ex opere operato*, a real gratification to the Deity securing a gracious acceptance to the worshipper. This delusion the Christians never ceased to protest against; they maintained the Sacrifice of Christ to be the one only acceptable offering to the Father, and all human rites either nugatory, or subordinate and spiritual, *i.e.* effective only through faith and devotion. To the heathen, it would have been essentially untrue to represent the Eucharist as a sacrifice, but there was no hesitation in employing the word among Christians, who were cognizant of the spiritual meaning.

Irenæus's statement that the Eucharist contains two things, an earthly and a celestial, has proved a sore trouble to the advocates of transubstantiation. Bellarmine gives the usual explanation, that the earthly thing means the accidents, and the heavenly thing the Body and Blood of Christ, the only substance really present after consecration. But, besides that accidents cannot contribute to 'the nourishment and increase of the substance of our flesh,' Irenæus, like Justin Martyr, expressly attributes this nourishment to the Body and Blood of Christ, *i.e.* to the earthly not the heavenly thing. Massuet tries to meet the difficulty by understanding the earthly thing of the Humanity, and the heavenly one of the Divinity, of Christ. But this would make the natural Flesh of Christ to be actually digested into the flesh of the communicant.

Other Romish expositions are refuted by Pfaff, but he is less successful in establishing the Lutheran interpretation (lately revived in the Objective theory) of a *union* between the bread and Christ's Body. For in that case the bread, as the earthly part, must supply the nourishment of our bodies, and the Body of Christ, as the heavenly thing, should be reserved to the soul; whereas Irenæus expressly says that the Body of Christ nourishes the substance of our flesh. It is plain that by the Body of Christ he meant the bread itself, and not another substance in union with it. So in the Liturgies the Invocation to which he refers does not call upon God to *unite* the Body and Blood to the bread and wine, but to *make* them the Body and Blood. Plainly then, whatever be the interpretation, it is the bread and wine—remaining such—which are the Body and Blood. It follows that the 'heavenly part' is not another substance united to the earthly, but a new and spiritual *power*, or condition, communicated to it.

What Irenæus affirms is a *communion and oneness*[1] of flesh and spirit; the word is taken from the apostle who calls the bread the *communion of the Body*.[2] Not that the bread holds the Body in union with it, but it is gifted with the power of communicating the Body; just as, in a lower way, the memorial of the peace-offering communicated the body of the holocaust to the Israelite who feasted on the remnant. The doctrine both of Justin and Irenæus clearly is, that the same bread which nourishes our flesh is the Body of Christ: and this is utterly inconsistent with its conversion, or union, to another substance.

The phrase, 'unbloody sacrifice,' is as old at least as Athenagoras, (A.D. 177,) though it is by no means certain that he applies it to the Eucharist. It occurs, in fact, in a passage where he is answering the reproach of *not* sacrificing.

'The Framer and Father of this universe does not need blood, nor the odour of burnt-offerings, nor the fragrance of flowers and incense,' (none of which therefore, it may be inferred, formed any part of the Christian worship,) 'but the noblest sacrifice to Him is for us to know who stretched out and vaulted the heavens, and fixed the earth in its place like a centre;—Who gathered the water into seas, and

---

[1] κοινωνίαν καὶ ἕνωσιν.   [2] 1 Cor. x. 16.

divided the light from the darkness;—Who adorned the sky with stars, and made the earth to bring forth seed of every kind;—Who made animals and fashioned man. When holding God to be this Framer of all things, Who preserves them in being, and superintends them all by knowledge and administrative skill, we lift up holy hands to Him, what need has He further of a hecatomb?' The gods of the heathen are represented in Homer as soothed by libations and burnt-offerings. 'But what have I to do with holocausts which God has no need of?—though indeed it does behove us to offer an unbloody sacrifice, and present the reasonable service.' (καίτοι προσφέρειν δέον αναίμακτον θυσίαν, και την λογικήν προσάγειν λατρείαν.') [1]

This passage seems to identify the 'unbloody sacrifice' with the 'reasonable service' of the apostle. Possibly both expressions originated with the philosophers; they were adopted into the Liturgies to express the self-immolation of the worshipper, which the Eucharistic oblation was understood to present. In this sense Athenagoras may have alluded to the Eucharist, but his words can hardly be referred to an oblation of the sacrament alone.

Tertullian regards the offering of the Church as prefigured in Abel's lamb, and those of the Jews in the fruits of the earth presented by Cain.[2] He is clear to the bread and the Body being but one substance.

'The bread which He took and distributed to His disciples, Christ made His Body, saying, This is my Body, that is, the figure of my Body. . . . He who then (Gen. xlix. 11.) used the figure of wine for blood, hath now consecrated His own Blood in wine.'[3]

---

[1] Ath. Leg. xiii.   [2] Adv. Jud.   [3] Adv. Mar. iv. 40.

To some who abstained from the prayers of the sacrifices on station days, through fear of breaking their fast by receiving the Body of Christ, Tertullian suggests that they might take the Eucharist and keep it by them till the fast was over.[1] It is clear, then, that none could be present at the sacrifice without receiving the communion; moreover, that what they received as the Lord's Body, was still bread, since their fast would have been broken by eating it.

A similar reservation of the elements is mentioned by S. Basil in the next age, as observed at Alexandria and in Egypt, where the people were in the habit of carrying away part of what they had received to communicate by themselves at home:[2] probably it was to prevent this abuse that the priests first began to put the bread into the mouth of the communicant. It must be obvious that what was so carried away, and consumed in private, could not have been *adored*, as the host now is in the Church of Rome.

Origen, the only Hebraist of the early fathers, compares the memorial ($\dot{a}\nu\dot{a}\mu\nu\eta\sigma\iota\varsigma$) of the shew-bread with the Eucharist.

<blockquote>
Christ is 'the Bread which cometh down from Heaven and giveth life unto the world; the shewbread which God hath set forth to be a propitiation through faith in His Blood.' Hence 'the memorial ($\dot{a}\nu\dot{a}\mu\nu\eta\sigma\iota\varsigma$) of which the Lord hath said, Do this in remembrance of Me, is the only memorial which makes God propitious to men'; *i.e.* applies the propitiation set forth through faith in His Blood.
</blockquote>

---

[1] De Orat. xix. [2] Bas. Ep. 289.

Again, referring to the priests eating the shewbread in the holy place as 'the most holy of holocausts,'[1] (though none of it was actually consumed in the fire,) Origen writes:

'Now we being accepted of the Creator, do also eat the loaves presented with thanksgiving, and the prayer over the gifts, having become by the prayer a certain Holy Body, hallowing those who receive it with sound devotion.'[2]

The loaves are still bread when they are eaten, though by prayer made a certain Holy Body profitable to the receivers.

Again:—

'It is not the matter of the bread, but the Word said over it, which profits him who eats it not unworthily of the Lord. No wicked man is capable of eating the Word made flesh, for if it were possible that a wicked man so continuing should eat Him that was made Flesh, seeing He is the Word and the Living Bread, it would not have been written, That whosoever eateth this Bread shall live for ever.'[3]

None of the Fathers carried the doctrine of the Eucharistic Sacrifice higher than S. Cyprian. (*d.* A.D. 258.) He expatiates on the analogy of the New Testament offerings with those of the law, using the words 'sacrifice,' 'priest,' and 'altar,' equally of both, and even quoting the Levitical rules of sacerdotal purity as binding on the Evangelical ministry. He describes the public worship as 'meeting together with the brethren in one place, and celebrating divine

[1] Lev. xxiv. 9.
[2] Contr. Cels. viii.; Pfaff de Cons. Vet. 375.
[3] In Matt. xv. 15.

sacrifices with God's Priest.'¹ He cites the prohibition against carrying any of the paschal lamb out of the house, as showing that 'the Flesh of Christ, the holy of the Lord, cannot be sent abroad,' by which he means that schismatics cannot celebrate a true communion.²

Yet that Cyprian conceived the oblation of the Eucharist to be a very different sacrifice to that of the cross, is plain from his exhortation to the confessors at the mines.

'There cannot be felt any loss either of religion or faith, most beloved brethren, in the fact that now there is given no opportunity there to God's priests for offering and celebrating the divine sacrifices; yea, ye celebrate and offer a sacrifice to God *equally precious and glorious*, one that will greatly profit you for the retribution of heavenly rewards, since the sacred Scripture speaks, saying, The sacrifice of God is a broken spirit, a contrite and humbled heart God doth not despise. You offer this sacrifice to God: you celebrate this sacrifice without intermission day and night, being made victims to God, and exhibiting yourselves as holy and unspotted offerings, as the Apostle exhorts and says, I beseech you, therefore, brethren, by the mercies of God, that ye present your bodies a living sacrifice, holy and acceptable unto God.'³

In applying the expressions used in the Liturgies of the Eucharistic elements, to the bodies and souls of the martyrs, Cyprian clearly indicates that both were conjoined in the Christian sacrifice, which was therefore vastly inferior to that of Christ. It would have been blasphemy to extol the self-sacrifice of the martyrs as 'equally precious and glorious' with that of the Cross.

¹ De Orat. Dom. iv.   ² De Unit. viii.   ³ Ep. lxxvi. 3.

Again, of the sacrifice for the dead, Cyprian quotes a canon, not now found in the African Code, that if a bishop leave a presbyter executor of his will, (a burden which the Roman law did not allow to be declined,) 'no offering should be made for him, nor any sacrifice be celebrated, *pro dormitione ejus.*'[1]

This canon exactly corroborates the language of the Liturgies produced in our last section, and proves the sacrifice to be totally different from that of the Tridentine Mass. The deceased is supposed to be in peace, and would be included in the general commendation of the departed. A canon against reciting his name in the diptychs could not be meant to operate as an excommunication in the grave where there is no repentance. It simply withheld a discretionary honour in the church from one who had violated the church's injunctions. In enforcing this canon, Cyprian writes:—

'It is not allowed that any offering be made by you for his repose, *nor any prayer be made in the church in his name.*'

Supplications of this kind were not *limited* to the Eucharistic Office. This is expressly stated in the African canon before quoted, which provides that when a bishop or other person dies in the evening, the commendation shall be performed with prayers only, without the Eucharist.[2] The commendations, first made immediately after

[1] Ep. lxv. 2; (Oxfd. ed., Ep. i.) [2] Conc. Carth. Can. xliv.

death, were repeated on the anniversary, but there is no hint of any remission of sins, much less of deliverance from pain, being communicated to the departed from the Eucharistic celebration. Indeed, the commendation was equally beneficial without the sacrament.

Cyprian, like the rest of the Fathers, supposes all present at the sacrifice to communicate in both kinds. The delivery of the cup by the deacon was a thing not to be avoided by anyone present at the celebration.[1] Of one who ventured to receive with the rest unworthily, he writes:

'He could not eat or handle the Holy of the Lord, but found in his hand when opened that he carried a cinder. Thus by the experience of one it was shown that the Lord *withdraws when He is denied;* nor does that which is received benefit the undeserving of salvation, since saving grace is changed by the departure of the sanctity into a cinder.'[2]

This implies that the unworthy do not receive the Lord's Body. Private masses must have been also unknown, since Cyprian's chief objection to evening celebrations, is that

'we cannot call the people together to our banquet so as to celebrate the truth of the sacrament in the presence of all the brotherhood.'[3]

Cyprian was a sturdy opponent of all tradition against the letter of Scripture. On this ground he stoutly resisted the decree of the Roman Pope on the subject of heretical baptism. In the

---

[1] De lapsis, 25.   [2] Ibid. 26.
[3] Ep. lxii. (Oxfd. lxiii.) ad Cæc. 16.

Eucharist he insists on the necessity of following strictly the example of Christ. He has no doubt (though it was denied at the Council of Trent) that our Lord offered a sacrifice in the Institution, nor that the cup which He offered was mingled of wine and water. Still, he observes that the wine alone was that which He called His Blood, adding an explanation of the water curiously contrasting with his profession of strict adherence to the original Institution. Observing that in the Apocalypse, the waters signify peoples and multitudes,[1] Cyprian expounds the water in the chalice as a symbol of the *people*, whom our Lord associated with His own Body in the Sacrifice.

'For because Christ bore us all, in that He also bore our sins, we see that in the water is understood the people, but in the wine is showed the Blood of Christ. But when the water is mingled in the cup with wine, the people is made one with Christ, and the assembly of the believers is associated and conjoined with Him on whom it believes, which association and conjunction of water and wine is so mingled in the Lord's Cup, that that mixture cannot any more be separated.'[2]

Cyprian was famous for discovering 'hidden and obscure sacraments,'[3] and we may perhaps credit him with the *invention* of this allegorical use of the water. He was so pleased with it, as to declare that in consecrating the cup of the Lord, water alone cannot be offered *even as wine alone cannot be offered*. Now, though it is probably

[1] Rev. xvii. 15.   [2] Ep. lxii. (Oxfd. lxiii.) ad Cæc. 18.
[3] Ep. lxxvii. 1.

true in fact, that our Lord blessed a mixed chalice, it is certain that He *spoke* of nothing in the cup but His Blood. That He designed to symbolize the people by the water is assuredly not revealed in Scripture, nor was it ever generally the belief of the Church. This is one of those numerous explanations which are invented after the fact, to account for the origin of traditional usages. Other explanations of the mixture, devised in later times, have been repeated with equal confidence; but all are pure conjecture, and clearly extraneous to the sacrament. The Catholic doctrine is, that 'wine alone is that which Christ called His Blood,' and whatever the water may have symbolized in the Paschal chalice, it was clearly His Blood, and nothing else, which Christ gave in the mystery of the cup. We may observe further that as Cyprian held the water to be the *symbol*, not the real bodies, of the people, so he must certainly have held the wine to be the symbol and not the real Body of Christ in the sacrifice.

To Cyprian belongs the further discovery of Melchisedek's typical sacrifice; the argument resting entirely on the Eucharistic oblation being of the same substance with his.

'For who is more a Priest of the most High God than our Lord Jesus Christ, who offered a sacrifice to God the Father, and offered that very same thing which Melchisedek had offered, that is, bread and wine, to wit, His own Body and Blood. . . . In Genesis, therefore, that the benediction in respect of Abraham by Melchisedek the priest might be duly celebrated, the figure of Christ's sacrifice precedes, namely, as ordained in bread and wine; which thing the Lord completing and fulfilling, offered bread and the cup mixed with wine, and so He who is the fullness of truth fulfilled the truth of the image prefigured.'[1]

This good pope of Carthage knew how to help out a tradition quite as well as his rival at Rome: in the celebration itself, however, he insists on exact conformity to the original institution.

'For if Jesus Christ our Lord and God is Himself the Chief Priest of God the Father, and has first offered Himself a sacrifice to the Father, and has commanded this to be done in commemoration of Himself, certainly that priest truly discharges the office of Christ who imitates that which Christ did: and he then offers a true and full sacrifice in the Church to God the Father, when he proceeds to offer it according to what he sees Christ Himself to have offered.'[2]

All this evidently refers to what was done in the *supper*, not on the cross: but as Cyprian considers both Sacrifices to be exhibited in the Eucharist, he must have held the one to be symbolical of the other; otherwise, Christ would have sacrificed Himself twice. The Melchisedekian type, therefore, requires the bread and wine of the supper to be retained in the Eucharistic Sacrifice, mystically to exhibit the Body and Blood of the cross. Hence he affirms that the

'Lord's Passion is the Sacrifice which we offer, and we ought to do nothing else than what He did, for Scripture says: As often as ye eat this bread and drink this cup ye

---

[1] Ad Cæc. 4.   [2] Ib. 14.

do show forth the Lord's Death till He come. As often, therefore, as we offer the cup in commemoration of the Lord and His Passion, let us do what it is known the Lord did.'¹

This conclusion implies not only communion in both kinds by all present, but the entire consumption of the elements. Cyprian alludes indeed to the practice of the communicants taking part of the gifts home for private daily reception,² but he has no trace of their adoration, or of any other use than manducation.

Eusebius, like Athenagoras, refers to the 'unbloody sacrifices' offered in the 'mystical liturgies;' but in the same passage he mentions *prayer* as the offering presented for the Church, the emperor, &c.³

So again:—

'Who but our Saviour only ever commanded His disciples to offer unbloody and reasonable sacrifices, celebrated by prayer and mystical invocation (θεολογίας)? Hence through the whole universe of men are established altars, and consecrations of churches, and holy liturgies of intellectual and reasonable sacrifices.'⁴

The value of sacrifice is here placed in the faith and prayer of the worshipper, rather than the material of the gift. This, we have seen, was also the doctrine of Justin and Irenæus. It is absolutely contradictory of the idea that the oblation was the identical Body of Christ, since *that* is of inherent and infinite value, being

---

¹ Ad Cæc. 17.   ² De lapsis.   ³ V. C. iv. 45.
⁴ Oration in praise of Constantine, 16.

indeed the sacrifice which makes faith possible, and prayer effectual.

Again:—

'Of this Sacrifice, having been taught to celebrate the remembrance upon the holy table by symbols of His Body and saving Blood, according to the laws of the New Testament, we are instructed by the prophet David to say, Thou hast prepared a table before me, Thou hast anointed my head with oil. For in those words are signified the mystical anointing and the holy victims of the Lord's table, by which unblamably ministering we are taught of Him to offer all our life long to God over all, the unbloody and reasonable, and to Him acceptable sacrifices.'[1]

Commenting on Genesis, xlix. 12, Eusebius writes:—

'He Himself gave the symbols of His divine economy to His disciples, commanding the image of His Body to be offered; for since He no longer desired sacrifices of blood nor the slaughter of divers beasts, as under Moses, but commanded to use bread as the symbol of His own Body, He foreshadowed the purity and cleanness of this food in saying, His teeth are white with milk. And the same thing is mentioned by another prophet, who says, Sacrifice and offering Thou wouldest not, but a Body hast Thou prepared me.'[2]

Cyril of Jerusalem wrote a sort of Companion to the Altar, in which he explains the Liturgy much as we still find it in the Greek formularies. Commenting on the Thanksgiving, the Seraphic Hymn, and the Invocation, he says of the last:—

'We beseech God, the lover of men, to send His Holy Spirit upon the gifts lying before Him, that He may make

---

[1] Demonstr. Ev. Johnson's Unbloody Sacrifice, Appx.
[2] Ibid.

the bread the Body of Christ, and the cup the Blood of Christ. For that on which the Holy Ghost descends is sanctified and changed.' And, 'When we have finished the spiritual sacrifice, the unbloody worship in that propitiatory sacrifice, we pray to God for the common peace of the Church, &c. Then we also make mention of those who are at rest before us; first the patriarchs, prophets, deceased bishops, and fathers; lastly for all those who once lived with us, and are now departed; believing it to be a great benefit to their souls, for whom prayer is made while the holy and tremendous sacrifice lies before us.'

This passage seems conclusive on the faith of the fourth century. The benefit to the departed is not attributed to the oblation, (which was ended before the intercessions began,) but to the prayers of the Church while the sacrifice is on the Table. Nothing could more clearly demonstrate that the sacrifice on the Table is not identical with that of the cross, but representative of it. The next sentence, 'We offer Christ who was slain for our sins, that we may render Him who is the lover of men gracious and propitious to them and ourselves,' cannot mean anything else, though the language (if genuine) partakes of the dramatic. To offer Christ slain is to offer the symbols of His dead Body and Blood; but when this offering is compared to a crown sent to a king to induce him to remit a sentence of exile, the commentator indulges his figurative vein, far beyond anything to be found in the Liturgy itself.

On the exclamation, 'Holy things to holy persons,' Cyril observes:

'The oblations lying on the altar are holy, receiving the descent of the Holy Ghost. Ye also are holy, being also sanctified by the Holy Ghost. Then you answer, "There is One holy, our Lord Jesus Christ." Truly there is One Holy—holy by nature; but we are also holy, not by nature, but by participation, by exercise, and by prayer.'

Here a very decided distinction is drawn between Christ and the consecrated oblation on the altar. He proceeds to direct the communicant

'to make the left hand a support for the right, as being about to receive the King, and, keeping the palm hollow, take the Body of Christ, saying Amen. Then after communicating of the Body of Christ, to draw near and take the cup of His Blood, not reaching out the hands, but bowing down and in a posture of worship and adoration, saying, Amen.'

These directions are clear for the separate communion in both kinds. They further indicate the deep reverence due to the consecrated elements as sanctified by the Holy Ghost. In this respect, however, they hardly come up to our own practice of receiving *on the knees;* they are far from hinting at any adoration of Christ, or of His Body, in the material object received.

In another place Cyril writes:

'For as the bread and wine of the Eucharist before the holy invocation of the adorable Trinity (which, it will be remembered, was *subsequent* to the recital of the words of Institution) were simple bread and wine, but the Invocation being made, the bread becomes the Body of Christ and the wine the Blood of Christ, in the same manner the meats of the worship of Satan being in their own nature simple food, by the invocation of the demons become profane.'[1]

---

[1] Cyr. Myst.

This comparison is conclusive against all corporal, or co-existent, theories of the Sacramental Presence. So of the participation:—

'Let us with all confidence communicate, as of the Body and Blood of Christ, for in the figure (τύπῳ) of bread the Body is given thee, and in the figure of wine the Blood is given thee, that ye may be made one Body and one Blood with Him.'[1]

The elements are still but types, though the reception is real.

S. Ambrose, to whom many strong expressions are imputed without sufficient authority, expressly undertakes to prove that the Body of Christ which we receive in the Eucharist

'is not that which nature formed, but which the benediction has consecrated.' He calls it 'the sacrament of His Flesh; Christ is in that sacrament because it is the Body of Christ; adding, the Body of God is a spiritual Body, for the Body of Christ is the Body of the Holy Spirit, because Christ is Spirit.'[2]

These words attribute the presence of Christ's Human Nature to its hypostatical union with the Divine.

Again:

'Truly we offer, but so that we make a remembrance of His death. We offer Him always; or rather we offer a remembrance of His Sacrifice.' The Shadow in the law, the Image in the Gospels, the Truth in the heavenly places. Of old a lamb was offered, a calf was offered, now Christ is offered. Here in image, there in truth, where He intercedes for us with the Father as our Advocate.'

Hence the sacrament is an image of the Body, which in truth is in heaven.

[1] Myst. iv. [2] De his qui initiantur, c. viii. [3] In Heb. x.

The language of Ambrose with respect to the sacrifice of Christ in the sacrament is explained by his disciple, S. Augustine, who often affirms that Christ is immolated in the sacrament, but with this explanation subjoined:

'that is, the immolation of Christ is represented, and a remembrance of His Passion is made.'[1] 'Christ is slain to anyone when he believes Him to be slain.'[2] 'Christ is daily immolated to us when out of the relics of this very thought we believe in Christ.'[3] 'The Flesh and Blood of this sacrifice, before the Advent of Christ, was promised through victims of similitude: in the Passion of Christ it was exhibited in the very truth; after His Ascension it is celebrated through a sacrament of remembrance.'[4]

This most learned father insists that every true body consists of parts, containing greater and lesser spaces of place:

'Take away local extent from bodies, and they will be nowhere; and since they are nowhere, they will not be at all..... We are not to doubt that whole Christ is present everywhere as God ... and in one certain place of heaven, by reason of the nature of His True Body.'[5] 'He is always with us by His Divinity, but if He were not *corporally absent from us—nisi corporaliter abiret a nobis*—we should always carnally behold His Body, and never spiritually believe.'[6]

And again:

'Our Lord is above, but also the truth of the Lord (*veritas Dominus*) is here. For the Body of the Lord in which He rose must be in one place; His truth, or the truth of it (*veritas ejus*) is everywhere diffused.'[7]

---

[1] De Consec. Dis. ii.
[2] Quæst. Evan. II., xxxiii. 5.
[3] In Psalm lxxiii.
[4] Cont. Faust, xx. 21.
[5] Ad. Dard. Ep. lvii. cap. vi. 8.
[6] De Verb. Dom. Serm. lx. (al. cxliii.) 4.
[7] Tract in Johann. xxx. 1.

'According to His corporal presence Christ is in heaven, at the Father's right hand; according to the presence of faith, He is in all Christians.'[1]

Of the sacrament he says:

'Our Lord hesitated not to say This is My Body when He was giving the sign of His Body.'[2]

After mentioning a number of types which were bare signs, having no force of the truth annexed, he continues:

'We do not call these the Body and Blood of Christ, but that only which, being taken from the fruits of the earth and consecrated by the mystic prayer, we solemnly receive to spiritual health, in memory of our Lord's Passion for us. And this, though brought by the hand of man to its visible species, yet is not sanctified to become so great a sacrament without the Holy Ghost working invisibly.'[3]

From this it appears that the African Liturgy agreed with the Greek in the prayer of Consecration. Further, *species*, as in all the Latin fathers, means the whole substance, not the forms and accidents, of bread and wine: the Greek fathers use εἶδος in the same sense. On the Gospel of S. John, Augustine writes:—

'The signs are varied, faith remaining. There the Rock was Christ, to us that which is placed on the altar is Christ. They for a great sacrament of the same Christ drank water from the rock; we drink what the faithful know. If you regard the visible species it is different; understand the signification, we drink the same spiritual drink.'

Chrysostom and his disciple Theophylact, (whom Baronius rightly places in the eleventh

[1] Serm. cxx. [2] Cont. Ad. xii. 3. [3] De Trin. III. iv. 10.

century rather than the ninth,) have already been cited.[1] The former does not hesitate to describe the Eucharist as a sort of re-enacting of the spectacle of the cross.

'Christ lies before us slain.[2] His death is celebrated,[3] the Sacrifice is brought forth, the Lord's Sheep is slain.[4] The Blood is emptied out of His spotless side into the cup,[5] all the people are purple-dyed in that precious Blood.[6] He has given us to be filled with His Flesh, He has offered Himself to us *sacrificed.*' (killed.)[7]

In these rhetorical speeches the object exhibited in the sacrament is not the risen Christ, or His glorified Humanity, but His dead Body and Blood, 'the carcase,' as he elsewhere speaks, 'to which the eagles mount up and fly.'[8] Now the corpse of Jesus Christ cannot be present to anyone, after the resurrection, save by faith and in representation. If it were, He must again be slain, and, as Chrysostom says, the communicants would be really purpled with His Blood. But then how could this be an 'unbloody sacrifice'? That phrase, wherever it originated, is a standing denial of the real sacrifice of Christ's Body and Blood in the Eucharist, and was probably so intended from the beginning.

It is needless to carry our citations further. Enough has been produced to show that in the

[1] Sect. 1. p. 7. [2] Hom. de Prod. Jud. 1. 6.
[3] Hom. in Act. xxi. 4. [4] In Ep. ad Eph. [5] De Pœn. in Euc.
[6] De Sac. iii. 4. [7] Hom. ii. 3. in Matt. xiv. 23.
[8] Homily on the Worthy Receiving.

undivided Church, according to the concurrent evidence of Liturgies and Fathers—

1. The Eucharistic Sacrifice is a sacrifice of praise and prayer, in which the bodies, souls, and spirits of all present are offered unto God in union with the Sacrifice of His Son on the cross.

2. That the material oblation expressing this sacrifice is bread and wine, commemorative and symbolical of the Body and Blood of Christ, and made the real participation of His Body and Blood to the faithful communicant.

3. That to join in this sacrifice it is necessary to receive the communion in both kinds, and that no other use of the consecrated gifts is acknowledged or permitted.

These are the main propositions, and in these the Fathers are unanimous. It is not pretended that no expressions of theirs admit of any other interpretation. The Fathers were not infallible, even if we could accept as genuine all that bears their names. Their language, and possibly their views, were not always rigidly consistent; nor do we charge on the Council of Trent the absolute *invention* of all the errors and superstitions which it unhappily bound upon the Roman See. Practices, at first innocent, or even laudable, became abused in course of time. Figurative and mystical language was confounded with literal. The decay of letters, after the triumph of the barbarians in the West, favoured the growth of superstition; while Scripture was unhappily neglected, the schoolmen employed their logic, and the Church its authority, to elaborate into dogma the misconceptions of a darker age.

A reform was inevitable, when the fall of Constantinople covered Europe with the wreck of Greek literature, and the invention of printing rescued the Bible from the seclusion of the cloister. The Word of God was then again seen to be the true standard of the Church's faith; they who believed its promises to the Church herself sought to discard the accretions of superstition, without relinquishing their hold on the Catholic body. This was pre-eminently the aim of the English Reformation. The conservative instincts of our nation combined with its strong practical good sense, to shape a middle way between blind obedience and unnecessary innovation. The task might have been easier but for the notorious corruptions of the fathers, through the dishonesty of the later copyists, and the suspicion thus attaching to the productions of antiquity. Still the Church of England learned to speak with no uncertain sound, and her voice deepened and grew firmer as she felt her hold upon antiquity more assured.

The true churchman may be thankful to receive, from the greater light of modern learning, a further confirmation of her appeal to the old godly doctors. Still it is not the Fathers, but the Scriptures and the Church, which claim our allegiance. The Anglo-Catholic stands related to the Fathers through his own mother Church, not by private choice. It is by membership with her that he has communion with the Catholic Church; and far from seeking to supplement her utterances by his own selections from antiquity, he sits at her feet, and hopes to die in her arms, as the *only* Church that to him 'hath power to decree rites and ceremonies, and authority in controversies of faith.'[1]

X.—THE ANGLICAN LITURGY.

THE two great landmarks of the Church of England, in holding her middle way between the Tridentine and the ultra-Protestant errors, were the apostolical succession and the Catholic Liturgy. An eminent divine of the Roman obedience declares that

'There are not more than three possible modes of a Christian form of worship. Either the sermon constitutes the main portion and centre of the worship, so that the remainder, hymn and prayer, are merely subservient assistants; or the main act of worship is a Liturgy, in which there is a reading aloud of passages of Scripture and forms of prayer; or in the third the worship is an actual celebration of the whole work of Redemption;—a communion in which

---

[1] Article XX.

all who are present participate in the complete act of the Lord's Supper, and in which each of the whole community offers himself up with Christ, a victim to the Father, as the most perfect form of adoration to the Almighty God.

'The first form (he continues) is indisputably the most suitable to the old and true Protestantism; the second is that which has been chosen by the English Established Church, and though pleasing to the higher classes, is not so universally acceptable to the populace; the third is the form of worship of the ancient Church, and of the ecclesiastical communities which have maintained their continuity, either without interruption or essential change; such as the (Roman) Catholic, the Greek, the Russian, and the Monophysite Churches in Asia and Africa.'[1]

In this classification the place assigned to the Church of England will be accepted by no one who impartially studies her liturgical formularies. On the contrary, it may be affirmed, that as this Church most unquestionably 'maintained her continuity' at the Reformation, so the ancient worship, described in the third alternative, is more truthfully exemplified in our Book of Common Prayer, than in any of the ecclesiastical communities enumerated by Dr. Döllinger. The Churches of the Roman obedience are those which have most widely departed from the Catholic form of worship. The foreign language, the non-communicating attendance, the denial of the cup, the adoration of the host, and the almost entire disappearance of the self-oblatory feature,[2] in the impossible endeavour to repeat

[1] 'The Church and the Churches,' by Dr. Döllinger, McCabe's Translation, p. 304.

[2] The Canon of the Mass contains but the faintest possible allusion to any sacrifice by the people. 'Be mindful,

the vicarious sacrifice of the Cross, make the Roman Mass very different from 'a communion in which all who are present participate in the complete act of the Lord's Supper, and in which each of the whole community offers himself up with Christ a victim to the Father.'[1]

On the other hand, no words could more exactly describe the purport and effect of the Anglican Liturgy. So far from subordinating the Eucharistic worship to the preliminary Lessons and Prayers, the very first reform in our ritual was

---

O Lord, of Thy servants and handmaidens N. and N., and of all here present, whose faith and devotion are known to Thee, for whom we offer Thee, *or who offer Thee this sacrifice of praise for themselves and all theirs*,' &c. Even here it is not a sacrifice of *themselves*, but of something *for* themselves; while everywhere else the sacrifice is distinctly limited to the celebrant. Contrast this with the eucharistic prayer in our own Post-Communion, 'And here we offer and present unto Thee, O Lord, ourselves, our souls and bodies, to be a reasonable, holy, and lively sacrifice unto Thee,' and it will be obvious which answers best to Dr. Döllinger's description of the ancient, Catholic, and most perfect form of adoration to the Almighty.

[1] On most of these points the Greek and Russian Churches are less corrupt than the Roman; still, Dr. Döllinger represents the first as 'in the most shameful and perishing condition to which an ancient and venerable Church has ever yet been reduced.' p. 125. 'The Russian Church (he says) is a dumb one; there is no singing by the congregation, and there is no sermon. . . . There are neither Prayer-books nor ascetic writings in the hands of the people, . . . and no remedies against the overwhelming mass of superstition which cannot fail to be engendered by a purely ceremonial religion in the absence of doctrine and of the living word.'—p. 135, 136.

an English Office for Communion in both kinds.¹ The first Book of Common Prayer, compiled the year after, placed the Eucharistic rite in the front and centre of public worship. It contemplated daily celebration in cathedrals and other places, and in all parish churches on Sundays and Holy Days *at the least*.² The only condition was the requirement of a genuine communion, in place of the nominal one approved by the Council of Trent, and every effort was made to fulfil this condition, by exhorting the people to communicate.³

From these views our Church has never receded.⁴ In cathedral and collegiate churches,

¹ A.D. 1547, Bishop Sparrow's Collection.

² 'In Cathedral Churches, or other places where there is daily Communion, it shall be sufficient to read this Exhortation above written once in a month; and in Parish Churches, upon the week-days, it may be left unsaid. And if upon the Sunday or Holy Day the people be negligent to come to the Communion, then shall the priest earnestly exhort his parishioners to dispose themselves to the receiving of the Holy Communion more diligently, saying these or the like words unto them.'—*Rubric*, 1549.

³ The intention of the Sermon in this Office (still the only Sermon prescribed in the Book of Common Prayer) was shown by the Rubric: 'After the Creed shall follow the Sermon or Homily, or some portion of one of the Homilies, as they shall hereafter be divided, wherein if the people be not exhorted to the worthy receiving of the Holy Sacrament of the Body and Blood of our Saviour Christ, then shall the Curate give this Exhortation to those that be minded to receive the same.'

⁴ Archdeacon Wilberforce's opinion (Euch. p. 138.) that 'Cranmer abandoned his belief in the Real Presence' between

where there are many clergy, the rule is still that all shall communicate with the celebrant every Sunday *at the least.* Every parishioner is required to communicate three times in the year, of which Easter is to be one. The Church lacks power to enforce her discipline in England, as in Rome and every other part of Europe, but if the 'complete act of communion' be taken as the test of Catholic worship, it will be found far more fully realized in the Anglican Churches than in any other whatever.

The moral and spiritual unfitness of the multitude for 'the most perfect form of adoration to the Almighty,' has been the common difficulty from the third century downward. How Chrysostom dealt with it has been seen at p. 139. The Tridentine Churches cut the knot by directing the priest to offer it by himself, in the presence of a prostrate but non-participating

---

the publication of the First and Second Books, is refuted by the Archbishop's own words before cited. (p. 53.) They were given in to the commission of which he was a member, certainly before the First Liturgy, if not before the earlier Communion Office. On the same occasion Cranmer contended that no man could receive the sacrament for another; that the solitary communion of the priest, with the reservation and hanging up of the sacrament, were corruptions later than the sixth century; and that satisfactory Masses ought not to be continued. He was supported on all these points by Ridley and Ferrars, and opposed by Holgate of York, with other bishops, holding the views soon after sanctioned at Trent.— *Collier, Eccl. Hist.* Part ii. Book iv.

audience.¹ The Calvinists fell back upon prayer and sermon, in which the officiating minister is still the sole performer, the people joining only in the hymn. Standing between these vicious extremes, the Anglican Liturgy refuses either to desecrate, or to withdraw, the Eucharistic Sacrifice. It not only maintains the Holy Eucharist in its character of the chief means of grace,—the privilege acquired by Confirmation, the sanctification of Matrimony and Holy Orders, the consolation of mourners at funerals, the rite which unites the sick and dying believer, in the body of the Church, with the great Sacrifice of the cross;—but it persistently presents it as the supreme act of worship in the Christian congregation. It does not harden and debase the non-communicant, by a fictitious participation in the sacrifice of another, but after preparing the altar and the sacrifice in the presence of all, and exhorting all to their duty, it proceeds to the complete act with as many as are ready, in the exercise of their Christian priesthood, to eat of the holy things in the holy place.

So far from forsaking the ancient form of

[1] It must be remembered that in these Churches it is only the celebrant who *ever* 'participates in the complete act' of the Christian Sacrifice. The subsequent ministration of the communion in one kind (*i. e.* without the blood of the sacrifice) to the clergy and a few pious laity, is manifestly a means of grace rather than an act of worship; nor is it followed by any self-oblatory prayer, as in our own Post-Communion. The *placeat tibi*, said by the priest, is limited by the singular pronoun to the sacrifice offered by himself alone.

divine service, the Church of England has formally disclaimed any intention of departing even from modern branches of the Church Catholic, except where they had themselves departed from Catholic antiquity.

'So far was it from the purpose of the Church of England to forsake and reject the Churches of Italy, France, Spain, Germany, or any such like Churches, in all things which they held and practised, that, as the Apology of the Church of England confesseth, it doth with reverence retain those ceremonies which doth neither endamage the Church of God, nor offend the minds of sober men; and only departed from them in those particular points, wherein they were fallen both from themselves in their ancient integrity, and from the Apostolical Churches which were their first founders.'[1]

With regard to the Eucharist in particular, the Homily declares it to be necessary

'before all things that this Supper be in such wise done and ministered as our Lord and Saviour did, and commanded to be done; as His holy apostles used it; and the good fathers in the primitive church frequented it.

Again, at the Savoy Conference, previous to the last Review, the commissioners were charged 'to advise upon and review the Book of Common Prayer, comparing the same with the most ancient Liturgies which have been used in the Church in the primitive and purest times.'

This principle restored at once the 'complete act' of communion in both kinds and by all present, together with the use of the vernacular tongue; at the same time it excluded the adora-

[1] Canon xxx.

tion of the host, with all other consequences of the modern error of transubstantiation.

Still, the Church of England has not hesitated to assert that authority in decreeing rites and ceremonies, without which the ancient Liturgies could never have existed. The power exercised by S. Basil and S. Chrysostom, and by innumerable bishops and abbots after them, was not to be denied to the rulers of the English Church in reducing the numerous 'uses'—provincial, diocesan, and capitular—to one national Liturgy.[1] Extensive modifications were required by the necessities both of Church and State. With the Catholic instinct, which prompts the churchman ever to look to the 'pit from which he was hewn,' it was determined to adhere to the Western model in preference to the Eastern. Whatever the origin of Christianity in Britain, the English as a nation belonged to the Western Church; the Latin Offices were in possession, and there was no call to forsake them for the Greek.

[1] This measure was demanded, not only for the purity of the religious Offices, but for the consolidation of the State, then growing into a new consciousness of national life, after the decay of the feudal system from the fall of the nobles in the Wars of the Roses, and the loss of the foreign possessions of the Crown. The effect of these political changes, in enabling the English Church to complete its long struggle against the papal supremacy, is not always sufficiently considered. Henry VIII.'s was the first reign in which the national life found room to grow, and Elizabeth's was that which brought it to maturity. Hence the extraordinary popularity of those despotic sovereigns.

The Liturgy so compiled became, as in the primitive Church, the one complete standard of Eucharistic doctrine, no less than of worship. The Canon of the Mass is overlaid and distorted by the definitions of the Council of Trent: but with us the Articles and Catechism, like the ancient Councils, only correct particular errors; the full exposition of sacramental teaching is formally and synodically assigned to the Liturgy.

'The doctrine both of Baptism and of the Lord's Supper is so sufficiently set down in the Book of Common Prayer to be used at the administration of the said Sacraments, as nothing can be added unto it that is material or necessary.'[1]

These authoritative statements amply refute the charge of abandoning the ancient and most perfect form of worship. They are no less conclusive against a notion, recently taken up, that the Church of England invites, or permits, her children to supplement her liturgical work by their own private judgment of antiquity. In referring to 'the good fathers and godly doctors' of the primitive church, the intention was not to endorse *every* opinion and practice of antiquity, still less to send English churchmen to pick and choose from its multifarious stores at discretion. This is exactly the office which the Church claims to herself; and she has propounded the result in the Book of Common Prayer, as forming, in fact, that just temperament of antiquity, sobriety, and necessary truth, which it was her aim to secure.

[1] Canon lvii.

Whatever is not here set down, is judged either liable to objection, or at least not material or necessary. To the Church's judgment in this respect, she requires the absolute submission of her members. The canon declares it to be

'the part of every private man, both minister and other, reverently to retain the true use of the order prescribed by public authority; considering that things in themselves indifferent do in some sort alter their natures, when they are either commanded or forbidden by a lawful magistrate; and may not be omitted at every man's pleasure contrary to law, when they be commanded, nor used when they are prohibited.'[1]

It is true that this standard has undergone some modification in form, but the substance and doctrine have never varied. The synodical utterance of the Fifty-seventh Canon applied to the Liturgy established under Queen Elizabeth, which was substantially the same with the Second Book of Edward VI., (A. D. 1552,) and the final Recension made in 1661-2. These undoubtedly differed from the *First* Book of Edward VI., (1549,) but the nature and extent of the difference have been grossly misrepresented. By one party the First Book is viewed as an imperfect step out of the errors of the mass; by the other as the rightful standard of the English Reformation, which was grievously lowered in subsequent recensions.[2] Both imagine a doctrinal difference

[1] Canon xxx.
[2] This latter view is maintained by Archdeacon Wilberforce, and the author of 'The Liturgies of 1549 and 1662 Contrasted and Compared,' in *The Church and the World, First Series.*

between the First and Second Books of Edward VI., which is incompatible with the facts of history. The two Books were the production of the same persons within the short period of three years. The principal compilers laid down their lives at the stake rather than allow the Corporal Presence or the Sacrifice of the Mass. These were the 'burning articles,' as Collier calls them throughout the reign of Mary: they were also the prime articles in dispute before the rejection of the Papacy in 1545, and indeed more than a century earlier, under Archbishop Arundel. It is absurd to suppose that any shelter would be designedly left for such errors in 1549; indeed, we have the most direct evidence to the contrary. Not only were these very corruptions distinctly opposed by Cranmer, Ridley, and Ferrars in 1547, but the preamble of the Act, which substituted the book of 1552, pronounces the previous Liturgy to be

'a very godly order, agreeable to the Word of God and the primitive Church, very comfortable to all good people desiring to live in Christian conversation, and most profitable to the estate of this realm.'[1]

The Second Book is declared to be set forth 'in *explanation*' of 'divers doubts that had arisen for the fashion and manner of the ministration'— doubts expressly ascribed 'rather to the curiosity of the minister and mistakers than to any other worthy cause.'[2] This language is decisive against

[1] Act 5 and 6, Edward VI.
[2] The 'mistakers' were the *Romanizing* party. (See Cranmer's Answer to Gardiner, presently.)

any doctrinal difference. The authors of both books declare the true meaning of each to be the same. The second is only a more accurate 'explanation' of things mistaken and misrepresented in the first.

When we hear it argued that this Second Book—and by consequence the existing Liturgy, which we have all subscribed—was a surrender of our 'Catholic inheritance' to the baneful influence of a few German Protestants, one cannot but wonder that neither party should have been in the least aware of the parts they were playing. They who had the chief hand in both books deny that the latter at all departs from the former; and in a letter to Calvin we find Peter Martyr complaining, that the archbishop would not tell him what alterations were concluded upon, 'neither durst he take the freedom to inquire.'[1]

Neither is it true that the animadversions of Bucer had the effect which has been ascribed to them. Many of his suggestions were rejected, while other changes were made of which there is no trace in his censure. He himself pretended no actual error, but only urged the propriety of avoiding misconceptions, by a populace still deeply imbued with Romish views; to this danger the bishops were quite as much alive as the foreigners. At all events, Bucer's views could have little influence with Queen Elizabeth, and none at all

[1] Collier's Eccl. Hist. ii. 4.

with the Convocations of 1661, who completed the present Liturgy. The deliberate preference of the Second Book of King Edward on those two critical occasions ought to silence for ever the 'foreign Protestant' theory.[1]

In point of fact, both Edward's Liturgies emanated, in strictness, from the State, setting aside for the time the constituted ecclesiastical authorities. The Archbishop of Canterbury, with a few others selected out of the two Houses by the Crown, superseded the regular action of Convocation, in which the vast majority were known to be Papists. The Royal Supremacy was the only national authority that could be exerted against Rome; its usurpation may be justified by the necessity of overthrowing the previous usurpation of the Pope; but of all the paradoxes in which private judgment ever revelled, none was ever more palpably absurd than this erecting into a standard of Catholic doctrine or ritual, the arbitrary acts of a boy king, or rather of his church-robbing council, enforced by secular penalties on a recalcitrant clergy, and in a few years unanimously repealed.

The ecclesiastical authority of the Anglican Liturgy rests neither on Henry VIII., Edward VI., or their servile, time-seeking parliaments,

---

[1] Martyr and Bucer both defended the episcopal and sacerdotal habits against the scruples of Hooper: even the latter wished them to be altered only to avoid contentions between Protestants.

but on its canonical reception in the English Church. The first royal Liturgy lost all the sanction it ever had, when repealed in 1552 by the power which gave it existence; it has never since had a shadow of authority in Church or State. The second shared the same fate on the accession of Queen Mary, but being revived, with modifications, by Elizabeth, and further explained by James I., it was then canonically recognized in the Synods of both Provinces, and made the Church's standard of sacramental doctrine. This long reception and final synodical sanction gave it an authority never acquired by the state formularies of the Tudors. Still it is in the existing Liturgy of 1662 that we now hear the 'voice of the Church.' The most deliberate and final utterance of the English Church and State were combined in its promulgation, and its authority is now sole and complete. To go back to the Parliament of Edward VI. in quest of our 'Catholic inheritance,' or to pretend that any point of doctrine then enjoyed has been since lost, is to erect a naked Erastianism on one of the most perverse contradictions of historical truth.

The authors of the two books affirm that the doctrine of the First was not altered, but more fully explained, in the Second; and this last is the basis of our own. The variations were adopted to resolve 'doubts rising rather by the curiosity of the minister and mistakers than of any worthy cause;' so that if the authority of the First book were greater than it is, we should still have to seek its meaning in the Second, unless we choose to explain the explanation by the very mistakes it was intended to correct.

The truth is, that the Eucharistic Office of 1549, while correcting the chief errors of the Roman Missal, followed its arrangement too closely to be either liturgically correct, or doctrinally free from ambiguity. What it aimed at was the removal of four principal corruptions—the Corporal Presence, the sacrifice of the Mass, the suppression of the cup, and non-communicating attendance. The first, implying the adoration of the host, was met by a rubric prohibiting any elevation, or showing of the sacrament to the people; the second, by placing the intercessions before the consecration, (as in the Liturgy of S. Mark,) and changing the oblation after it to a 'Memorial;' the third and fourth, by enjoining communion in both kinds on all present,[1] reserving nothing for after uses, but only so much as would serve for the sick, who were to receive immediately after the public celebration. These changes amounted to an entire abrogation of the Tridentine Mass, and though the name was left in the title of the Office,—being in itself ancient and un-

[1] 'All other that mind not to receive the Holy Communion shall depart out of the quire, except the minister and clerks.' A similar departure is implied in the present rubric before the longer exhortation; hence the direction for *all* to communicate, before the minister returns to the Lord's Table with the remainder of the consecrated elements.

objectionable,—and some of the former vestments were retained,[1] both were summarily abolished the moment that the 'curiosity of ministers and mistakers' raised a 'doubt' of the intention.

While thus excluding the chief corruptions, the Reformers were less anxious about liturgical arrangement. The real essentials to the Eucharistic Sacrifice are consecration and communion, and there was no call to desert the Western form for the Eastern, even if the more ancient. The consecration of the bread and wine into the mystical Body and Blood of Christ was still, therefore, held to be complete on the recital of the words of Institution, though the effect was now ascribed to the prayer and whole action, rather than, as in the Roman canon, to the utterance of the five words by the priest. To judge of the entire effect, and of the subsequent changes, the prayer of consecration shall be given at length, divided into paragraphs for the convenience of after reference.

1. 'O God, Heavenly Father, which of Thy tender mercy didst give Thine only Son Jesu Christ to suffer death upon the cross for our redemption, Who made there (by His one oblation once offered) a full, perfect, and sufficient sacrifice, oblation, and satisfaction for the sins of the whole world, and did institute, and in His holy Gospel command us to celebrate, a perpetual memory of that His precious death, until His coming again: Hear us, (O merciful Father,) we beseech Thee:

2. 'And with Thy Holy Spirit and Word vouchsafe to bless and sanctify these Thy gifts and creatures of bread

---

[1] See Note on Vestments in the Appendix.

and wine, that they may be unto us the Body and Blood of Thy most dearly beloved Son Jesus Christ:

3. 'Who in the same night that He was betrayed, took bread; and when He had blessed and given thanks, He brake it, and gave it to His disciples, saying, Take, eat, this is My Body which is given for you: do this in remembrance of Me. Likewise after supper He took the cup; and when He had given thanks, He gave it to them, saying, Drink ye all of this, for this is My Blood of the New Testament, which is shed for you and for many, for the remission of sins: Do this, as oft as ye drink it, in remembrance of Me.'

These words before rehearsed are to be said turning still to the altar, without any elevation, or showing the sacrament to the people.

4. 'Wherefore, O Lord and Heavenly Father, according to the Institution of Thy dearly beloved Son our Saviour Jesu Christ, we Thy humble servants do celebrate and make here before Thy Divine Majesty, with these Thy holy gifts, the Memorial which Thy Son hath willed us to make: having in remembrance His blessed passion, mighty resurrection, and glorious ascension, rendering unto Thee most hearty thanks for the innumerable benefits procured unto us by the same,

5. 'Entirely desiring Thy Fatherly goodness mercifully to accept this our sacrifice of praise and thanksgiving, most humbly beseeching Thee to grant, that by the merits and death of Thy Son Jesus Christ, and through faith in His Blood, we and all Thy whole Church may obtain remission of our sins, and all other benefits of His passion.

6. 'And here we offer and present unto Thee O Lord ourself, our souls and bodies, to be a reasonable, holy, and lively sacrifice unto Thee, humbly beseeching Thee that whosoever shall be partakers of this holy Communion, may worthily receive the most precious Body and Blood of Thy Son Jesus Christ, and be fulfilled with Thy grace and heavenly benediction, and made one body with Thy Son Jesu Christ, that He may dwell in them, and they in Him.

7. 'And although we be unworthy (through our manifold sins) to offer unto Thee any sacrifice, yet we beseech Thee to accept this our bounden duty and service, [and command these our prayers and supplications, by the ministry of Thy

holy angels, to be brought up into Thy holy tabernacle, before the sight of Thy Divine Majesty,'] not weighing our merits, but pardoning our offences, through Christ our Lord: by Whom and with Whom in the unity of the Holy Ghost, all honour and glory be unto Thee O Father Almighty, world without end. Amen.'

This was beyond question a very noble prayer, and a vast improvement on the Canon of the Mass. Besides expunging the rubrics which in that Office are more corrupt than the words, it expanded the whole recital, more after the ancient models, and in particular introduced a prayer for the Spirit to bless the gifts, of which the Roman Canon was destitute. Still, when this formulary is held up as our Catholic inheritance, and our

[1] These words, taken from the Roman canon, are here distinctly restrained to the prayers. They were omitted in 1552, from a reasonable doubt whether this office is authoritatively to be ascribed to the *angelic* ministry. The ancient liturgies attributed it to the mediation of Christ. The petition itself seems to have been based on the action of the Levitical priests, who carried the memorials from the great altar of sacrifice into the holy place, and burned incense on the golden altar before the vail. The smoke of the incense ascending within, at the same time with that of the sacrifice without, was symbolical of the prayers of the people. Compare Luke, i. 10, and Rev. viii. 3, 4. There is no trace, however, in antiquity of this Levitical symbol being retained in the commemoration of the True Sacrifice. In the visions of S. John the incense indicates, no doubt, the acceptance in heaven of the services below; but it is a confusion of the imagery to unite a literal use of this material drug with the spiritual sacrifice. The apostolical canon forbids any other material oblation than the bread and wine ordained by Christ; Tertullian tells us that frankincense was particularly objected to as being used in the heathen rites.

present Office is disparaged as mangled and misplaced, it is necessary to remind the unwary that in every one of the portions altered, the Office of 1549 was entirely *new and unprecedented*. The true effect of the subsequent alterations, and the real meaning of the original, which they were designed to explain, must be considered in detail.

The first paragraph remained unchanged in the Second book, and so continues in the existing Liturgy. The second was removed, possibly in consequence of Bucer's animadversion. Bucer's objection, however, was not to the petition for the Holy Ghost, but to the remainder of the clause, which, being a translation of the Roman *ut fiat nobis*, might be twisted, (*detorqueatur,*) he feared, to the support of the Corporal Presence. The objection is futile enough; as Archbishop Laud observed, 'it were for the good of Christendom if this were the worst error in the Mass.' Nevertheless, this construction was actually attempted by Gardiner, and Cranmer's answer was as follows :—

'We do not pray absolutely that the bread and wine may be made the Body and Blood of Christ, but that *unto us*, in that holy mystery, they may be so: that is to say, that we may so worthily receive the same that we may be partakers of Christ's Body and Blood, and that therewith, in spirit and in truth, we may be spiritually nourished.'

This, he adds, was always the meaning of the petition in the ancient Liturgies. Hence it is clear that in substituting this very explanation of Cranmer's in the book of 1552, the Reformers gave expression to their own original meaning, and not to any different conception of the 'foreign Protestants.'[1]

It is true that the petition for the Spirit disappeared in the change, an omission which may for good reasons be regretted; but in stigmatizing this loss as a 'mutilation,' in violation of all liturgical precedent, it is overlooked, first, that no such petition is found in the Roman Canon, nor in any of the Western Offices framed on its model; and secondly, that, as inserted in the Office of 1549, the petition did *not* accord with the Invocation of the Holy Ghost in the Eastern Liturgies, either in form, substance, or position. The difference was enough not only for its own authors to abandon it in 1552, (apparently without objection,) but to induce Johnson to denounce it as 'imperfect and preposterous,' and the Nonjurors to reject it from their New Communion Office of 1718.

Dr. Brett censures it as

'a plain deviation from Catholic practice; for whereas in all the ancient Liturgies, except the Roman, the words of *Institution*, the *Oblation*, and the *Invocation*, always follow one another in the order I have named them; in this Liturgy the last is put in the first place, and God is petitioned to bless and sanctify the elements by the Holy

---

[1] The Scotch Liturgy of 1637 contained the petition of 1549, but qualified it by inserting the word *so* before 'bless and sanctify,' and adding at the end, 'so that we, receiving them, may be partakers,' &c. This was satisfactory to Laud, but not to the Nonjurors.

Ghost, before we have recited the words of Institution, and thereby declared or set forth our commission and our duty to perform that service.'¹

It is true the Doctor thinks this mistake 'by no means so material as the total exclusion of the Invocation;' but it was a mistake which could only be remedied by substituting the Eastern form of consecration for the Western; and that was a greater change than our Reformers were prepared to attempt. Hence when the difficulty came to be felt, they determined to omit the petition altogether. It is certain that the action of the Holy Ghost is implied in all consecration, and if the omission of an express petition for His blessing be a liturgical loss, it is one which all the churches of the Roman obedience suffer with us, and which the Church of England has only escaped during the three famous years when her Liturgy was ruled by the first impressions of King Edward VI. and his advisers.

The third paragraph is still retained, and with it, in all reasonable construction, the prohibition of elevation, though not now expressed in the rubric. The fourth was omitted, and the remainder transposed to the Post-Communion.

These alterations, which appear to have excited little or no discussion at the time, were certainly not suggested by Bucer. There is no trace of them in his animadversions, nor a particle of

¹ Dissertation, p. 383.

evidence to impugn their being the unbiased determination of the English Reformers.[1] Neither do we hear of much debate at the accession of Elizabeth, when it was determined to restore the Second Book in preference to the First. It was not the Protestants who disliked the 'explanations' of 1552; but the papal party, who, for their own purposes, had endeavoured to fasten on the older formulary a meaning which it was never intended to bear.

The first expression of dissatisfaction was heard at the compiling of the Scottish Liturgy of 1637, when, against the advice of Laud, it was resolved to revert to the Office of 1549, as more truly expressing the Eucharistic Sacrifice. The issue of that experiment was not such as to encourage its renewal at the Restoration; but in the next century the Nonjurors revived the complaint of there being no proper oblation; and Wheatley went so far as to stigmatize the alterations of 1552 as a 'mangling and displacing' of the office. These complaints are now reiterated with still greater bitterness, and less discrimination.

The chief grievance is the omission of the fourth clause in the Consecration Prayer of 1549. This is called in the Scottish Liturgy the Memorial, or *Prayer of Oblation;* but not only is the word 'oblation' not in the original, but whoever will compare the clause with the corresponding portion

---

[1] Some discussions took place in Convocation, of which no particulars are extant.

of the Roman Canon, must perceive that this word was precisely what was *rejected*. The Roman Canon, as we have seen, contained *two* formal oblations of the elements, both of which are omitted in the Liturgy of 1549. Of the first, before consecration, the petition remained for the sanctification of the Spirit, but all words of oblation were carefully eliminated. The second, after consecration, was altogether omitted, and a new form substituted in its place. The words of the Roman Canon are, 'We offer unto Thy glorious Majesty, of Thine own gifts and presents, a pure host,' &c. The English runs, 'We do celebrate and make here before Thy Divine Majesty, with these Thy holy gifts, the Memorial which Thy Son hath willed us to make,' &c. The words 'offer' and 'oblation' are scrupulously expunged; and it is impossible to compare the English with the Latin, and not see that the oblation of the gifts was the very thing rejected. And with good reason, for this oblation of the *consecrated* elements was, in fact, the peculiarity of the Roman Canon, differing from all the Greek Liturgies.

It is true that in them the oblation followed the words of Institution, but it was followed in turn by the Invocation, which effected the consecration. Indeed it was *in order* to the benediction, implored in the Invocation, that the oblation was made. In the oblation the bread and wine are but symbols; the Invocation makes them the

Body and Blood, and of these *communion* is the sole remaining use.

In the Western Church, where the consecration into the Body and Blood was held to be perfect on the recital of the words of Institution, the oblation was necessarily thrown back to an earlier stage; and the second oblation of the Roman canon was an error, arising from a corrupt following of the Eastern Office. This error, when coupled with the later mistake of transubstantiation, gave birth to the sacrifice of the Mass;—a dogma resisted by our Reformers even to the death. To avoid it in their own Liturgy, they changed the second oblation into a Memorial; and when 'the curiosity of ministers and mistakers' rendered further 'explanation' necessary, they expunged the clause altogether. As matters stood, this was the wisest thing to do. In a liturgical point of view the clause was erroneous as well as novel. The 'memorial' is the name of the *oblata before* consecration, and is not so properly applicable to the holy gifts after the benediction, in virtue of which they are to us 'verily and indeed the Body and Blood of Christ.' To insert the word in this place was, in fact, to peril the reality of the consecration, seeing that nothing follows to change the symbolical into the real.

This grave consequence is overlooked by those who now want to return to the 'Memorial' of 1549, in a sense disclaimed by its authors. It has severely exercised, however, the divines who from time to time endeavoured to restore the oblation. The Scotch Liturgy of 1637 made an oblation out of the 'Memorial,' by interpolating the new title, 'Prayer of oblation.' Even so, however, the oblation was the whole sacrifice of praise and thanksgiving, together with the reasonable sacrifice of bodies and souls, more than the material gifts; for, as we have seen, this is not the proper place for offering the gifts, and in fact they are actually offered at an earlier part of the Scotch Liturgy.

The Nonjurors found the confusion was only to be remedied by altogether abrogating the arrangement of 1549. In their 'New Communion Office,' after reciting the words of institution, the priest proceeded thus:—

'Wherefore, having in remembrance His passion, death and resurrection from the dead, His ascension into heaven and second coming with glory and great power to judge the quick and the dead, and to render to every man according to his works, we offer to Thee our King and our God, according to His holy institution, this bread and this cup; giving thanks to Thee through Him, that Thou hast vouchsafed us the honour to stand before Thee, and to sacrifice unto Thee. And we beseech Thee to look favourably on these Thy gifts which are here set before Thee, O Thou self-sufficient God; and do Thou accept them to the honour of Thy Christ, and send down Thine Holy Spirit, the witness of the passion of our Lord Jesus, upon this sacrifice, that He may make this bread the Body of Thy Christ, and this cup the Blood of Thy Christ; that they who are partakers thereof may be confirmed in godliness,' &c.

Here we have a clear, unambiguous oblation of the gifts, but they are offered before consecration as 'bread' and 'cup'; and these names are continued in the following clause, where the Holy Ghost is invoked to make them the Body and Blood. The *sacrifice* is distinctly of the bread and wine, not of the Body and Blood, and the Tridentine mass is thus effectually excluded. But then not only is the Liturgy of 1549 wholly discarded, but the doctrine of the Western Church with regard to consecration is abandoned for the Eastern, and the words of Institution are denied the power of effecting the Sacramental Presence.

A similar result was arrived at in the revision of the Scotch Liturgy made in 1765.[1]

[1] I am indebted to the present Bishop of Aberdeen for an authentic copy of this Liturgy as collated by Bishop Horsley, and attested by Bishop Skinner, for the information of Parliament, A.D. 1792. This office agrees with the English up to the sermon, except that in place of the Ten Commandments it is permitted to substitute a summary of the Law taken from Mark, xii. 29-31; Matt. xxii. 40. After the sermon the materials are for the most part taken from the English, but entirely re-arranged. The presbyter, (as he is called,) on returning to the altar, begins with our long Exhortation; then follows the Offertory, in which the devotions are termed 'oblations,' and presented upon the holy table with the thanksgiving in 2 Chron. xxix. 10-12, 14. After this, the presbyter is to 'offer up and place the bread and wine prepared for the sacrament upon the Lord's Table;' but for this, the true oblation, no words are provided. The service opens with the *Dominus vobiscum, Sursum corda, Vere dignum, Preface,* and *Trisagion.* Then comes the Prayer of Consecration, and then that for the whole state of Christ's Church, omitting the words 'militant upon earth,' and with an unimportant amplification of the concluding clauses. The Lord's Prayer, the

The prayer of consecration opens with the words,

'All glory be to Thee, Almighty God, our Heavenly Father, for that Thou, of Thy tender mercy, didst give Thine only Son Jesus Christ to suffer death upon the cross for our redemption, (Who by His *own* oblation of Himself, once offered,) made a full, perfect, and sufficient Sacrifice, Oblation, and Satisfaction for the sins of the whole world, and did institute, and in His holy gospel command us to continue, a perpetual Memorial of that His precious Death and Sacrifice until His coming again. For in the night that He was betrayed He took bread,' &c. (as in our own Liturgy.)

After the words of the Institution, the priest proceeds with the 'Oblation' as follows:—

'Wherefore, O Lord and Heavenly Father, according to the Institution of Thy dearly beloved Son our Saviour Jesus Christ, we Thy humble servants do Celebrate and Make here before Thy Divine Majesty, with these Thy holy Gifts, WHICH WE NOW OFFER UNTO THEE, the Memorial Thy Son hath commanded us to make; having in remembrance His blessed Passion and precious Death, His mighty Resur-

---

short Exhortation, Confession, Absolution, Comfortable words, and Collect of humble access, introduce the Communion, in which the first half only of the English words of distribution is retained. The post-Communion consists of our second prayer of thanksgiving, the *Gloria in Excelsis*, and the Benediction. The concluding rubrics, in the printed copies now in use, sanction the mixing of the chalice *before it is presented on the altar*, and direct a reservation of the consecrated gifts for the communion of the sick, aged, and infirm, who could not be present. The remainder is to be reverently eaten and drunk after the Blessing. None of these rubrics were included in Bishop Horsley's Collation, or in the attestation of Bishop Skinner, which, if these directions are authoritative, cannot be considered so accurate as it appeared to be at the time.

rection and glorious Ascension; rendering unto Thee most hearty thanks for the innumerable benefits procured unto us by the same.'

The *Invocation* :—

'And we most humbly beseech Thee, O merciful Father, to hear us, and, of Thy Almighty Goodness, vouchsafe to bl✠ess and sanct✠ify with Thy Word and Holy Spirit these Thy gifts and creatures of bread and wine, that they may become the Body and Blood of Thy most dearly beloved Son.'

This ends the Consecration: the celebrant proceeds :—

'And we earnestly desire Thy Fatherly goodness, mercifully to accept this our sacrifice of praise and thanksgiving; most humbly beseeching Thee to grant that by the merits and death of Thy Son Jesus Christ, and through faith in His Blood, we and all Thy whole Church may obtain remission of our sins, and all other benefits of His passion. And here we humbly offer and present unto Thee, O Lord, ourselves, our souls and bodies, to be a reasonable, holy, and lively sacrifice unto Thee, beseeching Thee that whosoever shall be partakers of this Holy Communion may worthily receive the most precious Body and Blood of Thy Son Jesus Christ, and be filled with Thy grace and heavenly benediction, and made one Body with Him, that He may dwell in them, and they in Him.

'And although we are unworthy, through our manifold sins,' &c. (as in our Post-Communion Office.)

This form of consecration has been adopted in the 'Book of Common Prayer according to the use of the Protestant Episcopal Church in the United States of America,'[1] (1790,) with the verbal correction of *own* to *one*, and with the alteration in the Invocation of the words that 'they may

[1] The Bishop of Illinois (my esteemed friend Dr. H. J. Whitehouse) supplied my copy of this book.

become the Body and Blood of Thy most dearly beloved Son,' to the English form, 'that we, receiving them according to Thy Son our Saviour Christ's holy institution, in remembrance of His death and passion, may be partakers of His most blessed Body and Blood.'[1] The Scotch expression, it will be observed, is more absolute than the Roman Canon itself, (ut fiat *nobis*,) still the petition plainly relates to Communion only, since no other use of the gifts is authorized, and the *doctrine* of that Church is identical with our own and the American.

It should be observed that, both in the Scotch and American rubrics, the manual action of the celebrant is used as in our own, along with the words of Institution, but it is *not* repeated (as in the Nonjuring Office) at the Invocation, which effects the consecration. For it will be noted that the Scottish and American Churches have taken the serious step, not ventured upon by the Church of England, of exchanging the Western doctrine of Consecration for the Eastern. In their Office the 'Memorial' is a true oblation, which it was not, and could not be, in the English book of 1549. The 'holy gifts' are offered as bread and wine, and they continue to be so called down to the end of the Invocation, when they are

---

[1] With the exception of the Consecration Prayer, the American Office is nearly the same with the English of 1662: it omits, however, the references to John vi. and 1 Cor. xi. in the Exhortation.

sanctified to become the Body and Blood to the receivers. The whole prayer is thus at once primitive and consistent. All that can be said against it is that it involves a wider separation from the churches of the Roman obedience than has yet been deemed necessary in England. It may be assumed that the Scotch and American Churches, being in full communion with our own, have no intention to impugn the validity of our Eucharistical consecration, yet it is a serious reflection for ourselves, that if the words of Institution do not effect the presence of the Body and Blood, (as the two daughter Churches have the temerity to indicate,) there are no others in our Liturgy, or in the Roman Canon, to constitute the sacrament at all!

Returning now to the 'explanations' of 1552. The concession really made to Bucer was not the omission of the Memorial clause, (on which his animadversions contain no censure) but the expunging of the rubric after the Offertory, which directed the priest to set forth the elements on the altar previously to the sacramental service. This act constituted the real oblation of King Edward's First Book, as it does of our own, and as such it was most unreasonably objected to in the fourth chapter of Bucer's *Censura*.[1] Its omission left the Office without any other oblation than is always implied in consecration, and this was beyond question a

[1] Collier's Eccl. Hist.

departure from the uniform order of the older Liturgies, based on our Lord's own action in the Institution. The defect remained when the Fifty-seventh Canon was passed, and was only supplied at the last review.

Not only is this oblatory act now restored and enjoined, but a voice is put into it, by the insertion of the proper words in the beginning of the prayer that immediately follows : ' We humbly beseech Thee most mercifully to accept these our alms and *oblations*,[1] and to receive these our prayers, *which we offer unto Thy Divine Majesty*, beseeching Thee,' &c.

The priest subsequently recites over the *oblata* so lying upon the altar (τὰ προκείμενα) the perpetual memory of the Cross, and perfects the

[1] An attempt has been made to explain this word of the 'other devotions,' presented together with the alms ; but this is to give a new and unnatural meaning to a familiar liturgical term. The mistake was indeed committed, and still continues, in the Scotch rubric, but there is no pretence for charging it on our own. 'The *alms* signifying that which was given for the relief of the poor, the *oblations* can signify nothing else but, according to the style of the ancient Church, the bread and wine presented to God.'—(*Patrick's Christian Sacrifice.*) To scruple at giving this name to the ordained symbols of bread and wine, and yet divert it to money or other gifts, is strangely inconsistent. Observe further that the words, 'which we offer unto Thy Divine Majesty' express the main feature of the action, and include both the oblations and the prayers. For the same reason this offertory prayer ought, surely, to be said in the same place and posture as the oblations are presented in, viz. standing before the altar. There is no authority for the common practice of separating the action from the prayer by removing to another place.

consecration, not, as in the Roman Canon, by the bare recital of the words of Institution, but by prayer that, in receiving them according to His Institution, we may be partakers of that most blessed Body and Blood which those undying words reveal. This arrangement, though differing in form, is full and true to the substance of the ancient Liturgies, and will be found closer than any other to the precedents of Holy Scripture.

In removing the remaining petitions from the Consecration Prayer to the Post-Communion, the Reformers (who must be allowed to know their own meaning) 'explained' beyond question that no oblation of the gifts had ever been here intended. The 'bounden duty and service' of the seventh clause related to the whole celebration, and is most appropriately presented when the act is completed by communion. So, too, the reasonable sacrifice of ourselves, our souls and bodies, is most suitably offered when we have verily and indeed received the Body and Blood of Christ, and are so united with Him in the Sacrifice of the Cross. This self-oblation is a rich addition to the Anglican Office, not found in any ancient Liturgy, but expressing, in a less questionable form, the thought which Cyprian aimed at in his fanciful exposition of the mixed chalice.

On the whole, the pretended 'mangling and displacing' of the older form not only gave the true interpretation of its own meaning, but supplied a remedy for some not unimportant liturgical mistakes. Two great practical improvements resulted from the new arrangement:—

1. The Eucharistic Sacrifice, which the Romanists would restrain to the mere oblation of the gifts, is more distinctly extended to the whole celebration, including the self-oblation of the communicants.

2. The Communion itself is brought into immediate connection with the words of Institution, as in the original Supper, where nothing whatever intervened.

These simple provisions cover the whole ground of the controversies we have been examining. The first exhibits the Sacrifice as all the Fathers held it, and as neither Lutheran nor Calvinist need demur to. The second cuts away by the roots the whole series of scandals and controversies, which a perverse ingenuity had crowded into an interval, unauthorized by Scripture, and in the first celebration impossible. It is true that these practical common-sense arrangements are found in no Liturgy but our own; nevertheless they represent more exactly than any other the Institution of Christ, and the acknowledged purport of the Sacrament. We owe them neither to fathers nor councils, but to the good Providence of God over a Church which, taking Holy Scripture for her guide, was not afraid to exercise her own authority in the sphere that belongs to it.

When such an arrangement is stigmatized as 'liturgically unique,' 'absolutely without support from the whole family of liturgies,'[1] it is enough to answer that this is part of the evil wrought by the schism of East and West, for which the Church of England is not responsible. The Roman Canon is unique; the First Book of Edward VI. was unique; and so must every English Office be, unless, like the Scottish and American Bishops, we separate further from Rome, and seek a more Catholic model among the Greek Liturgies. If the churches of antiquity had been restrained by this puerile objection, no 'family of Liturgies' could have sprung into existence.

Two particulars still remain to be noticed. In the alterations hitherto considered, our Church was dealing only with her own novelties of the year 1549; but that Liturgy contained two provisions of undoubted antiquity, the omission of which may be thought a more questionable exercise of power in a particular Church. These were the mixed chalice, and the commemoration of the dead.

With respect to the first, there is no question of its antiquity or catholicity. The tradition of the Church, which held the original cup of our Lord to contain a mixture of water, is confirmed by what is known of the paschal usages; it is in no degree invalidated by wine alone being men-

[1] Church and the World.

tioned in Scripture, since in the Liturgies also the mixture is often called 'wine.' Moreover, in the Old Testament type referred to in the Eucharistic Institution, Moses is only related to have taken blood, while we learn from the apostle that water also was in the bason.[1]

The point to be observed is that in neither case is any *significance* attached to the water. It is the *blood* to which the purifying power is assigned, both by Moses and the apostle; and it is the *wine* which our Saviour gave to be the communion of His Blood. Neither the early Fathers, nor the Liturgies, ascribe any special signification to the water: the later symbolism is varying and unauthorized, while all agree that the wine is the Blood.[2] Even the Trullan Canon, which censured the Armenians for omitting the water, treats it as a departure from established usage, rather than an essential defect in the sacrament. However strong, therefore, may be the argument from antiquity, there is no pretence for supposing that anything beyond bread and wine is *necessary;* consequently the Church has power to regulate this usage, as well as others in which the commemoration lawfully varies from the original Institution.

[1] Compare Exod. xxiv. 6 with Heb. ix. 19.

[2] S. Cyprian made the water to signify the people: others see a reference to the blood and water issuing from the Lord's side on the cross; and before the Commission on Ritual the mixture has been held to symbolize His Divine and Human Natures. (*Evidence, Qu.* 1990.)

It is to be further observed that in the Institution the cup was mixed, if at all, before the Saviour took it. The mixing itself formed no part of His action, and has no necessary place in the Church's ritual; in fact, it is not mentioned in Justin's account. Now, the only change made in 1552 was to omit the rubric which in 1549 directed the priest to add 'a little pure and clean water' to the wine at the time of the oblation. Wheatley is 'apt to suspect that this direction was thrown out on some suggestion of Calvin and Bucer;' but no such suggestion has been produced. What Bucer objected to was the act of oblation made in setting the elements on the altar. To meet this objection the entire rubric was expunged, but there is not a trace of any intention to alter the contents of the chalice, much less to *prohibit* the water. The omission of the rubric, though made for a totally different reason, rendered it possible to exclude the water without violating the Act of Uniformity, but neither the Act, nor any canon, article, or injunction, gives the lightest hint of any direction, or even permission, to do so.

The Church of England has neither committed herself to any theory of the mixture, nor disapproved the practice. She has only withdrawn the direction to mix the cup as a ritual act. The most that can fairly be inferred is that she is willing to indulge the scruple of any who insist on the letter of Scripture. The mixing is no longer part of the ritual, nor is there any reason why it should be; but it is too much to infer that the use of a mixed chalice is forbidden.[1]

Much the same kind of remark applies to the omission of departed Christians from the Eucharistic Intercessions, save that no one pretends to include such intercessions in the original Institution. Neither are they mentioned (like the mixed chalice) in the earliest accounts of the celebration. That our own Church considers prayer for the dead *unlawful* it must be absurd to assert, in the absence of any canon, article, or rubric to that effect, and in the teeth of the statute affirming the doctrinal purity of the Liturgy which prescribed it.

On the other hand, it is equally impossible to contend for its being 'material or necessary' to the Eucharist, in the face of the original Institution, and the language of the Fifty-seventh Canon of our own Church. It is, as it always was, a question of Church order. Wherever such intercessions have been used, they were varied at the discretion of the bishop; and why may not the living Church close the diptychs altogether as well as enter or expunge particular names? There is a time to speak and a time to keep silence. Sometimes a seeming defect in

---

[1] A judicial opinion to this effect has been pronounced since these remarks were written; but the suit is still under Appeal. It is marvellous that anyone cares to litigate a question so absolutely without controversial significance. What harm can there be in a little pure water being in the chalice before the wine is poured into it for consecration?

form is required to redress the balance of a truth violently disturbed from an opposite quarter. It is precisely for this ever-varying duty that the Church 'hath power to decree rites and ceremonies.' The power is the same in one century as in another, and must be exercised for edification in all.

The original object of such prayers, we have seen, was to exercise communion with the departed saints, as equally living in Christ with their brethren upon earth. The benefits expected were those that flow from mutual intercession; but when these became exaggerated, on the one side into a mediation of the saints in heaven, and on the other into masses upon earth for the deliverance of souls from purgatory, it was high time to reconsider the practice. Mr. Palmer well observes on this head that

'The true justification of the Church of England is to be found in her zeal for the purity of the Christian faith, and for the welfare of all her members. It is too well known that the erroneous doctrine of purgatory had crept into the Western Churches, and was held by many of the clergy and people. Prayers for the departed were represented as an absolute proof that the Church had always held the doctrine of purgatory. The deceitfulness of this argument can only be estimated by the fact that many persons at this day, who deny the doctrine of purgatory, assert positively that the custom of praying for the departed infers a belief in purgatory. If persons of education are deceived by this argument, which has been a hundred times refuted, how is it possible that the uneducated classes could ever have got rid of the persuasion that their Church held the doctrine of purgatory, if prayers for the departed had been continued in the Liturgy? Would not this custom, in fact, have rooted the error of purgatory in their minds? If, then, the

Church of England omitted public prayer for the departed saints, it was to remove the errors and superstitions of the people, and to preserve the purity of the Christian faith. ..... The happy consequence was that all the people gradually became free from the error of purgatory..... And when the doctrine of purgatory had been extirpated, the English Church restored the Commemoration of saints departed in the Liturgy, which had been omitted for many years, from the same cautious and pious regard to the souls of her children.'[1]

In fine, necessary truth and local church authority constitute *all* that was ever requisite to a Catholic Liturgy. The first of these conditions is certainly wanting to the Roman Canon, as expounded by the Council of Trent. The Anglican Liturgy, fulfilling both, is in every respect as Catholic as any of the old Greek or Latin, and more so than most of their modern representatives. When we add that it comes the closest of any to the standard of Holy Scripture, it is not too much to pronounce it the best and truest in the world.

Twice purified in the scorching fires of the Reformation and the Rebellion, it is now stamped by a national acceptance of two centuries as the great religious settlement of the English people;—the deed of union between Church and State at home;—the heart's bond of countless wanderers in foreign lands;—and the daily manual of our mission churches throughout the world. The old

[1] Palmer's Orig. Liturg. c. iv. s. 10. The 'Commemoration' is contained in the last clause, added to the Offertory prayer in 1662, where the petition that 'we *with them* may be partakers,' &c., is a brief summary of the supplications in the ancient Liturgies.

Romish taunt of isolation has passed away; the Liturgy, once stigmatized as the peculiarity of a little island, now reverberates in many languages, and gathers at this day around the throne of grace more Christian souls than any other, in 'the most perfect form of adoration to the Almighty.'

To disturb this settlement would be to shake English Christianity to the foundation: hence all parties in Church or State deprecate above all things any alteration in the Liturgy. Yet what is it but alteration which is aimed at, when repealed formularies are commended in preference to existing ones? or when it is attempted to over-ride the present ritual with the provisions of pre-Reformation canons? Such suggestions are incompatible with a loyal subscription to the existing Liturgy, and with the express declaration of the Fifty-seventh Canon. The only questions that can be now honestly raised are questions of interpretation on the Book of 1662; and of these it must be remembered that a power of interpretation is practically a legislative power. The Liturgy does not consist merely of the words prescribed to be uttered, but of the whole action of the sacramental service. The Church's doctrine, and the national settlement arrived at in the Book of Common Prayer, may be even more vitally affected by variations in the received method of celebration, than by an alteration of the prayers themselves.

Hence the Church has retained the all-important power of interpretation in the hands of the bishops, from whom originally emanated the liturgical legislation. It is provided that,

'Forasmuch as nothing can be so plainly set forth, but doubts may arise in the use and practice of the same; to appease all such diversity (if any arise) and for the resolution of all doubts, concerning the manner how to understand, do, and execute the things contained in this Book; the parties that so doubt or diversely take anything, shall alway resort to the Bishop of the Diocese, who by his discretion shall take order for the quieting and appeasing of the same, so that the same order be not contrary to anything contained in this Book. And if the Bishop of the Diocese be in doubt, then he may send for the resolution thereof to the Archbishop.'

A bold attempt is now made to transfer this power from the bishop to the officiating minister. The latter (it is argued) is bound in conscience to minister according to his own view of the Church's directions. If he has no doubt in his own mind, he is under no obligation to resort to the bishop; and if the bishop take any order, contrary to what the priest supposes to be the direction of the book, it is *ipso facto* invalid, and not to be obeyed. The clergyman is to take his own course, and leave the bishop to punish him (if he can) in the legal courts. If this argument were generally adopted, the Church of England could never escape the heavy censure pronounced by a living prelate of being an 'eminently contentious and litigious' body.[1] The provision just

[1] Bishop of Lichfield and New Zealand's Sermon before the University of Cambridge.

quoted would be either inoperative, or operative only where it is least required. The bold offender, who takes the law into his own hands, would be released at once from his oath of canonical obedience, and allowed to revel in all the chances of the law.

That such a position should be taken up by a party laying special claim to the designation of *Catholic*, is one of the inconsistencies which to those who come after us will be well-nigh incredible. It simply reverses the Catholic relations of bishop and priest: the latter instead of the former becomes the voice of the Church, and the bishop is reduced to a public prosecutor. This is to confound the Establishment with the Church, forgetting that, while the tribunals are only for the correction of offenders, there is an interior and far higher discipline, which claims the obedience of the genuine churchman. Where the tribunals have spoken, the bishop is concluded no less than the priest; but till then it is the bishop, not the priest, to whom the Church has committed the interpretation of her Liturgy.

The Courts, as they themselves anxiously explain, have no power to declare the mind of the Church: they simply pronounce on the penalties incurred by the accused. The reasons which guide their decision have no authority in the Church, or in the conscience; it is open to anyone to challenge a new decision on his own case. But the Bishop speaks for the

Church; he is entitled to canonical obedience, his authority binds the conscience. For no Catholic rule is more certain than that a priest cannot celebrate divine offices against the will of the bishop, without sin.

Such an authority no bishop can permit to be set at nought, without abandoning a most important part of his trust. The purity and integrity of liturgical offices throughout the diocese is especially in his keeping; both Church and State look to him to defend them. Neither can it be allowed (till the fact has been ascertained by experience) that the provision above quoted is incapable of being readily and effectually executed. If the priest will not resort to the bishop, those who 'diversely take' the matter may, and a citation would bring the other.

To talk as some now do of 'the liberty which has in such matters been always allowed to the clergy and people,'[1] is to gainsay the most notorious

[1] Memorial to the Archbishop of Canterbury from twenty-one Clergymen. It is to be hoped that these respectable names are not committed to the full extent in which this liberty is sometimes asserted. We hear it claimed that one kind of ritual should be allowed to congregations of *æsthetic* tendencies, and another to puritan ones—to speak plainly, a Romanizing ritual for Romanizers, a lower ceremonial for Anglicans, and whatever they like best for Evangelicals. But then why not a creedless Liturgy for latitudinarians, and a philosophical one for philosophers? This may be Presbyterianism, or Independent Congregationalism, but it is certainly not Episcopacy, as the word is understood in the Catholic

features in the history of Catholic Liturgies, and of our own in particular. To the 'old godly doctors' such a 'liberty' would have appeared preposterous. Who can fancy a priest of the 'most pure and uncorrupt ages' proposing to S. Basil (for example) to enrich his Liturgy with some alleged Ante-Nicene use? or astonishing S. Chrysostom by exchanging his surplice for the last and most authentic edition of the Clementine 'splendid garment'? What would S. Athanasius have said to an invitation, from some Alexandrian Church Union, to try the legality of lights and incense before a count of the empire?[1] Or how would S. Cyprian have dealt with a priest of Carthage taking the liberty to carry an 'olive leaf' to Pope Stephen?[2]

Church. How long the doctrine of the Church, or even its Orders, can be maintained when such liberties are taken with its ritual and discipline, may be seen in the present state of the societies founded by John Wesley.

[1] Not long ago a general complaint among churchmen was the unecclesiastical character of the State-made tribunal of Final appeal. *Now* it would seem to be the only authority with some who are misnamed High Churchmen. Convocation and the Bishops are confronted by the 'opinions' of Queen's Counsel, and the grand bulwark of Catholic truth is the Judicial Committee of the Privy Council expounding the 'authority of Parliament in the second year of King Edward VI.' One clergyman coolly tells his bishop 'he has sent his lordship's instructions to Sir R. Phillimore, and shall be governed by his opinion in obeying them!'

[2] The 'Olive Leaf' is the title of a little book just published, relating the self-imposed mission of an English clergyman to the pope of Rome and the patriarchs of Constantinople and

Such extravagancies, however congenial to the democratic spirit of the nineteenth century, have neither parallel nor sanction in the Catholic Church. They could not be tolerated, even if it were certain that the eucharistic Liturgy would be improved by the uncontrolled action of each aspiring priest. For obedience is better than sacrifice: no Liturgy is so lovely and acceptable as the offering up of the Church, in the unbroken order of her many members in One Body. It remains to be shown, however, that bishops are less competent than priests and laymen to discern the beauty of holiness. More responsible they are, both to Church and State, for the preservation of the Reformed National Liturgy; hence they may be more suspicious of embellishments imported from other sources, and especially from the Church of Rome.[1] But

---

Jerusalem, for a reconciliation of the Churches. Armed with a certificate of character from the late Archbishop of Canterbury, and attired in a monastic garb, this quixotic pilgrim gained admission to the Roman pontiff, and was received with his usual affability. How much was known of his 'mission,' either to the English or the Italian primate, may be questioned; but beyond doubt they were both good-natured men, and the English are a very extraordinary people.

[1] For example, it being difficult (or rather impossible) to recover the exact make and colour of the 'ornaments' in use in the second year of Edward VI., the modern use of Rome is resorted to instead. See Evidence before the Royal Commission on Ritual. (p. 730-81,) where the witness, having pleaded 'the custom of the Western Church' as ruling the colours of vest-

a bishop may well deny that the Italian ceremonial is in any sense higher or nobler than the English. The Corporal theory from which it sprung is a low and unreal one; and whatever tends to materialize the Presence, to substitute adoration for communion, or to confound the commemorative sacrifice with the Real, is a return to the Corporal error, which only stains the brightness of a sacramental service. If the highest Ritual be the most truthful expression of the highest truth, the Anglican Liturgy would be lowered, not raised, by such uncongenial interpolations.[1]

---

ments and altar-cloths, adds that by the Western Church he means 'the Church of Rome and the Churches in communion with it,' which latter, nevertheless, have many customs different from those of Rome. Another witness who professes to 'retain the bolder features of ritual' without attending to 'its very great minutiæ,' takes his stand 'on the Church Catholic throughout the world,' and plainly says 'the Church of England must settle the question for herself.' He admits that he 'has been so much lately abroad, that he hardly remembers what a rubric is.' He thinks 'every individual clergyman must use his own discretion. It is a sad sight that any individual priest in the Church of England should be obliged to select, but, as things are, he is obliged to do so.' This witness constantly designates the parish church as 'my church;' perhaps because he *bought* it.—*Ev. Royal Commission on Ritual*, ques. 2053, 2054, 2135.

[1] Having attended and communicated at S. Alban's, Holborn, I must be allowed to declare my own opinion that the service was every way lower, less majestic, and less attractive, than the spiritual and really magnificent celebrations of Dr. Hook at Leeds, with their hundreds of devout, intelligent, and truly reverent communicants.

The solemn remembrance before God of the One Eternal Sacrifice; the Real Spiritual Presence of the great Bishop of souls, feeding His Church with the Bread of life which cometh down from heaven; the Blessed Communion, lifting these soiled and yearning hearts to the glorified Humanity on high; and the dedication of body, soul, and spirit as a living sacrifice, incorporate in His and by Him presented in Himself to His Father and our Father;—*these* are the truths of the Eucharistic Sacrifice. They find their best expression in full and frequent celebrations, in the united voice of intelligent prayer and song, in the priestly blessing, and the Eucharistic eating and drinking of all present. These have a fragrance and majesty far above perfumes and vestments. They constitute a ceremonial which is at once national, scriptural, and impressive. Instead of lingering in the Levitical court of the sacrifices, vainly grasping at shadows that have passed away, they lead the Christian forward, clergy and people together, to the very Presence above the Cherubim. They enable us all, as priests and kings unto God, to eat of the most Holy in the Holy Place; for the Memorial, which we there eat and drink for the remembrance of Christ, is to us the very Sacrifice—HIS BODY broken, and HIS BLOOD shed, unto forgiveness, remission of sins, and immortal life.

APPENDIX.

NOTE ON VESTMENTS.

THE controversy *de Re Vestiaria*, as now carried on, suffers on both sides from the want of a distinct enumeration of the several vestments alleged to be sanctioned or forbidden. This defect is not fully supplied in the two elaborate Cases lately submitted for the opinion of counsel, and published in the Appendix to the First Report of the Commission on Ritual.

To be complete, the inquiry should start from the Vestments in use before the First English Liturgy was enacted.

The canons in force at the accession of Edward VI. required the parish to provide for the *Vestimentum Principale* a chasuble, alb, belt, amice, stole, and maniple. This was the eucharistic vesture of the celebrant. The deacon and sub-deacon were to be provided with other proper vestments, according to the means of the parish or church: these appear from other sources to comprise the alb, dalmatic, tunicle, stole, and maniple. The parish was further bound to supply a silk cope for the principal festivals, with two other copes for the choir.[1]

The officiating vestments were put on over the clerical *habit*, consisting of a long black gown and tippet, with the hood and square cap.

On the colour, shape, and material of the several vestments, we have no general regulations; probably there was no uniform use in England. What appears is that the alb was of white linen, while the other vestments varied from '*baudekin*,' (*i.e.* cloth of gold or silver,) *velvet*, and *silk*, down to *woollen*, *linen*, and humble *fustian*. The colours given in our inventories are *white*, *red*, *blue*, *green*, *purple*, *tawny*, (or yellow,) *brown*, and *black*. They seem to have been worn in 'sets,' or suits of the same colour, according to the occasion, but no authoritative *sequence* of colours for the several seasons has been made out.

There is no reason to suppose that Roman usage was at all the rule in England. Cathedrals as well as abbeys observed their own rules: pious donors gratified their tastes according to their means; but as the parish was legally bound to supply what was necessary, there can be no doubt that any dispute would be determined by the ordinary of the place.

As a general description we may take it that the *alb* was shaped like the modern cassock, and girt with the belt, the sleeves being either straight, or gathered at the wrist like the present episcopal lawn. It was often adorned with embroidery, lace, and fringe.

The *cope* was a long cloak, fastened at the neck and open in front. It seems to have been derived from the ancient Pall, and is represented in the doctors' *cappa* still used at Oxford and Cambridge.

[1] Canons of York, Wilk. Conc. iv.

The *chasuble* was a shorter cope, closed in front, but having openings at the sides, or else scolloped up from the bottom, to allow the free use of the hands. It was embroidered with a cross on the back, and was so peculiarly the *Missatica Vestis*, that its common name was 'the vestment.'

The *amice* seems to have been a kind of hood. The *stole* was a narrow strip like the Roman pall, hanging from the shoulders to the knee, and fringed at the end.

The *tunicle* is described by Durand and Wheatley as 'a sky-blue silk vestment in the shape of a cope,' but our Inventories give them of various colours, like the chasuble. No English authority, I believe, can be produced for the sleeved jacket, recently introduced as a tunicle.

The *maniple* was originally a napkin to wipe the lips of the chalice during the Communion, but after the ministration of the cup had been suppressed, it was retained as a mere ornament on the left arm, decorated with embroidery and fringe.

The officiating vestments were solemnly delivered to the several orders of the clergy at their ordination, and taken away from them at deprivation. From a minute account of the deprivation of William Sautre by Archbishop Arundel, (A. D. 1401.) it appears that the accused, having been produced 'in the habit and apparel of a priest,' was first deprived of the paten, chalice, and *chasuble*, or 'priestly vestment,' in token of deprivation from the priesthood; then of the book of the Gospels and the *stole*, as the badges of a deacon; then of the *alb* and *maniple*, as of a sub-deacon; the candlestick, taper, and urceolum, as of an acolyte; the book of Exorcisms, as of an exorcist; the book of Lections, as of a reader; and finally, of the *surplice* and key of the church, as of an ostiarius. The erasure of the clerical tonsure having reduced the prisoner to a layman, he was then delivered to the secular arm to be burnt alive.[1]

Hence it appears that the *surplice* was common to all the seven orders, being worn under the alb by the higher three. In that use it would probably be without sleeves, like the present episcopal rochet. There is reason to think the surplice was worn at times out of church, as the rochet undoubtedly was, and in that use it is probable that both had sleeves.[2]

Such were the Vestments in use in the reign of Henry VIII.; the canons which enjoined them having received a parliamentary sanction in that reign which was not in terms repealed till the 5th and 6th Edward VI., it has been contended of late that *all* these vestments are still sanctioned by the 'Ornament Rubric' of the existing Liturgy, as having been 'in this Church of England by authority of Parliament in the second year of the reign of King Edward VI.' It has been ruled, however, by the Judicial Committee, that these much-contested words 'apply and *are to be confined* to the ornaments *prescribed* in the First Book of Edward VI.;' so that so much of the previous law as was not directly continued by that Book was in fact repealed by the statute 2nd and 3rd Edward VI. (1548.)[3]

Proceeding, then, to the directions of that book, we find a great reduction of the ecclesiastical vesture, eucharistic and otherwise.

[1] Hook's Lives of the Abps. of Canterbury, iv. 504.
[2] See Canon lviii. of 1603.
[3] Privy Council. Liddell *v.* Westerton. Martin *v.* Mackonochie.

1. In the first place, instead of the old Pontificals, the Bishop is assigned the altar vesture of the priest, leaving only the rochet and pastoral staff to mark the episcopal order.

2. In the eucharistic vesture of the priest the alb is to be 'plain,' not worked or fringed.

3. The vestment is not the entire *vestimentum principale* of the canon, but the chasuble, or priestly vestment, only.

4. A cope may be substituted for the chasuble.

5. The assistant 'priests and deacons,' who take the place of the 'deacon and sub-deacon' of the Mass, retain only the tunicle and alb of the ancient vesture.

6. The dalmatic, stole,[1] maniple, amice, with every other mass vestment, are altogether excluded, and never appear again in any subsequent document.

7. For other Offices, the cope with a surplice or alb is the altar vesture when there is no Communion.

8. The *academical* hood is substituted for the cope or other ornaments, over the surplice, as the choral habit of chapters and colleges.[2]

9. The surplice *only* is appointed in parish churches and chapels at Matins and Evensong, baptizing and

---

[1] The name of stole is now often given to the *tippet* which forms part of the clerical habit; but this is a misnomer of very recent date—in fact, within our own recollection. Archbishop Grindal, writing to one of his foreign correspondents, calls it, in derision, *stola quædam*, but he plainly makes it part of the ordinary *habit*, not of the officiating vestments. The stole was never black but in mourning.

[2] This hood is limited to degrees 'taken in any University within this realm.' There is no authority for *foreign* hoods, or for the hood (if there be one) of what is called a 'Lambeth degree.'

burying. Marriage, being concluded at the altar, would doubtless be solemnized in the altar vestments.

10. In 'all other places,' (*e. g.* processions, synods, visitations, and preaching, at least out of Divine Service,) the surplice is optional, but the hood is pronounced 'seemly' in preaching.

11. Finally, no vesture at all is sanctioned, except for bishops, priests, and deacons.

Such, upon the very largest interpretation, is the full extent of 'the authority of Parliament in the second year of Edward VI.' In the same year, it should be observed, a new Ordinal was brought out and put in force, (though not enacted by Parliament till 1552,) under which the pontificals and *missaticæ vestes* were no longer delivered in ordination. Deacons and priests were presented and ordained in plain albs, and bishops in surplices and copes, with the pastoral staff.

A still more sweeping change followed in 1552. A new Communion Office was then set forth, from which the words 'mass' and 'altar,' retained in the First Book, were scrupulously expunged, and the service itself was re-arranged with the avowed design of receding further from the Canon of the Mass. In perfect accordance with this design the *missaticæ vestes* were one and all abolished. The new Communion Office had no vestment rubric; it provided for no assistant ministers, and allowed no distinctive vesture. One general rule was set in front of the book in these words: 'And here it is to be noted that the minister at the time of the Communion, and at all other times in his ministration, shall use neither alb, vestment, nor cope, but being an archbishop or bishop, he shall have and wear a rochet, and being a priest or deacon, he shall have and wear a surplice *only*.' This was a parliamentary repeal of all acts, canons, and usages to the contrary, and it is certain that the parish has never since been required to provide any other vestment than the surplice.

Both Edward's Acts of Uniformity were repealed by Queen Mary, and the first remains repealed to this day: consequently *nothing* in that book is now of any authority, save in so far as it has been re-enacted elsewhere. The Second Book was revived *entire* by 1 Elizabeth cap. ii. sec. 3. (1558.) But the twenty-fifth section contained a proviso that 'such ornaments of the church, and of the ministers thereof, shall be retained and be in use as was in this Church of England by authority of Parliament in the second year of King Edward VI., until other order shall be taken by the authority of the Queen's Majesty, with the advice of the Commissioners appointed and authorized under the Great Seal of England for Causes Ecclesiastical, or of the Metropolitan of the realm.' This 'other order' was taken in the 'Advertisements' of 1564, though a question has been made of the legal publication of that document. This question is now of little moment, since it is agreed that the Advertisements were practically in force down to the Rebellion, and were superseded at the Restoration by the 'ornament rubric' of the present Liturgy. The Advertisements are now of use only as illustrating the construction of the Act of Uniformity.

Now the first question is whether the Proviso above quoted from 1 Elizabeth cap. ii. sec. 25, extended to the alb, chasuble, and tunicle, mentioned in the Liturgy of 1549, or was limited to the other ornaments named in the 'Certain Notes' at the end of that book? This question, though strangely overlooked of late, is the first great pivot of the whole controversy, and was always so regarded by our older ritualists.

It is to be observed, then, that the first-named class of vestments are continued in the Book of 1549 as part of the ancient vesture of the Mass. They are ordered only in the special rubrics of the Eucharistic Office, (which then retained the word Mass in the title,) and in the vesture of the Bishop with reference to the same Office. Further, this order itself allowed the cope to be substituted for the chasuble, the proper and principal mass vestment.

Now this Eucharistic Office of 1549 was the thing chiefly altered in the book of 1552. In the other Offices the two books were much alike, but in the Communion the difference was considerable, and in one avowed direction. The words *mass* and *altar* were expunged, the consecration prayer was altered and transposed, avowedly to make it more unlike the sacrifice of the Mass, and the mass vestments were expressly forbidden. The prohibition was extended even to the *secondary* eucharistic vesture of 1549, no difference of vesture being now allowed between the Communion and other Offices.

These differences were seriously debated at the accession of Elizabeth, and mainly on account of them it was determined to restore the Second Book in preference to the First. The First would have been more popular, as more nearly resembling the Mass restored by Queen Mary; and there was no essential difference of doctrine between the two. It was entirely a question of form; and it is inconceivable that the same persons should openly prefer the Office which repudiated the name and form of the Mass, and in the same moment, by a side wind, covertly bring back the vestments of the Mass. So strange and inconsistent an enactment would require to be expressed in unmistakeable terms: it is not to be inferred from a general Proviso for 'ornaments,' when an equally probable and more consistent interpretation is at hand.

Further, it is to be observed that by the terms of the Act the Book of 1552 was restored *entire*, including the rubric against vestments, subject to the Proviso before quoted. Now that rubric comprised three particulars. 1. That the minister should use neither alb, vestment, nor cope. 2. That he should have a rochet or surplice. 3. That he should have this *only*—*i.e.* with no other ornament. That this last particular 'only' was the subject of the Proviso is more natural than that it should supersede the vesture positively *enjoined*, by one which was positively *forbidden*.

On the other hand, it is alleged that the *rubric*, substituted in Elizabeth's book for that of 1552, contemplates a distinctive eucharistic vesture, which can only be that of 1549. The rubric was in these words: 'And here it is to be noted that the minister at the time of the Communion, and at all other times of his ministration, shall use such ornaments in the church as were in use by authority of Parliament in the second year of the reign of King Edward VI., according to the Act of Parliament set in the beginning of this Book.' It certainly cannot be held that this separate mention of the Communion does of itself imply a separate vesture, because these words are retained *verbatim* from the old rubric, where they were used to *forbid* that distinction. And for the remainder of the rubric it refers us back to the Act of Parliament, which has *no* separate mention of the Communion.

Granting, however, that some distinctive vesture

was perhaps in contemplation, (for the final ordering was left to the Queen,) it by no means follows that it should be the vesture of the Mass. On the contrary, the *cope* was a eucharistic vestment in 1549, and that specifically 'by authority of Parliament in that year,' whereas the chasuble, alb, and tunicle were of ancient and ecclesiastical appointment. Moreover, the cope would be properly an 'ornament,' being worn over the surplice positively prescribed in 1552, whereas the chasuble and alb constituted a different vesture, either without a surplice, or with a different kind of surplice beneath.

If it be objected that the single word 'ornaments' cannot be thus divided into two classes, so as to restore some and not all of the vestments prescribed in the Book of 1549, the answer is that this division is made in that very Book. The mass vestments occur in the rubrics of the Eucharistic Office, which expired with the Office itself; the others in general directions contained in the 'Certain Notes' at the end of the book. The former are referred to as of ancient appointment, the latter are newly ordered by authority of Parliament. When to this we add that the Mass vestments, as such, were opposed to the spirit and intent of the reformed Communion Office enacted in the Statute, it is not too much to suppose that they were regarded as legally extinct, and never included in the purview of the Proviso for ornaments.

Certainly this was the construction of the Act at the time, and down to 1661. The 'Interpretations' issued by the Bishops in the same year contain the following, under the head 'Concerning the Book of Service:'—

First, that there be used only but one apparel, (by all degrees? or in all churches?) as the cope in the ministration of the Lord's Supper, and the surplice in all other ministrations.' There is not a word of chasubles, albs, or tunicles. This is decisive on the intention of the law as understood by the Bishops who passed it, before any other order had been taken.

Further, six months after the passing of the act, Archbishop Parker, the chief adviser in the whole settlement, was consecrated to the metropolitical see referred to in the Proviso. His register particularises rather minutely the vestments of himself and the bishops who consecrated him. The Archbishop elect entered the chapel dressed in a long scarlet gown and hood, obviously the doctor's *cappa*, worn by the bishops in Edward the Sixth's reign, and still retained in Convocation and Parliament.[1] After the sermon he retired with the four bishops to the vestry, and on their reappearance the archbishop elect was attired in a linen surplice, the chief bishop '*in a silk cope, ready to administer the blessed sacrament;*' two others 'in linen surplices,' and the fourth 'in a long woollen gown.' The last was Miles Coverdale, who, holding no charge, and having determined to retire from the active duties of the episcopate, appeared in the ecclesiastical habit only.[2]

These are incontestable proofs that the 'ornaments' retained by Queen Elizabeth's Act of Uniformity, in

---

[1] The parliament robe now used by the bishops is the full dress of a doctor at Cambridge: the convocation robe is the doctor's convocation habit at Oxford. Parker is said to have been the first who substituted for the latter the black satin chimere commonly used ever since. All seem to be modifications of the cope, the lawn sleeves properly belonging to the rochet beneath.

[2] Mason's Vindication, book iii. c. 9.

addition to the surplice, were the cope and hood, not the alb, chasuble, or tunicle, of 1549. Accordingly the former three alone are the subjects of the further order taken by the Queen in the Advertisements of 1565. By these, (1) The cope was to be used by the celebrant, epistoler, and gospeller at the Holy Communion, in cathedral and collegiate churches; (2) The surplice and hood by deans and prebendaries in the choir and pulpit; and (3) The surplice only (with sleeves) by all other ministers in any public prayers or ministering of the sacraments, such surplice to be provided by the parish.

Under James I., A. D. 1603, the twenty-fourth and twenty-fifth Canons re-enacted the Advertisements, while the fifty-eighth added the hood to the surplice in parish churches, and a black tippet *not* of silk for non-graduates. This last regulation is explained by the seventy-fourth Canon, where the tippet is shown to be part of the ordinary clerical habit, as before stated. Deans, dignitaries, doctors, and *beneficed* clergymen of the degree of M.A. or B.C.L. are allowed to wear it of silk, and it seems they displayed it above the surplice, like the hood, of which it was perhaps originally a part. This ornament, 'so it be not of silk,' the canon allows to be worn by non-graduates not entitled to the hood. The words in the seventy-fourth Canon—'except tippets only'—were probably intended to apply to *silk* tippets, not to deprive the unbeneficed clergy of this part of the habit altogether. The ambiguity of the expression, however, joined with the natural dislike to marks of inferiority, induced the clergy in the universities to drop the tippet and remain content with their hoods.

Such was the law of vestments when James I. issued

his edition of the Liturgy with the very same Ornament Rubric as Queen Elizabeth, clearly showing that the latter was not understood to revive the alb, chasuble, or tunicle, but only the cope, surplice, and hood.

At the Savoy Conference of 1661, a different construction was first heard of. The Puritans objected that the rubric, as it had stood ever since the accession of Elizabeth, 'seemeth to bring back the cope, alb, and other vestments forbidden by the Common Prayer Book, 5th and 6th Edward VI.' This language by no means implies that such was then the force of the rubric, or that any intention existed of making it so for the future. On the contrary, the objection assumes that the vestments were at the time illegal, and desires they may not be 'brought back' by an undesigned construction. And there was good reason for such an apprehension, if Elizabeth's rubric, hitherto limited by the Advertisements and Canons, should be now re-enacted *absolutely* by Parliament. The remedy, of course, was to alter the rubric, but this was not what the objectors wanted. They demanded its entire *omission*, which would have left the Liturgy with no provision for any officiating vestments at all. It was, in fact, a further attempt to get rid of the *surplice*, to which they had before excepted unsuccessfully; and the bishops accordingly insisted on retaining the rubric for the sake of the surplice, without condescending to notice the *ad invidiam* argument about other vestments.

In point of fact, however, the rubric was *not* retained after all. It was exchanged for another framed in the very words of the Proviso in Elizabeth's Act of Uniformity. But it is often overlooked that these words were not adopted without inserting a limitation directly to the point of the Puritan remonstrance. The insertion is shown in the italics:—'And here it is to be noted that such ornaments of the church and of the ministers thereof, *at all times of their ministration*, shall be retained and be in use as were in this Church of England by authority of Parliament in the second year of the reign of King Edward VI.' Brief as this insertion is, it cannot be supposed to have been made without a motive, at a time when all change was so jealously resisted. Neither will anyone, who has observed the nice and marvellous accuracy of the revisers in their choice of words and the composition of sentences, overlook the importance due to the precise terms and place of the interpolation. If the intention had been to restore the eucharistic vesture of 1549, the wording should have been 'at the *several* times of their ministration,' or at least, 'shall be retained and be in use at all times of their ministration.' Rather, indeed, the old rubric would have been left as it had stood ever since the accession of Elizabeth, and as the bishops at first declared that it should still stand. The subsequent alteration is of itself evidence that on further consideration some different order was felt to be requisite.

By substituting the words of the Act for that of the rubric in the old Book, three changes were effected at once. (1) The 'ornaments' became the nominative case, instead of the 'minister;' (2) The separate mention of the Communion Service was omitted; (3) The words 'in use,' inserted in the old rubric before 'authority of Parliament,' were removed. But this was not all: having made the ornaments the subject of the sentence, the revisers proceeded further to define them by introducing words of limitation. These, again, (after the invariable manner) are taken from the old rubric, but still rejecting the separate mention of the Communion which there preceded them. Lastly, the words were introduced at the exact part of the sentence where, by the laws of grammar, they refer to the *ornaments*, and not, as in the old rubric, to the *services* at which they are to be used.

Coupling all this nice and careful recasting with the objection which we know to have been made at the Savoy Conference, and the force which really belonged to it, apart from the artifice of the objectors, we cannot escape the construction, that what is really enacted is that the ministerial ornaments *at all times of ministration*—as distinguished from the *special* vesture of the Communion—shall be retained and be in use; *viz.* as directed by the canons then and still in force. These are the proper ecclesiastical authority, and there was no occasion for the rubric to say anything more. For the vestment itself a parliamentary enactment was required to oblige the parish to provide it.

This view is strengthened by the ornaments being restrained to such as '*were* in this Church of England by the authority of Parliament,' instead of to such as '*were in use* by authority of Parliament' in the second of Edward VI.

On any other construction it is impossible to understand the motive, object, or even existence, of this rubric. It conceded nothing, guarded nothing, explained nothing; but only wasted a good deal of pains to say what was already more clearly said in the rubric it supplanted.

Again, too, we must insist on the contemporaneous exposition. The Puritans did not cease to scruple at the surplice, nor were the bishops more inclined to humour their prejudices. Diligent inquiry was made at every Visitation for the legal vestments, but it was always the surplice, never the cope, alb, or chasuble, that was enforced. Even in cathedrals no new copes seem to have been provided as the old ones wore out, the canons which enjoined them having lost their statutory basis. It is true that Bishop Cosin and a few others are cited as holding that *all* the Edwardian vestments were included in the rubric; but this was a speculative opinion contrasting strongly with their authoritative acts. At his visitation, Cosin, like the other bishops, inquired only for the surplice, and in his own practice we hear of nothing beyond a white silk cope in Durham Cathedral.

The Appendix to the Second Report of the Commission on Ritual contains a series of Visitation Articles, extending from 1561 to 1730, issued by upwards of one hundred Archbishops, Bishops, and other ordinaries. Some of these are very full and minute, urging every point of conformity with the strictest rigour, and often specifying the law relied upon in the margin. The ornament rubric is thus quoted, but *never* as requiring any other Vestment than surplice and hood. Bishop Gunning (A. D. 1679) inquires minutely whether 'the Minister duly and reverently administers the Holy Sacrament of the Body and Blood of Christ our Lord,' urging every particular of the Consecration, the several delivery to the communicants, bidding of Holy days, &c. Yet of the Vestments his demand is, 'Doth your Minister always at the reading or celebrating any Divine Office constantly wear the Surplice and other Scholastical Habit according to his degree if he be a Graduate, and without a Hood (only instead thereof a Tipet of black stuff (not silk) being permitted him) if he be no Graduate;' putting 'Can. 58' in the margin. Cosin (1662) inquires for 'a large and decent Surplice (one or more) for the Minister to wear *at all times of his public Ministration in the Church;* and further, for 'a Hood or Tippet to wear over his Surplice.' Between 1662 and 1685, as many as twenty-six bishops and other ordinaries issued articles in a common form, with particular variations. All agree in the question, 'Doth your Minister at the reading or celebrating any Divine office wear the Surplice?' the majority adding, 'together with such other scholastical Habit as is suitable to his Degree.' Finally, the *Dean of Arches*, visiting the Peculiars of Canterbury A.D. 1703, asks for the 'Communion-plate, cloths, *Minister's surplice*, Pulpit Cloth, with other usual Ornaments.'

Now, to say that other vestments were legal but not imperative, is to contradict the express words of the rubric, 'shall be retained and be in use.' And to imagine that the ordinaries uniformly put up with less than the law enjoined, is to belie the whole temper and history of the times. Such mere conjectures cannot stand against the historical fact that for two centuries no single ordinary can be shown to have enjoined, and no one parish to have provided, anything but the surplice and hood, which Archbishop Sheldon called 'the priestly habit.'

The conclusions arrived at in this Review are as follows :—

1. That the ancient canonical vesture of the Mass was considerably reduced by the Eucharistic Rubric of 1549.

2. That a secondary or alternative Eucharistic vesture of cope and surplice, was introduced 'by authority of Parliament' in that book.

3. That both these vestures were repealed by the 5th and 6th Edward VI., and the first was never restored.

4. That the cope was provisionally restored by the 1st Eliz. cap. ii. sec. 25, and afterwards regulated by the Advertisements and Canons.

5. That the present rubric applies only to the vestments common to all ministrations, not repealing the canon for copes in cathedrals, but leaving it without its former statutory support to the proper vigour of the ecclesiastical arm.

The last conclusion (or at least the former part of it) is supported by L' Estrange, Bingham, Sharp, and a whole stream of commentators. What is more, it is the only construction which harmonises the law with itself, and with the universal practice of the ordinaries and their tribunals. It would be too much to say, after the legal opinions lately published, (imperfect as are the Cases on which they are founded,) that a contrary view might not be sustained by a common law judge; but when the Final Court of Appeal is claimed as having actually so ruled in the case of Liddell against Westerton, it must be remembered that the judgment in that case is confined to the ornaments of the *church*, not of the *ministers*. The more recent judgment in the case of Martin *v.* Mackonochie, pronounced since the foregoing was in type, proceeds entirely on the principles here contended for, and would probably conduct to the same conclusion should the Vestments come before the Court.

To the tribunals, however, the law has entrusted only the awarding of criminal penalties; the Church has never authorized them to supply the general interpretation of the Liturgy. Those who doubt are directed to resort to the bishop, and those who without doubting 'diversely take,' and yet refuse to resort to the appointed arbitrator, the bishop is *bound* to reduce to conformity. Every day increases the serious responsibilities already weighing on the bishops from their neglect of this plain duty. The appointed order might have taken without difficulty, when the innovation was young; a united explanation by all the bishops, such as was once issued with respect to a baptismal rubric, might have appeased the controversy at a later period; but at present a new canon, or a re-enactment of the old canon, would be the most effectual remedy. On offering this suggestion, some years ago, I was told that a canon cannot over-ride a rubric; yet the Convocations of both provinces straightway plunged into a hopeless struggle to over-ride the rubric on Godfathers and Godmothers. To meet the objection I submitted to a leading member of the House of Lords, the draft of a Bill empowering the Convocations to explain the required vesture, but I was answered—and far more justly—that it was for Convocation to act, and ask the concurrence of Parliament when necessary.

THE END.

www.ingramcontent.com/pod-product-compliance
Lightning Source LLC
Chambersburg PA
CBHW022112230426
43672CB00008B/1353